354.421 GRA -

Devolution, Regionalism and Regional Development

Devolution, Regionalism and Regional Development provides an assessment of the development of devolution, regionalism and regional development in the UK from the late 1990s to the end of the Blair Goverments. It provides a research-based analysis of issues central to the development of devolution and regionalism, focusing equally on politics, governance and planning.

This multidisciplinary book brings together leading researchers in political science, geography, regional planning, public policy, management, public administration and sociology. The three parts of the book focus on: the development of devolution in Scotland, Wales and Northern Ireland; the general development of English regionalism and specific developments in London and the South East and Yorkshire and the Humber; and finally approaches to regional development both across the UK as a whole, and specifically in Scotland, Wales and England. A concluding chapter seeks to assess the changing regional capacity of the UK and place analysis of the UK into comparative perspective.

This will be an important book for those researching and studying devolution, regionalism and regional development as well as those involved in their practice.

Jonathan Bradbury is Senior Lecturer in Politics at Swansea University. His research interests focus on devolution and regional governance. He is the founding joint convenor of the UK Political Studies Association specialist group on British and Comparative Territorial Politics.

Regions and Cities

Series editors: Ron Martin, University of Cambridge, UK; Gernot Grabher, University of Bonn, Germany; Maryann Feldman, University of Georgia, USA

Regions and Cities is an international, interdisciplinary series that provides authoritative analyses of the new significance of regions and cities for economic, social and cultural development, and public policy experimentation. The series seeks to combine theoretical and empirical insights with constructive policy debate and critically engages with formative processes and policies in regional and urban studies.

Devolution, Regionalism and Regional Development

The UK experience

Edited by Jonathan Bradbury

Routledge
Taylor & Francis Group

LONDON AND NEW YORK

First published 2008
by Routledge
2 Park Square, Milton Park, Abingdon, Oxon, OX14 4RN

Simultaneously published in the USA and Canada
by Routledge
270 Madison Ave, New York NY 10016

Routledge is an imprint of the Taylor & Francis Group, an informa business

Transferred to Digital Printing 2009

© 2008 selection and editorial matter: Jonathan Bradbury; individual
chapters: the contributors

Typeset in Bembo by
Keyword Group Ltd

British Library Cataloguing in Publication Data
A catalogue record for this book is available from the British Library

Library of Congress Cataloging in Publication Data
Devolution, regionalism, and regional development: the UK experience /
edited by Jonathan Bradbury.
   p. cm. – (Regions and cities)
   Includes bibliographical references and index.
   ISBN-13: 978-0-415-32361-1 (hbk : alk. paper)
   ISBN-13: 978-0-203-35667-8 (ebk)
   ISBN-10: 0-415-32361-4
   1. Regionalism–Great Britain. I. Bradbury, Jonathan, 1963-
JN297.R44D49 2008
   320.441'049–dc22
   2007023606

ISBN10: 0-415-32361-4 (hbk)
ISBN10: 0-415-57864-7 (pbk)
ISBN10: 0-203-35667-5 (ebk)

ISBN13: 978-0-415-32361-1 (hbk)
ISBN13: 978-0-415-57864-6 (pbk)
ISBN13: 978-0-203-35667-8 (ebk)

Contents

Tables and figure

Tables

Figure

Contributors

Jonathan Bradbury is Senior Lecturer in Politics at Swansea University. He is the joint convenor of the UK Political Studies Association specialist group on British and Comparative Territorial Politics. He is the author of *Union and Devolution: Territorial Politics in the United Kingdom* (forthcoming, 2008) as well as a number of articles and chapters on devolution, political parties, representation and elections in the UK. He is the editor of *British Regionalism and Devolution* (Taylor & Francis, 1997) and has been a guest editor for the journals *Regional and Federal Studies* and *Regional Studies*.

Peter John is the Hallsworth Chair of Governance at the University of Manchester, where he is director of the Institute for Political and Economic Governance (IPEG). He is an expert on public policy and decentralised politics, and is the author of *Analysing Public Policy* (1998) and *Local Governance in Western Europe* (2001). Recently, he has been working in the area of citizenship in the UK, and is the co-author of *Re-Energizing Citizenship* (2006).

Simon Lee is Senior Lecturer in Politics at the Department of Politics and International Studies, University of Hull, England. His research interests are principally in the field of political economy, with special reference to national economic performance and the politics of England. His recent publications include *Best for Britain?: The Politics and Legacy of Gordon Brown* (Oxford: OneWorld, 2007); 'Gordon Brown and the British Way', (*The Political Quarterly*, 77, 3, 2006, 369–78); and (co-edited with Stephen McBride), *Neo-Liberalism, the State and Global Governance* (Dordrecht: Springer Kluwer, 2007).

Patrick Le Galés is Director of Research, CNRS at CEVIPOF (Centre de recherches Politiques de Sciences Po), and Professor of Public Policy and Sociology at Sciences Po, Paris. His main fields of research are comparative public policy (France, UK, Italy and Finland), governance, urban sociology and political economy/economic sociology. He currently works on the middle classes in European cities, the restructuring of the British state, corruption and governance in the Paris region and the instruments of public policy at the national and EU level. He is one of the co-ordinators of the 'Cities/metropolis/cosmopolis' research unit at Sciences Po Paris and the Research Training Network 'Urbeurope'. He has published a number of books, including *European Cities, Social Conflicts and Governance* (OUP), which won the Stein Rokkan Prize in 2002. He is a past editor of the *International Journal of Urban and Regional Research* and is currently a member of the editorial boards of the *British Journal of Political Science,* the *Socio-Economic Review* and the *Journal of Public Policy*.

Greg Lloyd is Professor of Planning in the Department of Civic Design at the University of Liverpool. He has served as an Adviser to the House of Commons in the Scottish Affairs Committee and the Tayside Economic Forum. He is currently a member of the Scottish Executive's National Planning Framework Advisory Group. His research interests include the relations between public policy, planning and real property developments and institutional innovation in spatial planning practices. His recent publications focus on the technocratic and demo-cratic aspects of modernisation of land use planning in Scotland.

Neil McGarvey is Lecturer in Politics in the Department of Government at the University of Strathclyde, Glasgow. His main research interests are Scottish politics, public administration and local government. He has published widely on these subjects in journals such as *Public Administration, British Journal of Politics and International Relations, Policy Studies, Public Money and Management, Public Policy and Management* and *Local Government Studies*. His new book (co-authored with Paul Cairney) on Scottish politics will be published by Palgrave in 2008.

Kevin Morgan is Professor of European Regional Development in the School of City and Regional Planning at Cardiff University. His research interests revolve around three themes: the theory, policy and practice of territorial development; political devolution and economic development; and sustainable food systems. His recent publications include *Worlds of Food: Place, Power and Provenance in the Food Chain* (OUP, 2006); *The School Food Revolution: Public Food and Sustainable Development* (Earthscan, 2008); and *The Polycentric State: New Spaces of Empowerment and Engagement?* (Regional Studies, 2007).

Steven Musson is Lecturer in Human Geography at the University of Reading. His research interests are in regional and local government in the United Kingdom with a particular focus on the geography of capital investment and organisational networks of regional governance. He has worked extensively on devolution and regional government in England, including two major ESRC funded projects on the evolution of regional identities in the South East of England and on the North-East referendum of November 2004. Findings from these projects have been published in *Environment and Planning A, New Political Economy* and *The Political Quarterly*.

Graham Pearce is Senior Lecturer in the Aston Business School. His main areas of research interest are regional planning, governance and policy evaluation. He has written widely on English regionalism and recently completed a project on are 'Emerging patterns of governance in the English regions', as part of the Economic and Social Research Council's Devolution and Constitutional Change Programme.

Deborah Peel is Lecturer in the Department of Civic Design at the University of Liverpool where she teaches planning and development at undergraduate and postgraduate levels. Deborah is active in the professional planning community. Her research interests span the modernisation of planning practices and the associated implications for skills, knowledge and learning. She has developed a particular research expertise in development management, new state-market dynamics in regeneration, the role of spatial planning in public policy, and marine spatial planning.

Peter Roberts is Professor of Sustainable Spatial Development at the Sustainability Research Institute at the University of Liverpool. He is also Chair of the Academy for Sustainable Communities, an agency of UK central government, and was appointed OBE for services to regeneration and planning. Peter also advises Addleshaw Goddard on planning, regeneration and environmental matters. He is active in a range of organisations including Urban Mines and is past Chair (now Vice-President) of the Town and Country Planning Association. He is also past Chair and Honorary Vice-Chair of the Regional Studies Association, Vice-President of the Council of Europe ISCOMET Group, Chair of the Best Practice Committee of the British Urban Regeneration Association, a member of the Scientific Committee on the Regions of Europe, Chair of the Planning Exchange Foundation and an adviser to the Local Government Association. His research has been supported by research councils and foundations, and by a wide range of UK, European and regional governments, partnerships and local authorities on matters related to governance, planning, regeneration and the spatial dimension of environmental management and sustainable development.

Adam Tickell is Dean of the Faculty of History and Social Sciences at Royal Holloway College, University of London. He has completed research on the recent attempts to devolve power to the English regions, relating both to region-building in the South-East region and the referendum in the North East of England. Findings have been published in *Regional Studies, New Political Economy, Environment and Planning A* and *Local Economy*. His current research explores the ways in which free market ideas became the 'common sense' during the 1970s and 1980s, subsequent changes in political economy, and the role of contemporary conservative think tanks and advocacy groups, particularly in the US. The book of the project will be published by Oxford University Press.

Rick Wilford is Professor in Politics at Queen's University, Belfast. Since 1999 he has been the joint co-ordinator of the team, funded by the ESRC, Leverhulme (until 2005) and several Government Departments, established to monitor devolution in Northern Ireland under the aegis of the Constitution Unit at University College London. He has written extensively on devolution and politics in Northern Ireland, including his edited collection *Aspects of the Belfast Agreement* (OUP, 2001), annual chapters in the *State of the Nations* series (2000-) and articles in *Government and Opposition*, *Regional and Federal Studies* and *Representation*. His most recent publications include 'Inside Stormont: The Assembly and the Executive' in P. Carmichael *et al.* (eds), *Devolution and Constitutional Change in Northern Ireland* (MUP, 2007) and *Power to the People?: Assessing Democracy in Northern Ireland* (TASC New Island, 2007). He is a regular commentator on politics in Northern Ireland for the regional, national and international media.

Preface and acknowledgements

Ten years ago I co-edited a book for Jessica Kingsley publishers (later Taylor & Francis) called *British Regionalism and Devolution: The Challenges of State Reform and European Integration*. The book was a record of developments and debates during the years of the Thatcher and Major Governments. Devolution and regionalism were then largely opposed by government policy, but they formed key parts of an alternative agenda by which it was argued the UK might re-settle its identity politics, modernise its system of government and improve public policy. In 1997 a Labour Government was elected under Tony Blair, which duly introduced devolution in Scotland, Wales and Northern Ireland, reformed English regional governance and applied new regional development strategies across the UK. This book returns ten years on at the end of the Blair Governments to assess the development of these reforms and their implications for the UK's stateless nations and regions.

The organising principle in this volume, as with its predecessor, is to provide a multi-disciplinary approach. It is to be expected that political scientists, geographers and specialists in regional planning and policy might focus on related issues; equally it might be expected that they rarely combine their efforts. The book seeks to bring together the fruits of their research in a manner that is hopefully complementary and accessible. The volume also aims to capture the main features of the UK experience for purposes of comparative analysis. This most frequently means comparison within the experience of European regionalism. But the interest in state regional capacity is international. It is also ten years since I formed part of a team led by Dr Suranjit Saha that delivered papers on state change and regional planning at a conference of academics and policy-makers in Recife, Brazil. I realised then that a book-length study on these issues in the UK would be a useful addition to the international literature; hopefully, this book goes some of the way to achieving that aim.

The book brings together a wide range of leading researchers on their respective topics. I thank all of them for their commitment and assistance in bringing the book to fruition. I also thank Professor John Mawson for his assistance in commissioning three of the chapters, and Professor Ron Martin, series editor, for his comments on the book at various stages of completion. The publishers add their acknowledgement to Oxford University Press for permission to re-print Kevin Morgan, 'Devolution and development: territorial justice and the North–South divide', *Publius, the Journal of Federalism*, 36, 1, 2006, 189–206.

Jonathan Bradbury
Swansea and Cardiff, June 2007

1 Introduction

Jonathan Bradbury

To study the changing fortunes of regional politics and policy in the UK is to take a case of apparently significant contradictions. On the one hand the United Kingdom of Great Britain and Northern Ireland, with a population of over 55 million, an economy among the top ten in the world and an imperial past that still gives it a global reach, may initially appear a highly stable consolidated state. On the other hand, the UK incorporates a territorial complexity that should be obvious from its title. The UK is a composite state made up of a union of England, the biggest nation by territory and population, with three other nations/regions: Wales (since 1536), Scotland (since 1707) and Northern Ireland (since 1921, previously Ireland 1800–1921). Prior to 1997 this territorial dimension was accommodated for by a variety of constitutional, political and administrative arrangements. There had been a phase of political devolution only in Northern Ireland, when an elected assembly sat between 1921 and 1972. Between 1997 and 1999, however, following proposals made by the Labour Government, led by Tony Blair, referenda votes led to a transformation of political representation and government across the UK. Scotland was granted a devolved Parliament with primary legislative and tax varying powers; Wales a devolved assembly with secondary legislative powers; and Northern Ireland new legislative and executive structures based on a devolved assembly. In England, a directly elected mayor and authority were introduced for Greater London, and in all nine English regions development agencies were established. In each region these were to work in conjunction with central government offices of the regions, as well as regional chambers (later assemblies), representing the regional stakeholders.

Consequently, while regional politics and policy has always been a significant dimension of the UK, recent changes have been of profound importance in accentuating that fact. This book seeks to chart and explain the implications of these recent developments. It starts from the initial proposition that analysis is best explored by addressing three conceptual foci which are often taken as interchangeable but in fact refer to related but different phenomena, namely devolution, regionalism and regional development. First, devolution is an explicitly constitutional act, which involves 'the transfer to a subordinate elected body, on a geographical basis, of functions at present exercised by ministers and Parliament' (Bogdanor 1999: 2). The hallmark of devolution is legislative decentralisation, be it of primary legislative powers or of secondary powers. In the latter case primary powers remain with Parliament but the powers to make secondary laws through statutory instruments and orders are devolved.

Regionalism, in contrast, is a governmental process involving the 'formulation of public policy for, and the administration of policy in, large territorial units consisting usually of a numbering of neighbouring counties defined by geographical, sociological, administrative and political criteria' (Smith 1964: 2). Such governmental capacity may involve the development of an elected tier of government but not necessarily so. Even if it does, it will not compromise the legislative powers of central government. It is simply an executive capacity. Thirdly, closely associated with such developments, whether of devolved institutions with legislative powers or regional institutions with executive powers, is consideration of how such developments allow for 'the spatial co-ordination of many different policies' (Hall 1989: 8) at a level between the local and the state levels. Recent debates have seen narrow economic conceptions of regional co-ordination replaced by more holistic concerns with regional development, where sustainable economic development is considered in terms of wider social and environmental regional agendas (Townroe and Martin 1992). Both devolution and regionalism can be considered for their impact on regional development strategies.

The institutional changes wrought in the UK between 1997 and 1999 clearly introduced devolution to Scotland, Wales and Northern Ireland, albeit on different bases. They also consolidated governmental regionalism in England, with a new elected body being introduced for London, and political debates about the journey for the other English regions. Equally, the changes provided new potential for the spatial co-ordination of public policies at the regional level across the UK. For analysts of devolution, regionalism and regional development the study of the UK became of particular interest. The implications of these reforms for politics, governance and public policy in the nations/regions of the UK by the end of the Blair governments in 2007 provide the subject of this book.

As a prelude to substantive discussion this chapter has five principal aims. First, it will seek to explain the origins of the United Kingdom as a territorial state and the place of the nations/regions in it. Second, it will explain the pressures that led during the late twentieth century to new regional approaches, and in turn the implications of Thatcherism, the key state reform project of the late twentieth century. An analysis of both of these issues is essential to an understanding of contemporary developments. Third, the chapter will address how the 1997–1999 reforms introduced devolution and regionalism, and how the 1990s more broadly saw the development of new paradigms in regional development. Fourth, it will consider a number of key contexts affecting the operation of devolution, regionalism and regional development up to 2007. Finally, the chapter will explain the rationale of the book. There is a concern to understand the implications of the 1997–1999 reforms for overall regional capacity in the UK, which in turn raises key questions that contributors will address in framing their analyses.

Nations, regions and origins of a United Kingdom

The United Kingdom first emerged as a unified state in 1800, originally as Great Britain and Ireland. The *raison d'être* for the state rested initially on history and geography.

Waves of Roman, Anglo-Saxon and Norman invasion from the mainland continent of Europe had established the English as the dominant people with the indigenous Celtic Welsh, Scots and Irish thrown back into the peripheral areas of the British Isles archipelago. The Welsh never successfully created their own independent kingdom, leading to a process of incorporation by English monarchs over several centuries. The sixteenth century acts of union were the consolidation of a reality that had pertained for some time. The Scottish, however, did establish their own independent kingdom, leading to tensions between the English and the Scots for much of the early modern period. Ultimately, English views rested on strategic concerns about Scotland's relations with potential enemies from mainland Europe; Scotland in turn always felt vulnerable against its overwhelming neighbour to the South. The chance fusion of the English and Scottish Monarchies paved the way for a full act of union in 1707, negotiated between the respective political elites. Similar strategic concerns fuelled English interests in controlling Ireland, although here religious differences between predominantly Protestant Britain and Catholic Ireland, and British interests in land settlement, also played a key part. The 1800 Act of Union reflected the ultimately decisive influence of British security fears and the desire for political stability (for a range of perspectives see Colley 1992; Davies 1999; Bulpitt 1983).

The results of this English imperialism were not, however, a simple coercive English-centric state. Multiple sources of grievance notwithstanding, a number of scholars contend that the UK developed constitutionally in a manner consistent with the union state model (Mitchell 2004; Mclean and McMillan 2005). It is important to recognise that such a conception still recognises that 'administrative standardisation prevails over most of the territory'; simply that 'the consequences of personal union entail the survival in some areas of pre-union rights and institutional infrastructures which preserve some degree of regional autonomy and serve as agencies of indigenous elite recruitment' (Rokkan and Urwin 1982: 11). Consequently, until the late twentieth century, the UK was predominantly governed as a unitary state. This rested on the central principle of the sovereignty of the UK Parliament at Westminster with sole right to make legislation and enact taxation. The development of the franchise and popular politics led to a party system that in the main was British-wide. The Liberal–Conservative dominated system before 1914 and the Labour–Conservative dominated one after 1945 both spanned Scotland and Wales as well as England. There was a unified civil service based in Whitehall. Experience of relative economic success and Empire in the nineteenth and early twentieth centuries cemented London and the South East of England as the financial and economic power house of the state, not to mention its principal cultural centre. Equally, it consolidated presumptions of Westminster as the principal locus of power to which aspiring politicians from all parts of the UK would descend.

Nevertheless, the politics of union encompassed quite distinct territorial issues and political differentiation (for more detailed summaries see McGarry and O'Leary, 1997; Griffiths 1996; Brown *et al.* 1998). Throughout this period, territorial politics in the United Kingdom was deeply troubled by the Irish Question. During the nineteenth century a movement for Irish national autonomy emerged, and after three efforts at home rule within the context of the UK, the 1920 Government of Ireland Act effectively divided Ireland. This established a process that gradually led to the South, with an overwhelming Catholic majority, forming its own state as the Republic of Ireland. Meanwhile, a rump Northern Ireland, with a majority of pro-union Protestants, remained in the UK albeit with a devolved Parliament. The Stormont Parliament lasted until 1972, presided over by a succession of Protestant unionist leaders, dependent upon UK finance but governing in a manner largely free of UK central government control. While it engendered fierce support from the unionist community, the Stormont Parliament was deeply opposed by Catholic, nationalist and republican minorities. The institutions of Protestant unionism and nationalist republicanism marked out the distinctiveness of the political-cultural life of Northern Ireland. Orange orders harked back to William of Orange, the Protestant pretender who took the British throne in 1688, and asserted the Protestant ascendancy in Ireland with victory at the Battle of the Boyne in 1690. Catholic nationalists identified with the Republic of Ireland's constitutional claim on Northern Ireland. Schools and community associations were organised by this religious-political division, and each summer there was a marching season during which the Protestant–Catholic battles of the late seventeenth century were commemorated. A distinctive party system also emerged, ranged between Protestant unionist parties, by the 1970s led by the Ulster Unionist Party and the Democratic Unionist Party, and nationalist republican parties, principally the Social Democratic Labour Party and Sinn Féin.

Northern Ireland may have been particularly distinctive, but during the nineteenth and twentieth centuries the territorial dimension of the UK remained apparent in four other key ways. First, the saliency of national or regional identity was reflected in distinctive civil institutions. By the 1707 Act of Union Scotland sustained its own established Church of Scotland, its own system of education and its own system of civil law. Wales sustained a separate language distinct from the English spoken throughout the British Isles. By the late twentieth century surveys indicated that approximately 20 per cent continued to speak the language with areas of West and North Wales having it as a working language. The introduction of a Welsh language television station – S4C – the growth of Welsh language radio media and the requirement from 1988 that all school pupils take Welsh up to the age of 14 cemented the language in modern Welsh culture.

Second, differences in national culture stimulated differences in national politics. During the twentieth century the Scottish and the Welsh increasingly came to distinguish themselves by their support for social collectivism or national autonomy in contrast to the individualistic values attributed to the English. As a result, the Labour Party through most of the twentieth century enjoyed a clear advantage over both the Conservative and Liberal/Liberal Democrat parties. This contrasted sharply with party fortunes in England, where, with the exception of certain landmark elections like 1945, the Conservative Party was dominant. Scotland and Wales also saw the rise of nationalist parties – the Scottish National Party and Plaid Cymru (Party of Wales) – to take parliamentary seats in the 1960s. In Scotland the SNP, which campaigned clearly for independence, regularly polled around 20 per cent of the vote.

Third, the saliency of territorial politics was reflected in notions of economic territory. During the post-Second World War era, when ideas of state responsibility for the management of the economy became orthodox, notions of the Scottish, Welsh and Northern Irish economies as distinct entities emerged. They became 'standard regions' for the UK, used as a basis for the collection of statistical data, and considered in aggregate terms when planning economic policy. There were also ramifications from British relative economic decline when confidence in the British state to deliver high levels of employment began to diminish. Campaigns emerged in Scotland to argue that North Sea oil was 'Scotland's oil' rather than Britain's. In Wales, activities of English corporations to use Wales as source of water supply had a similar, if somewhat more limited, effect in encouraging a sense of national economic self-consciousness. The notion of Scotland, Wales and Northern Ireland as economic territories led to the creation of development agencies during the 1970s. Subsequently, their general brief to promote economic development, combined with the efforts of other 'national' lobbies such as the Scottish or Welsh tourist industry, consolidated the economic institutionalisation of the UK's nations and regions.

Fourth, territory also *came* to define public policy institutions. This occurred in an overtly political sense in a number of ways. UK Government developed the modern principle of the territorial department of state. From 1885 UK Government decided to organise the services of many central departments of state as they applied to Scotland from a new central department called the Scottish Office. A minister of government was put in charge, who conventionally was a Scottish MP, and from the 1920s he/she was given Cabinet rank. The Scottish Office had both London and Edinburgh headquarters and whilst entirely being part of the UK central system of government came to be a focus for the debate of Scottish public affairs. The principle was subsequently applied in Wales with the creation of the Welsh Office in 1964, and was forced upon UK Government in the case of Northern Ireland when devolution had to be abandoned in 1972 to be replaced by UK direct rule.

In each of these cases, debate of public policy focused around the policies promoted by the secretaries of state and the critiques of their political opponents. From the 1970s this principle of territorialising central government was exacerbated by the explicit territorialising of public expenditure allocation to these departments. Through the Barnett formula, the Scottish, Welsh and Northern Irish Offices received block grant allocations that were based on proportionate ratio calculations to English levels of expenditure. Generally, these allocations were judged to be generous in per capita terms in recognition of the special demands placed by identity politics on the politics of the UK.

Distinctive territorial institutional arrangements extended to forms of political organisation in the UK Parliament. Patterns of over-representation developed in the number of MPs relative to population for both Scotland and Wales relative to England. The Scottish and Welsh Grand Committees provided opportunities for general debates by MPs just from these countries, and the Scottish, Welsh and latterly the Northern Ireland select committees provided opportunities for the scrutiny of the relevant territorial departments. Special standing committees allowed Scottish MPs separate debate of Scottish civil law. Distinctive territorial arrangements also extended to the development of public policy institutions in the territories that were not overtly political. For example, Scotland and Wales amassed a number of 'national' cultural institutions such as 'national' libraries as well as distinctive national pressure groups. Scotland, Wales and Northern Ireland have long had their own sports teams in international competition. Scotland and Northern Ireland have distinctive pounds sterling notes. Each of these territories has its own distinctive national/regional media to comment on public affairs at a Scottish, Welsh or Northern Irish level. All of these institutions have developed for their own reasons, but nevertheless cumulatively have consolidated the idea of distinctive national or regional communities.

Although there were always dissident nationalist voices, especially in Northern Ireland, the United Kingdom for several decades after the First World War was a relatively settled entity. Some scholars stressed the integrative implications of the common experience of Empire and two world wars, and the relatively high levels of cultural, political and economic exchange between England, Scotland and Wales (Birch 1989; Garside and Hebbert 1989). Others stressed the continuing lack of strong ties that bind. Notably, Bulpitt argued that stability was the product of a dual polity in which central government and politics in the various territories of the UK generally operated in quite separate ways. In other words, the notion of a union state was a constitutional nicety; the reality was that the centre had more than enough to do, and simply allowed local collaborative elites the autonomy to govern on routine issues in these distinct parts of the state (Bulpitt 1983). Whichever was the case, in the mid twentieth century few inhabitants would have seriously questioned the territorial unity of the UK state. By the 1970s, however, a variety of movements had developed which questioned the very nature of the state.

Pressures for change and Thatcherism

The most dramatic changes occurred in Northern Ireland. Nationalist republican-ism grew stronger as criticism of the perceived abuses of unionist governments spawned a major civil rights movement. Paramilitary violence and growing civil disorder then led the UK Government to suspend the Stormont Parliament and impose direct rule in 1972. From this point onwards Northern Ireland was ruled as the rest of the UK from the centre, with the assistance of a territorial office of central government headed by a Cabinet minister.

Almost as soon as direct rule was established, debates developed about restoring devolved government in Northern Ireland, albeit this time on the basis of power sharing between the parties representing both the nationalist and unionist commu-nities. The Sunningdale agreement in 1973 provided for a power-sharing assembly accompanied by a Council for Ireland, which would also establish governmental co-operation between Northern Ireland and the Republic of Ireland. The arrange-ments did not last long, defeated by a Protestant workers' revolt against the idea of sharing power with nationalists. Direct UK rule was restored, accompanied again by unrelenting paramilitary action by the provisional Irish Republican Army (IRA) against unionist targets both in Northern Ireland and on the English 'Mainland', provoking in response violence by Protestant loyalist paramilitary groups. Such sectarian bitterness made the prospect of power-sharing devolution very unlikely, and by the time Mrs Thatcher, the most unionist of all Conservative leaders, was elected in 1979, direct rule and sectarian violence had became the norm in this bitterly divided and bloody part of the UK.

Campaigns for political change also emerged in Scotland and Wales, although it should be stressed that they were conducted almost exclusively on a peaceful and constitutional basis. Here there had been no devolution previously and the conventional view of British politicians had been that none was desirable. Political devolution potentially undermined the state by encouraging separatist nationalism. It was only to be accepted in Northern Ireland because political violence on such a scale undermined the state anyway. In the 1960s and 1970s, however, the popularity of the SNP reached new heights, specifically placing a pressure on one of the Labour Party's electoral heartlands, and generally placing considerable pressure on the political establishment. Plaid Cymru made less of an electoral breakthrough but nevertheless raised concerns that Welsh politics could become as divisive as that in Scotland. Following protracted debate, including the Kilbrandon Royal Commission, which advocated devolution in its final report in 1973, the 1974–1979 Labour Governments responded by legislating for devolution in both Scotland and Wales. It proved to be an enormously difficult issue in the Labour Party, dividing those who sympathised with national autonomy from those who valued central state power and its redistributive capacity more highly. Labour sceptics succeeded in gaining the crucial requirement that not only would public referenda be required, but that any 'yes' vote had to amount to more than 40 per cent of the registered electorate. The two referenda in 1979 returned a resounding 'no' in the Welsh case and a slim 'yes' majority in the Scottish case, but nevertheless not one that passed the 40 per cent rule. The fall of the Labour Government shortly after to be replaced by Mrs Thatcher's Conservatives meant that devolution was firmly off the agenda (Bogdanor 1999; Birch 1989).

In contrast to these dramatic territorial debates elsewhere in the UK, by the 1970s England as the largest country and the original host nation of the union did not exist overtly in any territorial political sense. English national identity as a political identity had largely been submerged in Britishness. The English economy was not a territorial unit that had any explicit meaning for policy planners. England was governed by field offices of UK central government departments. There was no English office, nor was there an English grand committee in the House of Commons. England only existed in the most routine of senses as the territory over which public bodies that had Scottish equivalents organised themselves; as the basis for sporting teams and cultural anthems. Politically, England did not exist as an idea distinct from Great Britain in the way that the other nations did. Partly as a result of this, while the English could look upon British institutions as benignly serving the needs of the whole state, Scottish, Welsh and Irish nationalism could envisage the UK state as one that was indelibly imprinted with English power.

The English phenomenon that was in any sense an aspect of territorial politics was instead English regionalism. This was expressed in regional consciousness in the North generally and the North East specifically, the South West and specifically in Cornish nationalism. The North of England was the strongest Labour voting part of England, and the South West during the last quarter of the twentieth century was a successful area for the Liberals/Liberal Democrats. This appeared to evoke a regional consciousness and party alignments that opposed the Conservative

Party as the perceived party of the Southern Home Counties. English regionalism also developed. From the 1960s public policy-makers worked with a notion of the standard regions of England for which economic data would be collected and economic performance judged. In the post-war period most domestic central government departments developed their own field administration based on the standard regions, though with varying administrative centres and sub-regional organisation (Hogwood and Keating 1982). Such developments did not, however, stimulate political movements for regional change. Overall, regional identity and politics remained relatively weak. As Harvie (1991) put it, English regionalism remained 'the dog that never barked'. During the devolution debates of the 1970s the question of what to do for England was actually put to one side. This was disastrous, as the resentments this aroused in Northern Labour MPs stimulated support for the blocking 40 per cent rule for devolution in Scotland.

Regional planning in the UK also received new impetus. In the immediate post-war period this had been limited to land use and infrastructure planning. It had its origins in inter-war legislation relating to the control of unregulated urbanisation and ribbon development, followed by the 1946 Town and Country Planning Act. Meanwhile other countries in this era, for example France, approached post-Second World War reconstruction with more all-embracing philosophies of indicative planning by which economic sectors and regional territories would be provided with targets on investment, production and consumption and planning instruments by which they could be achieved. In post-war Britain, where much was made of state nationalisation of key strategic industries, the state presided over a mixed economy where in fact only 20 per cent of the private sector went under public ownership. Despite appearances to the contrary, the market remained the principal vehicle for economic development; economic planning and its regional component remained a philosophy more discussed by advocates than one practised by government in the two decades after the war.

Finally, though, in the debate about the modernisation of the British economy from the late 1950s economic planning became a crucial component of progressive agendas for state-led economic renewal. The Wilson-led Labour Governments of the 1960s created a ministry for economic affairs and machinery for national economic planning. Given the importance of the territorial dimension to the UK, whether on the basis of identity politics in Scotland, Wales, Northern Ireland and parts of England, or more administratively driven policy considerations in most of England, regional development strategies emerged as a key new aspect of UK Government policy. During the 1960s regional economic planning councils were created as part of a national planning structure, based on the economic territories of Scotland, Wales, Northern Ireland and the English standard regions. This regional planning machinery remained in place throughout the 1970s and was accompanied by the development of the aforementioned development agencies in Scotland and Wales. Overall, UK regional economic expenditure was the highest in Europe by the mid 1970s.

Nevertheless, regional planning initiatives fell victim first to the mid-1970's economic crisis and then also to the change of government in 1979. UK regional expenditure collapsed between 1976 and 1979 and thereafter Margaret Thatcher's brand of Conservatism favoured the strictures of the market as a mechanism for economic recovery over state-led change. Regional economic planning councils were abolished. The only survivors were the Welsh and Scottish development agencies; both, however, were re-oriented towards free market policies with the latter being explicitly re-titled Scottish Enterprise. In England the regional field administration of central government departments that remained followed similar supply side approaches. The city challenge policy, by which local authorities were required to compete for limited public funds for regeneration projects, was typical of the state's limited and market oriented approach towards economic development up until 1997 (see Smith 1964; Hall 1989).

After such pressures towards devolution, regionalism and active regional development strategies, the long era of Conservative Government 1979–1997 pioneered a very different kind of state reform. It was marked by its combination of political conservatism and economic liberalism, both of which were entirely antithetical to devolution and regionalism (Gamble 1988). Adherence to the traditional institutions of the state meant that devolutionist aspirations for political change were given short shrift. The only differences really lay between Thatcher's confrontational attempts to persuade the British periphery to her way of thinking, and the attempts by John Major, her successor, to combine the underlying uniformity of reform agendas across the state with more mollifying styles in how they were presented. Devolution and governmental regionalism were also seen as all the worse for their potential relationship to European integration. Conservative Eurosceptics observed sub-state regionalisation to be an integral part of the pincer movement of European supra-nationalists that would seek to undermine the integrity of the UK from below as well as from above.

Adherence to economic liberalism meanwhile ensured a consistent stress on policies that left the level of unemployment to the market and sought to control inflation as the route to stable economic growth. Where possible, levels of public spending or the rate at which departmental budgets rose were to be cut. Large parts of the economy that had come under public ownership since 1945 were privatised, and attempts to stimulate the market were focused on deregulating state controls over land, labour and capital. Entrepreneurship was elevated to the status of an intrinsic social good. Reforms of the welfare state where possible were directed at reducing public dependency on state provision, with the sale of public built council houses to their owners underpinning the most significant reduction in state welfare responsibility. In this wind of change there was no place for regional economic planning, damned as inherently statist and oriented towards discredited forms of demand management.

Devolution, regionalism and regional development in the 1990s

The 1990s, however, marked a watershed in the significance of devolution, regionalism and regional development in the UK. A number of new pressures emerged: the stresses of global and European economic change on regional economies;

developments in civil society notably in Scotland; an emerging order of multi-level governance; institutional thickness at the Scottish and Welsh levels; and anti-Conservative electoral opinion. In Scotland and Wales nationalist opinion revived, and campaigns for devolution re-emerged. There were also critiques of Conservative policies that highlighted the considerable disparities of wealth and had territorial expression in a perceived North–South divide (Amin and Thrift 1994; Bradbury and Mawson 1997; Bache and Flinders 2004). During its long years in opposition the Labour Party became firm adherents to the principle of political devolution in Scotland and Wales. On the back of this Labour came into office in 1997 under Tony Blair pledged to a manifesto of sweeping territorial reform. It was made a priority with referenda bills passed in the first weeks of office and referenda successfully held in September 1997. The Scottish vote produced a 74.3 per cent yes vote for a Parliament, with 63.5 per cent also supporting tax-varying powers, on a 60.4 per cent turnout. Meanwhile, the Welsh vote for an Assembly only just succeeded, with 50.3 per cent voting yes on a 50.1 per cent turnout.

Long-standing campaigns for constitutional change in Scotland and Wales had realised their aims, with the new institutions holding their first elections and forming their first devolved governments in May 1999. The devolution settlements varied (see Bogdanor 1999 for more detailed summaries). In Scotland, a Parliament was introduced. It was made up of 129 members, elected by a mixed member proportional (MMP) electoral system, in which there were 73 single member constituency seats and 56 regional list seats. The latter were elected as top-up members in eight seven-member regions on the basis of the d'Hondt formula to make the overall result more proportional. The Parliament was given a general right to make primary legislation outside of certain prescribed areas that were reserved to the UK Parliament. These reserved areas included constitutional issues, foreign and defence policy, macro-economic policy, social security and sundry other matters. The scope across domestic issues for the Parliament was, however, considerable, including large areas of the welfare state – health and education, economic development, the control of local government, and agriculture, fisheries and land policy. The Parliament was to be funded by block grant allocated by Westminster, but there was also a power to vary income tax in Scotland by plus or minus 3p in the £. Theoretically, Westminster remained sovereign and there continued to be a post of secretary of state for Scotland, but in practice the Parliament was expected to have significant legitimacy as an autonomous law-making institution within the parameters of the UK state.

Wales received a rather different devolution settlement. It was provided with an assembly rather than a Parliament. This was composed of 60 members, 40 of which were elected from single-member constituencies and 20 from five four-member regional lists, again elected as top-up members on the d'Hondt formula. It was given no primary legislative powers, which remained at Westminster. Rather, it was given secondary legislative powers in those areas in which the secretary of state for Wales had previously had executive responsibility. These covered similar areas to the Scottish Parliament, including health care, education, housing and regeneration, economic development, rural affairs and arts and culture; but powers in these areas were defined by Westminster statute and there was no general power of legislative initiation. Simply, the decisions which had previously been taken by Welsh Office ministers with no direct accountability to debate within a Welsh forum were now opened up to development within the assembly. The assembly was also funded by block grant from Westminster, but unlike the Scottish Parliament had no potential tax-varying power. The Welsh Assembly much more obviously was to operate constitutionally as a junior partner to Westminster, and yet there was considerable potential discretion in secondary legislative and executive powers.

In Northern Ireland, there was a yet further different form of devolution introduced (see Wilford 2001). The inspiration for reform should be laid partly with the response of John Major's Conservative administrations, 1990–1997, to new moves in republican thinking. From the late 1980s a series of developments led to a new inclination among the Irish nationalist parties to collectively engage in a process that might lead to a cessation of paramilitary hostilities and agreement on a settlement on power-sharing government. The Downing Street Declaration, signed jointly by the UK and Irish Governments in 1993, declared the willingness of both states to set aside their selfish interests in Northern Ireland and to negotiate a peace and constitutional settlement that respected primarily the consent of the people of Northern Ireland themselves. On this basis and with IRA and loyalist paramilitary ceasefires in place from 1994, the unionist parties under promises of a more acceptable power-sharing settlement than that provided at Sunningdale, were reluctantly brought to the negotiating table. By 1997, however, the peace and constitutional talks process were in disarray as Major's Government had failed to broker agreements, and in the light of its parlous parliamentary position was seen as too close to the unionist MPs on whose votes it was thought to rely all too often. The potential for a revived peace process and a power-sharing devolution settlement was nevertheless still substantial, and a challenge that Blair, with a huge Parliamentary majority, was willing and able to address.

When Blair took office in 1997 the revival of the peace process and resumption of political talks were made priorities. With co-operation between the UK and Irish Governments and with the strong support of the Clinton administration in the USA, including promises of large financial investment, remarkable progress was made. By April 1998 agreement was achieved between all of the parties in Northern Ireland on a new form of political power sharing, with the exception of the Democratic Unionist Party who nevertheless agreed later to participate in the new institutions. The Belfast (or 'Good Friday') Agreement provided three strands to a new constitutional settlement. Strand one involved the establishment of a power-sharing assembly. It was made up of 108 members, elected under the single transferable vote electoral system. Its members, once elected, had to declare themselves to be unionist, nationalist, or non-aligned. Ministerial positions within the executive were then allocated to parties using the d'Hondt method, to produce a multi-party unionist-nationalist power-sharing executive. Decision-making within the executive required cross-party agreement, and votes within the assembly required either a weighted majority or parallel consent of the blocks of unionist and nationalist members to agree decisions. The assembly was at the heart of defining the new devolved Northern Ireland as not a majoritarian form of democracy, but a consociational one in which the divisions in the community were recognised and a mutual community veto was built intrinsically into the very existence of the assembly and any decisions it might pass. The powers of the assembly included primary legislative powers in a variety of domestic issues, which mirrored those at the heart of Scottish devolution, but these crucially did not include policing and security, and the assembly was given no fiscal powers. Given the political divisions, it was expected that the focus of the assembly would be on what executive decision making could be agreed over the expenditure of the block grant provided from Westminster. In this sense its practical capacity for decision making was more comparable to the Welsh Assembly than the Scottish Parliament, compromised even further by the requirements of and contexts to power sharing.

The second strand to the Belfast agreement provided for a North–South ministerial council in which representatives of the Irish Government and of the new Northern Ireland Assembly met for joint deliberation of issues of cross-border interest. The Agreement specified a minimum of 12 areas for such co-operation, including such matters as transport links, agricultural issues and European Union structural funds policy. The politics of the North–South link lay in providing the nationalist parties with an institutional expression of the potential for pan-Irish policy-making, within which lay the possible dynamics for developing towards the re-unification of Ireland. Unionist politicians had sought to limit the areas for cross-border deliberation by the ministerial council while nationalists had sought to expand them. The result was an uneasy compromise. At the same time to balance the North–South link in the eyes of unionists, the agreement included a third strand, the creation of the British–Irish Council, in which representatives of the UK and Irish Governments as well as of all the devolved institutions within the UK and crown dependencies would meet to discuss issues of common interests. Symbolically, this institutionalised the East–West links of Northern Ireland within the broad scope of the British Isles. Overall, the Belfast Agreement provided for a unity in the operation of all three strands. If any one of the institutions collapsed then so too did the others (see Bogdanor 1999).

In practice, while the Scottish Parliament and Welsh Assembly began their lives smoothly in 1999, the Northern Ireland Assembly and associated institutions developed in much more problematic ways. The first elections were held soon after the Belfast Agreement in 1998 but the power-sharing executive could not be finally agreed until late 1999. Even then devolution lasted only fleetingly into 2000 and while it was re-established later in 2000 there was a further suspension following the 2001 General Election. After an attempt at reconvening the assembly there was a further suspension in October 2002, which endured until 2006–2007. In short, devolution in Northern Ireland was suspended for longer periods than it existed. Indeed, following the elections in 2003 which delivered the anti-agreement DUP as the principal unionist party, and Sinn Féin, the party with close links with the provisional IRA, as the largest nationalist party, there appeared few hopes of future success. The DUP demanded the irrevocable and demonstrable giving up of arms by the IRA and Sinn Féin's support for the rule of law, while Sinn Féin refused to countenance anything that looked like the surrender of republican interests or values. However, long negotiations during 2004 to revive power-sharing devolution appeared to get tantalisingly close to a deal. Eventually, in 2006 the UK and Irish

Governments held make-or-break talks with party leaders at St Andrews in Scotland, which made the breakthrough. Following further elections a power-sharing executive, led by the DUP and Sinn Féin, was re-established in May 2007, and devolution of powers to devolved government in Northern Ireland was re-commenced. This gave great hopes of a new stability, although few were under any illusion of the paucity of trust between unionist and nationalist political parties that had historically represented the most uncompromising of opinions within their respective communities.

Such historic changes and controversies left developments in England again somewhat overshadowed. Nevertheless, England remained the largest part of the UK and here too regional politics and policy were on the move (Hazell 2006). The perceived North–South divide inspired some institutions in the north to seek to fill the vacuum left by a missing regional policy. There was also a desire to overcome the atomisation of local government experienced under Mrs Thatcher's governments. This included the abolition of the largest upper tier metropolitan county councils and the introduction of market-driven reforms to reduce the scope of local government and make it leaner and fitter. From the late 1980s there was a trend of local authorities creating regional associations to conduct joint lobbying over such matters as land use and transport planning as well as for grant aid and networking in the European Union. This joint regional working established a bottom-up pressure which highlighted the saliency of the regions as a tier of governance in England by the mid 1990s. At the same time, during the Major Governments there was a renewed interest in central policy co-ordination that expanded to the regional level. In 1994 the regional offices of a number of central departments were integrated into ten government offices of the regions, presided over by a senior civil servant and with a brief to bring co-ordination to the English regions. This created simultaneously a top-down executive regionalism along boundaries that closely resembled those of the regional local authority associations.

Labour's deliberations in opposition on how to develop the English regional agenda were now couched in a general sympathy with devolution and regionalism. Labour produced three policies. First, Labour was committed to the creation of new English Regional Development Agencies. These were introduced in 1998. Second, Labour developed a policy for the piecemeal democratisation of regional governance. This involved in the first instance the re-creation of an elected authority for Greater London with an elected Mayor to hold executive authority, and the creation of indirectly elected regional chambers across the rest of the English regions, made up of all the regional stakeholders including appointees from local authorities, and the business and voluntary sectors. The reform of London government was supported in a referendum and the first elections for an elected mayor and members of the Greater London Authority were held in 2000. The powers of the Mayor and GLA were not in any sense legislative, either primary or secondary, but executive. Nevertheless, within the constraints imposed by legislation and ministerial decisions, they still covered the power to create strategic policy across a wide range of issues including economic development, transport infrastructure and housing. The regional chambers were established in 1998 and formed the third and weakest part of a structure of regional governance in the rest of the country in which in each region the government offices and centrally funded Regional Development Agencies were the dominant bodies.

Labour's third policy, nevertheless, was to provide for the possibility of fully democratising regional governance across the rest of England if supported by the stakeholders and public opinion. This paved the way for possible elected regional assemblies in England on demand. In practice, such demand was not present throughout the first Blair Government and even after the case was finally put in a referendum in the North East of England in 2004 it was firmly rejected. Ultimately, the English regions did not experience the democratic reform seen in Scotland, Wales and Northern Ireland. Nevertheless, developments in regional governance were still significant.

Overall, devolution and regionalism developed asymmetrically across the UK in the late 1990s. There were three different devolution settlements for Scotland, Wales and Northern Ireland. England was characterised by the development of more instrumental regional governance, the form of which was also likely to differ between the regions of England as the precise roles and relationships developed by the government offices, Regional Development Agencies and regional chambers were open to variation. They all also had to confront a potential major sea change in ideas about regional development policy. During the 1990s there was strong support for revised approaches to regional economic development. These drew strength from regional development strategies successfully pursued in other European countries, which appeared to emphasise the importance of linking economic development instruments that largely emphasised supply side control with the development of social capital, environmental sustainability and institutional trust in successful restructuring. This maintained a focus on the notion that regional development policy should focus on a regional economic dividend, but potentially broadened the issues seen as important to providing a sustainable dividend over time (Cooke and Morgan 1998; Tewdwr-Jones and Allmendinger 2006). Labour's Commission on regional policy, chaired by former EU commissioner, Bruce Millan, attempted to harness some of this new thinking in the proposals for new Regional Development Agencies across England once Labour got to power, but disciples of the new regional development sought to influence the policies of the devolved institutions as well.

Contemporary contexts to regional politics and policy

The question was how did the new institutions of devolution and regionalism, and new strategies for regional development develop? (For analyses of aspects of these issues formulated on different bases see also Jeffery and Wincott 2006; Trench, 2004a). In assessing this we need to be mindful of a number of potentially major influences. These can be summarised under four headings. First, there was a common and highly influential domestic environment of state reform started under the Thatcher Governments and continued in revised ways by the Major and Blair Governments. From the 1980s the economy was significantly liberalised. This created a situation in which capital markets were deregulated and personal credit extended, the power of trade unions was significantly diminished and labour markets made more flexible, and the planning of land development compromised by free market policies. In the wake of the perceived failure of both Keynesianism and monetarism, prevailing political economy simply prioritised relatively low taxation, a budgetary approach based on fiscal and monetary prudence and supply side policies to enable economic factors of production.

In this approach the state privatised many previously publicly owned industries and sought partnerships with the private sector rather than direct control. This retrenchment of the state was also felt in welfare policy, where state housing provided through local government was significantly curtailed following right-to-buy schemes for council house tenants. There were also innovations to involve the private sector in education and health policy through direct finance schemes, competitive tendering, internal markets, and transfers of private sector personnel or private sector management techniques. This was combined with a greater readiness to control public expenditure and intervene where education and health bodies were perceived to be failing to meet performance targets. Such approaches, while reducing the scale of the North–South divide, still nevertheless sustained the broad relative economic positions.

The Conservative Governments of Thatcher and Major were led by the objectives of reviving the economy, re-inspiring the entrepreneurial spirit and reducing welfare dependency. The Labour Governments after 1997 brought a revised focus in welfare policy on the eradication of poverty and aspirations for equality of opportunity, but 'New Labour' principles were broadly in agreement with the modernisation objectives of modern Conservatism (see Heffernan 2000). They were also not at all shy of using instruments of neo-liberal political economy, the private sector or command and control strategies of target-setting in realising revised social democratic aims. Equally, despite having previously criticised the Conservative Governments, Labour also extensively used quangos, throwing up dilemmas between the demands of centrally led government and democratic accountability. On the issue of regional economic development Labour came to power sceptical of strongly interventionist area-based policies, based on demand management. Expectations of the power of the region to guide its own future were scaled down and policy was focused on enhancing supply side capacity. This created an environment for devolved and regional institutions in which there were fears of a contradiction between the spirit of political decentralisation and the encouragement of new holistic policy strategies at the sub-state level on the one hand and the strong UK central lead on what the role of the state should be on the other. In England, in particular, there were expectations that the Labour Government would use regional governance as simply improved mechanisms for policy delivery out from the centre through the regions to local authority area and public service agreements. Such central leadership was a double-edged sword. It created a highly dynamic atmosphere of state change, which was potentially helpful but it also potentially provided significant constraints on developing innovation and divergence from UK norms.

Second, there was a highly influential external environment from which also came both opportunities and threats. The European Union loomed large in several ways (see Jones and Keating 1995). It had established a new European economic space, to which there was a need for sub-UK regional and local responses to the challenges it posed. The EU was also a significant political context in which debates about the powers and capacity of devolved and regional institutions could be developed. EU structural funds were of major significance to the development of multi-level governance in all parts of the UK and specifically significant to regional development policy. However, such influences were not clear-cut in their implications, as the EU was as much a potential controller of regional strategies as it was a facilitator of locally set aims. At the same time, and on a broader scale, globalisation of the world economy involved penetration of regional as much as national markets. This required economic restructuring of labour, capital and land markets, and new approaches to the management of state relations with large, multi-national and foreign firms as well as encouragement of indigenous industry and commerce. Such phenomena posed considerable threats to long-standing sources of strength in regional economies but at the same time possible opportunities for seeking and attaining new forms of competitive advantage. The creation of new political institutions to make the nations and regions of the UK more flexible to meet these challenges was supposed to be one of their biggest justifications.

Third, in responding to these state-wide and external environments there were further influences suggesting continuity with British norms. The results of both the first and second elections to the Scottish Parliament and Welsh Assembly in 1999 and 2003 confirmed the Labour Party as the largest party in both institutions. Labour in Scotland governed in coalition with the Liberal Democrats, and in Wales as a minority government (1999–2000), as the largest party in coalition with the Liberal Democrats (2000–2003) and as a majority government (from 2003). Given that Labour were in power at the UK level throughout this period and thus determined central policy for all of the English regions as well, the early adaptation to devolution and regionalism in party political terms was largely influenced by the Labour Party. At the same time the public officials who served the politicians in Scotland, Wales and England remained part of a unified UK home civil service, servants of their distinct political masters but schooled in common ethics and part of a service-wide career structure.

There were also a number of mechanisms that structured developments in accord with centrally led or managed approaches. The mechanism for block grant funding was still determined on the basis of the Barnett formula, an automatic accounting mechanism that determined funding in the other parts of the UK on a ratio formula relative to centrally defined spending per capita in England. The political and legal recourses to the settlement of disputes were also not independent from central government: the concordats by which public officials routinely related to each other between the devolved and regional institutions and central government were drawn up by central government; the joint ministerial council for clearing up disputes was chaired by a UK Cabinet minister; and the final court of appeal over disputes was a committee of the privy council, an 'efficient' adjunct of the largely symbolic machinery of the UK crown. Northern Ireland, with its own party system and formally its own civil service stood out from this pattern but it was behaviourally highly influenced by UK norms and was subject to the same financial, intergovernmental and legal structures.

Last but not least, however, there was still considerable potential for the regional determination of new approaches to politics, governance and public policy. The devolution settlements gave considerable scope for autonomy. This was obvious in the case of the Scottish Parliament's primary legislative powers but much real autonomy also lay in the Welsh Assembly's secondary powers to implement broadly phrased primary legislation. The potential was there in the Northern Ireland settlement if agreement could be reached to not only sustain power-sharing devolution but also agree on strategies for government. Even in the case of English regionalism, the operational powers of government offices and Regional Development Agencies, as well as the relationships between them and regional chambers made for potential autonomy to shape governance and public policy to fresh regional priorities.

At the same time devolution came with a number of institutional innovations, not least of which was electoral reform: MMP systems in Scotland and Wales and use of the single transferable vote in Northern Ireland. Innovation in electoral systems encouraged innovation in party approaches both to the electorate and to each other, for example in the need for coalition or at the very least inter-party co-operation. In the period 1999–2007, the Labour-led administrations in Scotland and Wales both had the potential to depart from UK Labour approaches, and to work with other parties, notably the Liberal Democrats, and in Wales on certain occasions with Plaid Cymru. Following the 2007 elections, the potential for different approaches was given an even greater impetus. In Scotland Labour's hold on power was finally lost as the SNP narrowly became the largest party, and formed a minority government with the help of the Green Party. In Wales, after lengthy negotiations over a so-called 'rainbow coalition' of Plaid Cymru, the Conservatives and the Liberal Democrats, Labour remained in office but at the cost of a coalition with Plaid Cymru, Hence, with the opportunity for autonomy came the possibilities for fresh approaches to executive organisation and styles of politics.

Equally, the fact of distinct national and regional political cultures of the UK added much to the potential of regional assertion. Specifically, Scotland, Wales and the Northern regions of England were attributed with more collectivist community-minded values than the individualistic liberal South East of England. Where the latter might more easily conform to the tenets of neo-liberalism and the use of the private sector in public services, the former may be keen to amend the mix of policy priorities. This was possible even within the context of the Labour Party, where despite its formally unitary territorial character the party harboured potentially varied views on political ideology. For example, one of the key reasons why the Labour Party in Scotland and Wales had become so firmly pro-devolution between 1979 and 1997 was their opposition to Conservative state reforms. Continuities in the UK Labour Government's approach with Conservative reforms undoubtedly encouraged those who were not fully supportive of Labour modernisation to believe that devolution gave a chance to buck the approaches of UK central government, whether they were Conservative or Labour. In Northern Ireland difference in political culture was even more obvious, but had potentially different implications. For example, Northern Ireland alone had hung onto selective secondary school education since the 1960s and given that in part UK central policies since 1979s had sought reform through re-inventing old policies, governmental autonomy in Northern Ireland offered variations on the notion of 'forwards to the past'.

The economic and social needs of the different parts of the UK also varied, suggesting that devolution would allow the adoption of appropriate strategies to suit the needs of different nations/regions. Specifically, Scotland, Wales and the English Northern regions portrayed themselves as suffering from concentrated problems of de-industrialisation, and over-reliance on simplistic strategies of inward investment that led to branch plant economic effects. This created enormous vulnerability during downturns in the global economy. At the same time, there were concentrations of unemployment and chronic problems of employability, training, and social infrastructure that were inextricably linked with the experience of relative poverty. There was a desire to defend national and regional cultural heritages against the impact of state and global culture. All of these factors created possibilities for innovation and divergence.

The implications of any such innovation and divergence were inevitably, however, open to debate both as to whether they advantaged the nations and regions and as to whether they established variations across the UK which the state as a whole could accommodate. In evaluating the extent of autonomy it is important to recognise though that studies of the early years of devolution for Scotland and Wales have tended to emphasise the room for manoeuvre allowed by central government. Studies of the formal mechanisms of intergovernmental relations have emphasised the fact that on the whole they were little used (see, for example, Trench 2004b). Linkages between central and devolved government were instead strongly influenced by informal channels within the Labour Party. Undoubtedly the lead-up to devolution was characterised by central party intervention to attempt to influence electoral systems, leadership and candidate selection so as to influence the character of how devolved politics would work. Thereafter there was a strong degree of policy co-ordination and communication, evidenced, for example, by regular Monday morning liaison between Welsh Office and National Assembly ministers to set the agenda for the week. Nevertheless, a strong feature of the post-1999 period was the relative autonomy given to territorial Labour Party elites in Scotland and Wales to pursue their own strategies and policies. This appeared to reflect a recognition that perceived over-centralism could be counter-productive, the centre had its own preoccupations and that territorial leaders were generally best placed to see what was needed both in party and policy terms (see Bradbury 2006).

In seeking to shape the fortunes of stateless nations and regions in novel and divergent ways, therefore, devolution and regionalism in the UK had the potential to follow broader trends within the European Union (Sharpe 1993; Keating 1998). Most of the other leading member states of the EU have developed a strong meso level of government, either as part of federal or quasi-federal arrangements (such as Germany and Spain) or as a result of gradual regionalisation (France and Italy). The decision-making structures of the EU, notably the committee of the regions, reflected this trend, as did the demands of policy-making for a sub-state regional role, such as in the implementation of structural funds policies. Analysts of political decentralisation and regional development policy have developed cogent comparative analyses of the European experience. Yet, it was not expected that the UK in embracing devolution and regionalism would easily conform to EU-wide trends. The UK as a whole remained as much open to the influence of its transatlantic and global relationships, as it did to its EU membership. The readiness to embrace neo-liberal reforms of state and economy during the 1980s and 1990s also reflected these more divergent external contexts to UK politics and policy. All of this suggests that analysing the UK experience of devolution, regionalism and regional development would especially pay individual attention.

Analysing the UK experience: the development of regional capacity

The final key introductory issue is in what over-arching conceptual terms are we to assess developments? A current concern in the comparative literature is to focus analysis on the development of regional capacity. It is a widely accepted focus of analysis even if it is a concept that is still hard to pin down. Cole's (2005: 6) definition of it as 'an interactive process encompassing institutions and institutional processes, actors and their relationships, socially constructed identities and forms of overarching regulation' tells us much of the complexity of issues within the region as well as outside it that need to be discussed. It encompasses the ways in which a region develops capacity for the purpose of articulating the interests and concerns of the region as a whole, and for meeting the perceived needs of constituent electorates. It also accepts that regional capacity may include the delivery of strategies determined at UK or EU levels of government, which may or may not be to the liking of the regions themselves (see also Keating 1998; Le Galés 2002).

Despite such definitional complexities, an over-arching concern with understanding regional capacity does help us pull together two sets of questions for considering the various developments in devolution, regionalism and regional development in the UK: the first specific; the second more broadly evaluative. First, in each of the nations and regions what institutional and constitutional developments have occurred, and what powers and resources have developed within parties and bureaucracy at the regional level? What approaches to public policy have emerged and to what extent has devolution and regionalism been the crucible of autonomous and/or divergent approaches to public policy? Across the UK what have been the principal components of regional development policy given these new institutional, political and policy contexts? Second, what do such findings more generally mean? To what extent and in what ways has each constituent nation/region of the UK become a collective actor? To what extent has institutional innovation nurtured the development of common identities and interests, decision-making mechanisms, internal and external presentation strategies and established successful mechanisms of internal integration? To what extent has institutional innovation developed the capacity for broader political, governmental and policy innovation at the regional level across the UK?

To answer these questions the book is organised in three parts. Part I assesses the implications of devolution in Scotland, Wales and Northern Ireland. Each chapter addresses the development of institutional powers and resources, electoral politics and executive formation, institutional arrangements, styles of policy-making and substance of policy change. They appraise the principal interests, ideological values and political movements shaping the direction of politics and governance at the devolved level of government. Northern Ireland, of course, presents a special case, as for much of the period since 1998 devolution has actually been suspended. Consequently, there is a more fundamental issue to address in exploring how devolution was revived and what prospects it has for future success.

Part II focuses on the English regions. The first chapter provides an overview of the development of regional governance in England, assessing the development of institutional arrangements and relationships, and the possibilities for co-ordination within regions. Two chapters then look at individual regions. The first looks at the case of regional governance in the South East, where in Greater London an elected regional authority was created but where there are still a variety of institutions, each with different or overlapping responsibilities which confront major issues of co-ordination. The second looks at the case of an English region, Yorkshire and Humber, where structures of regional governance were achieved but the case for an elected assembly petered out. In both cases developments, achievements and problems are explored. All three chapters appraise the principal political and bureaucratic pressures shaping the direction of English regionalism.

Part III then provides an analysis of regional development policy across the UK. The first chapter provides an over-arching analysis of the relationship between devolution, regional reform and regional development and relates it to questions of territorial justice across the UK as a whole, as well as the economic dividend within each territory. The second chapter assesses the development of concepts of regional development, governance structures and development strategies in Scotland and Wales. The final chapter appraises the same issues in relation to England. Together they address the question of the extent to which new institutional capacities have led to different strategic regional development approaches.

The contributors to the book are all academic researchers who have been centrally engaged in analysing and informing the development of devolution, regionalism and regional development policy in the UK since the late 1990s. They are all broadly of a liberal-pluralist outlook in the analysis of politics and public policy, and within these assumptions the book is a chance to take stock and draw links. The concluding chapter seeks to reflect on the analysis and arguments presented in the book, what conclusions may be made overall about UK regional capacity and its broader implications for the UK state as a whole, and how it may be placed into comparative perspective. It is hoped that the book will be of value both to new students and practitioners of the subject as well as more experienced hands in the field. It is also intended to be of clear value to scholars and practitioners from other countries, wishing to know more about the UK experience, and learn what may be emulated as well as what are best understood as cautionary tales to be avoided at all costs.

References

Amin, A. and Thrift, N. (1994) (eds) *Globalisation, Institutions and Regional Development in Europe*, Oxford: Oxford University Press.

Bache, I. and Flinders, M. (2004) (eds) *Multi-level Governance*, Oxford: Oxford University Press.

Birch, A. (1989) *Nationalism and National Integration*, London: Unwin Hyman.

Bogdanor, V. (1999) *Devolution in the United Kingdom*, Oxford: Oxford University Press.

Bradbury, J. (2006) 'Territory and Power revisited: theorising territorial politics in the United Kingdom after devolution', *Political Studies*, 54:559–82.

Bradbury, J. and Mawson, J. (1997) (eds) *British Regionalism and Devolution: The Challenges of State Reform and European Integration*, London: Jessica Kingsley.

Brown, A., McCrone, D. and Paterson, L. (1998) (2nd edn) *Politics and Society in Scotland*, Basingstoke: Macmillan.

Bulpitt, J. (1983) *Territory and Power in the United Kingdom: An Interpretation*, Manchester: Manchester University Press.

Cole, A. (2005) *Beyond Devolution and Decentralisation: Building Regional Capacity in Wales and Brittany*, Manchester: Manchester University Press.

Colley, L. (1992) *Britons: Forging the Nation 1707–1837*, New Haven, CT: Yale University Press.

Cooke, P. and Morgan, K. (1998) *The Associational Economy*, Oxford: Oxford University Press.

Davies, N. (1999) *The Isles, A History*, London: Palgrave Macmillan.

Gamble, A. (1988) *The Free Economy and The Strong State: The Politics of Thatcherism*, London: Macmillan.

Garside, P. and Hebbert, M. (1989) (eds) *British Regionalism 1900–2000*, London: Mansell.

Griffiths, D. (1996), *Thatcherism and Territorial Politics: A Welsh Case Study*, Aldershot: Avebury.

Hall, P. (1989) *Urban and Regional Planning*, London: Unwin Hyman.

Harvie, C. (1991) 'English regionalism: the dog that never barked' in B. Crick (ed.) *National Identities*, Oxford: Blackwell.

Hazell, R. (2006) (ed.) *The English Question*, Manchester: Manchester University Press.

Heffernan, R. (2000) *New Labour and Thatcherism: Political Change in Britain*, Basingstoke: Palgrave.

Hogwood, B. and Keating, M. (1982) (eds) *Regional Government in England*, Oxford: Clarendon Press.

Jeffery, C. and Wincott, D. (2006) 'Devolution in the United Kingdom: statehood and citizenship in transition', special issue of *Publius, the Journal of Federalism*, 36, 1.

Jones, J. B. and Keating, M. (1995) (eds) *The European Union and the Regions*, Oxford: Clarendon Press.

Keating, M. (1998) *The New Regionalism in Western Europe: Territorial Restructuring and Political Change*, Cheltenham: Edward Elgar.

Le Galés, P. (2002) *European Cities: Social Conflicts and Governance*, Oxford: Oxford University Press.

McGarry, J. and O'Leary, B. (1997) *Explaining Northern Ireland*, Oxford: Blackwell.

Mitchell, J. (2004) *Governing Scotland*, Basingstoke: Palgrave.

McLean, I. and McMillan, A. (2005) *State of the Union*, Oxford: Oxford University Press.

Rokkan, S. and Urwin, D. (1982) 'Introduction: centres and peripheries in Western Europe' in S. Rokkan and D. Urwin (eds), *The Politics of Territorial Identity*, London: Sage.

Sharpe, L.J. (1993) (ed.) *The Rise of Meso Government in Europe*, London: Sage.

Smith, B. (1964) *Regionalism in England*, London: Acton Society Trust.

Tewdwr-Jones, M. and Allmendinger, P. (2006) (eds), *Territory, Identity and Spatial Planning*, London: Routledge.

Townroe, P. and Martin, R. (1992) *Regional Development in the 1990s, The British Isles in Transition*, London: Jessica Kingsley.

Trench, A. (2004a) (ed.) *Has Devolution Made A Difference?: The State of the Nations 2004*, Exeter: Imprint Academic.

Trench, A. (2004b) 'The more things change the more they stay the same: intergovernmental relations four years on', in A. Trench (ed.), *Has Devolution Made A Difference?: The State of the Nations 2004*, Exeter: Imprint Academic.

Wilford, R. (2001) (ed.) *Aspects of the Belfast Agreement*, Oxford: Oxford University Press.

Part I

Devolution in the UK

2 Devolution in Scotland

Change and continuity

Neil McGarvey

It was John Smith, the former Labour Party leader, in the early 1990s who first referred to devolution as 'the settled will of the Scottish people'. By the time of his untimely death, devolution had moved from being a secondary to a primary issue on the Scottish political agenda. In 1997 it was endorsed emphatically in a referendum, and through eight years of Labour–Liberal Democrat governments, led by Donald Dewar (1999-2000), Henry McLeish (2000-2001) and Jack McConnell (2001-2007) the revived Scottish Parliament appeared to consolidate its centrality to the future of Scottish politics. In 2007, with the election of Scotland's first ever nationalist administration led by Alex Salmond (as First Minister) the current devolution settlement is no longer looking so 'settled'.

The existing settlement, of course, stems from cross-party co-operation in the form of the Scottish Constitutional Convention (SCC) between 1989 and 1995. It was a body which allowed cross-party supporters of home rule a forum for discussion. The re-establishment of a similar type body was high on the agenda of Scottish politics after the May 2007 elections. The SCC's final report – *Scotland's Parliament, Scotland's Right* (1995) – was part of the blueprint for the implementation of devolution in 1999. The SCC proposals were particularly influential regarding the electoral system and the issue of gender representation. In the words of Ian Lang, the former Secretary of State for Scotland, the SCC came:

> to form part of that congealing consensus that presaged constitutional change and eventually form(ed) part of the foundation of such change. By 1997 devolution had become a catalyst for all political opposition (to the Scottish Conservatives).
>
> (Lang 2002: 174, 199)

Devolution has changed the institutional architecture of Scottish politics. The formal machinery and operation of democracy and government in Scotland is now, in David Steel's phrase, 'a world away from the old Scottish Office model' (Steel 2001). The election of the minority SNP administration has accelerated that shift. Most accounts of devolution inevitably take as a starting point the institutional powers and resources of the devolved body in order to give a context for subsequent discussion. This reflects a long tradition in political analysis in general – there is an underlying implicit assumption that political institutions are important.

This chapter reviews the impact devolution has made on Scotland's key political institutions. Prior to doing so, however, it is importance to acknowledge that much of the contemporary institutional architecture of Scottish politics and government pre-dates devolution. The pre-devolution legacy should not be under-appreciated. The 1999 settlement merely added on a Parliament to the executive, administrative and policy-making powers already devolved to the Scottish Office. After outlining the context to devolution, its impact on Scotland's key political institutions, and relations between them will be examined. The final section will then assess the continuities and changes that have taken place in both the processes and outputs of public policy-making in Scotland.

Devolution in context

Despite the union with England in 1707 Scotland has always retained certain elements of 'nationhood'. Scotland's distinct culture and institutional heritage, geography, civil society, religion, sporting institutions and media have all contributed to Scottish consciousness of a separate national identity. The historic nation of Scotland was not simply absorbed into the unitary UK State – it retained some key features of statehood. As James Mitchell (2006) has noted, the UK is a state of unions rather than a unitary state.

The Scottish Office, established in 1885, provided a powerful administrative apparatus that had a degree of decision-making and administrative autonomy in certain sectors until 1999. It was responsible for Scottish policy in areas such as education, housing, health, economic development, social services, planning, transport, agriculture, fisheries and law and order. These responsibilities are broadly concurrent with the non-reserved legislative responsibilities of the Scottish Parliament. Hence, it was the old Scottish Office that formed the basis of devolved government. It had a degree of discretion in the exercise of its responsibilities, as well as ability to develop and implement UK policy and policy guidance. There is some debate over the extent of its governing autonomy. Brown et al. (1998) emphasise how the Scottish Office and its associated policy networks were very important in promoting Scottish distinctiveness and identity as well as allowing administrative and policy autonomy within the Union. They emphasise the autonomous role political elites in Scotland enjoyed (Brown et al. 1998: 93) in the 'partial' union (Paterson 2000: 2). A number of writers highlight the fact that the associational life of civil society (i.e. the dense networks of voluntary organisations and institutions) was distinctly Scottish (see Kellas 1989, McCrone 1992). McCrone argues:

> Scotland's professional classes – lawyers, doctors, teachers, churchmen – while socially conservative, embody the institutional survival of distinctive Scottish 'civil society', and can be considered as keepers of native institutions.
>
> (1992: 143).

Brown et al. refer to 'the consensual decision-making process and negotiated compromises which typified the outcome of policy formation' and suggest that this

Scottish approach came under increasing strain during the Thatcher-Major years (1998: 93). Poor territorial management, the perceived imposition of alien policies by the Conservative run Scottish Office and the consequent 'democratic deficit' led to the increased support for constitutional change. The real problem was one of legitimacy – the outputs of the Scottish Office were being imposed by what was seen as an alien Conservative Government.

Meanwhile, Midwinter *et al.* (1991:78) emphasise a more limited picture of the autonomy of the Scottish Office and suggest that it generally took its lead from UK departments. They argue that the key question in Scottish politics was the extent to which the policy networks centred on the Scottish Office could make policy themselves, as opposed simply to adapting the policy initiatives coming from their Whitehall big brothers. For Midwinter *et al.* the phrase 'administrative devolution' was something of a misnomer as it conveyed the mistaken idea that the Scottish Office represented a form of self-government (see also Mitchell 2004: 210–14). They suggested that:

> In reality the Scottish Office is neither an example of devolution, which would involve a capacity to take authoritative decisions and responsibility to a Scottish constituency, nor merely a form of field administration for UK departments. Rather, it is an example of territorial division of administrative responsibilities, existing alongside the more familiar functional ones.
>
> (Midwinter *et al.* 1991: 61)

They argue that the scope for policy innovation in Scotland was limited by UK policies, leadership from Whitehall departments and the heavy demands on the time of the Secretary of State. Most Secretaries of State were content to function as managers and adopters of policies (Midwinter *et al.* 1991: 83).

No matter your view as regards the autonomy of the Scottish Office, it is difficult to argue with the idea that its existence still encouraged a conception of Scotland as a political, and not merely a cultural, entity (Mitchell 2004). From the 1970s onwards feelings of difference and identity in Scotland were re-cast with its political dimension remoulded and impacting more significantly on Scottish politics. In the 1980s and 90s all the opposition parties increasingly portrayed themselves as representing and defending Scotland's interests in Westminster and Whitehall. The Scottish Labour Party and Liberal Democrats enhanced the Scottish tone in their message and image. Indeed Jack McConnell, the Labour First Minister 2001–2007, was one of the founding members of Scottish Labour Action, a campaigning group within the party for more autonomy for the Scottish branch of the party and a more radical approach to home rule. The Scottish Constitutional Convention, established in 1989, claimed sovereignty rested with the Scottish people rather than the Crown in Parliament.

Scottish and UK political differences became particularly evident during the 18 years of Conservative Party rule (1979–1997). The Thatcher administrations were notoriously unpopular in Scotland with Conservative Party support declining dramatically (see Table 2.1). The Conservative Party achieved a minority of the vote in Scotland and perceptions of a 'legitimacy deficit' grew with Scottish

Table 2.1 General and Scottish election results 1945–2007

Elections	Labour seats	%	Cons seats	%	Lib/Alliance/Lib Dems seats	%	SNP seats	%	Other seats	%
1945	37	47.6	27	41.1	0	5.0	0	1.2	4	
1950	37	46.2	32	44.8	2	6.6	0	0.4	0	
1951	35	47.9	35	48.6	1	2.7	0	0.3	0	
1955	34	46.7	36	50.1	1	1.9	0	0.5	0	
1959	38	46.7	31	47.2	1	4.1	0	0.8	0	
1964	43	48.7	24	40.6	4	7.6	0	2.4	0	
1966	46	49.9	20	37.7	5	6.8	0	5.0	0	
1970	44	44.5	23	38.0	3	5.5	0	11.4	0	
1974 (Feb)	41	36.6	21	32.9	3	7.9	7	21.9	0	
1974 (Oct)	41	36.3	16	24.7	3	8.3	11	30.4	0	
1979	44	41.5	22	31.4	3	9.0	2	17.3	0	
1983	41	35.1	21	28.4	8	24.5	2	11.8	0	
1987	50	42.4	10	24.0	9	19.4	3	11.0	0	
1992	49	39.0	11	25.6	9	13.1	3	21.5	0	
1997	56	45.6	0	17.5	10	13.0	6	22.1	0	
1999 (Sco)										
Constituency	53	38.8	0	15.6	12	14.2	7	28.7	1	2.7
Region	3	33.6	18	15.4	5	12.4	28	27.3	2	11.3
2001	55	43.2	1	15.6	10	16.4	5	20.1	0	
2003 (Sco)										
Constituency	46	34.6	3	16.6	13	15.4	9	23.8	2	9.6
Region	4	29.6	15	15.5	4	11.6	18	21.6	15	21.7
2005	41	39.5	1	15.8	11	22.6	6	17.7	0	
2007 (Sco)										
Constituency	37	32.2	4	16.6	11	16.2	21	32.9	0	0.7
Region	9	29.2	13	13.9	5	11.3	26	31.0	1	14.6

government being run by a party that was perceived to be alien to Scottish interests. This placed a strain on support for the existing UK system of government.

From the perspective of the political parties, and other institutions represented in the Scottish Constitutional Convention, it appeared that devolution could alleviate that strain. After the Labour Party's landslide victory at the 1997 UK General Election the new UK Government's devolution proposals were subject to a referendum later that year and were overwhelmingly endorsed (Table 2.2). This was followed by the Scotland Act in 1998, specifying the powers to be devolved to the Scottish Parliament (Table 2.3).

Table 2.2 The 1997 Scottish referendum result

Should there be a Scottish Parliament?	%	Should it have tax varying powers?	%
Agree	74.3%	Agree	63.5%
Disagree	25.7%	Disagree	36.5%
Turnout 60.4%			

Table 2.3 Responsibilities of the new Scottish Parliament

Reserved areas (not devolved)	Areas not reserved (responsibilities of the Scottish Parliament)
Common market for UK goods and services	Agriculture, fisheries and forestry
Constitution of the United Kingdom	Economic development
Defence & national security	Education
Employment legislation	Environment
Fiscal, economic & monetary union	Health
Health (in some areas), Medicine	Housing
Media and culture	Local government
Professional regulation (in certain cases)	Law and home affairs
Protection of borders	Social work
Social Security	Training
Transport Safety & Regulation	Transport

Source: Mitchell, J. (2000)

The first Scottish parliamentary elections were held in May 1999 and the Scottish Parliament was established on 1 July 1999. These were undoubtedly key landmarks in contemporary Scottish politics. However, a sole focus on the Parliament neglects many of the other important changes that have taken place. In modern academic terminology we live in an era of multi-level governance. The introduction of the Parliament was undoubtedly of profound symbolic significance, particularly in a democratic sense; its broader impact on Scottish policy-making and governance is not so clear-cut.

Devolution has changed many of the institutional arrangements of Scottish politics: executive coalition politics is now the norm; the Parliament is elected by an Additional Member System (AMS) (or as Arbuthnott (2006) called it a Mixed Member System); there are distinctive working procedures for the Parliament; and the Parliament has in turn introduced the Single Transferable Vote (STV) method for local elections in 2007. Much of what has taken place in Scotland has fed directly into constitutional and policy-making debates at the UK level. However, to concentrate exclusively on change neglects much of the pre-devolution legacy and its continuing impact on Scottish politics. The next section seeks to review briefly Scotland's key political institutions examining both continuity and change in each case.

Institutions and relationships

The main executive branch of government in Scotland, the Scottish Office, was re-named 'Executive' in 1999 and 'Government' by the SNP in 2007. Section 51 of the Scotland Act states that service of the Scottish Administration (the official term) shall be service in the Home Civil Service. The Scottish Government is thus bound by the legislative framework governing the UK Home Civil Service. All of the civil servants in Scotland remain employed by the United Kingdom

Home civil service and subject to its personnel policies dictated by the UK Cabinet Office. This has no parallel in other intergovernmental systems such as Canada, Australia and Germany (Parry 2004). This arrangement is likely to come under increasing strain following the election of the minority SNP administration in 2007.

Richard Parry, in his work on the post-devolution civil service in Scotland, tells a story of incremental adjustment largely in tune with existing Whitehall practice. There has, however, been some restructuring most notably in 2001 and 2007. In 2001 a Department of Finance and Central Services was created, reflecting the Government's desire to strengthen the corporate centre in order to facilitate a more strategic approach to policy-making. Industry and Higher Education were linked in a new department of Enterprise and Lifelong Learning. The Development and Agriculture departments were renamed but were not aligned with their ministers – the organisation of departments did not parallel that of ministers. The link between transport and environment was not carried through at official level (Parry and Jones 2000: 54).

However, in 2007 a major restructuring took place with the new SNP administration seeking to slim down the Government's structure. This was coupled with a cut-back in the number of ministers from 18 to 16 and a slimmed-down Cabinet, from 11 to 6 (renamed 'Cabinet Secretaries'). Figure 1 outlines the new structure.

The civil service in Scotland remains part of the UK home civil service. This provides the opportunity for the maintenance of a common civil service ethos. Internal civil service policy learning, policy networks and interpersonal connections will result in clear threads of communication being retained between

First Minister: Alex Salmond

Cabinet Secretaries (6)
Office of First Minister
Cabinet Secretary for Finance & Sustainable Growth
Cabinet Secretary for Education & Lifelong Learning
Cabinet Secretary for Health and Wellbeing
Cabinet Secretary for Justice
Cabinet Secretary for Rural Affairs and the Environment

Ministers (10)
Minister for Parliamentary Business
Minister for Europe, External Affairs and Culture
Minister for Enterprise, Energy and Tourism
Minister for Transport, Infrastructure and Climate Change
Minister for Schools and Skills
Minister for Children and Early Years
Minister for Public Health
Minister for Communities and Sport
Minister for Community Safety
Minister for Environment

Figure 2.1 The 2007 Scottish ministerial structure

Edinburgh and London. This is a thread/legacy that possibly continues to inject the unitary centralist culture into territorial policy-making. During the inital period of devolution Nelson commented on how the civil service in Scotland continued in 'regurgitating work done in London and passing it off as its own' (Nelson 2001). Within the civil service Parry and Jones suggest, 'The balance between innovation and replication (of UK structures) has on the whole been tilted in favour of the latter' (Parry and Jones 2000: 62).

The new legislative branch of Scottish politics, in the form of its own Parliament, represents a more radical break from the previous Westminster arrangements. It is undoubtedly different from the arrangements at Westminster. Indeed in many ways the House of Commons appears to have acted as a negative template for the constitutional designers of the new Scottish Parliament. The outdated voting system, adversarial politics and weak executive and legislative scrutiny were all cited as negative features of the House of Commons. In contrast, the Scottish Parliament would have a more proportional system, coalition politics and stronger committees. These features, together with its modern architecture, shape and standing orders, all emphasise its distinctiveness.

The Scottish Parliament, on occasion between 1999 and 2007, has gone beyond Garret's caricature of the House of Commons as 'heckling the steamroller' (Garret 1992: 6) of executive drafted legislation. However, when it has defeated the Government, 'victory' has often been transitory. For example, in March 2001 the Parliament defeated the Government over compensation payments to fishermen but the vote was subsequently overturned. In 2000 the Scottish Socialist Party's then leader, Tommy Sheridan, sponsored an Act banning warrant sales, but it was not implemented after the Government passed its own Act. The oft cited instance of the introduction of care for the elderly was more to do with Scottish Government division. The Parliament has on occasion amended Government policy on detail. For example, in 2000 the Equal Opportunities Committee demanded a question on religion to appear within the census. Some broader assertion of Parliamentary power is evidenced by the fact that 11 out of 61 bills were non-Government bills in the Parliament's first session. In 2001 the then deputy presiding officer, George Reid, prohibited a Government minister from addressing the Parliament with a statement that had been leaked to the media beforehand, suggesting that it could be 'taken as read' in the day's media. However, the Scottish legislative and policy process remains Government dominated. Indeed despite a much slimmer majority the McConnell administration suffered fewer parliamentary defeats than the Blair administration! This said, Government defeats are likely to become increasingly common with the establishment of a minority SNP administration in 2007.

Equally, the newness of the Parliament building and its standing orders should not mask some rather 'Westminster and Whitehall-like' arrangements that remain in place. First Minister's question time and the Scottish Ministerial Code (Scottish Government 1999) are both remarkably similar to the practice and documents in Westminster and Whitehall respectively. Moreover, there are post-devolution initiatives designed to retain clear linkages between Edinburgh and Whitehall. For example, the Memorandums of Understanding between the Governments established a series of joint ministerial councils (JMCs), including one on health. There have also been a series of 'concordats' as well as less formal meetings in which the relevant ministers in England, Scotland and Wales discuss issues of common interest. Nevertheless, although there was much fanfare in the early days of devolution about these docu-ments and meetings, there is little evidence, to date, of them impacting on policy processes in any significant manner. However, JMCs may well become more promi-nent forums, with the resolution of disputes between the Scottish Government and the UK Government likely to figure more prominently now that the Labour Party is no longer the dominant party in each administration.

A key theme of the Constitutional Convention and Consultative Steering Group (CSG), which designed the Parliament's initial standing orders, was how the new Parliament was going to facilitate public access, transparency, participation and delib-eration in the legislative and policy-making processes. Much effort went into the devising of different or new procedural values to govern policy-makers in Scotland. The committees were accorded an emphasised role in the legislative process with the expectation that, over time, they would develop a life of their own and new forms of politics would emerge (Brown 2000: 553). Alice Brown, a member of the cross-party CSG, was among the key exponents of the notion of a 'new politics' in Scotland – a move away from the adversarial, zero-sum politics associated with Westminster to a more plural and inclusive form of politics (Brown 2000: 556). Bradbury and Mitchell (2001: 257) refer to the aspiration that the innovations in institutional procedures would lead to a more open and collaborative style of decision-making. Equally, Roberts suggested that Scottish devolution had been accompanied by a new emphasis on bottom-up policy development (2000: 260).

It should be acknowledged that empirical research undertaken into the role of committees within the Scottish Parliament has shown some evidence of 'new poli-tics' (see Arter 2002, 2004; Shephard and Cairney 2004, 2005). However, there does appear to be a caricature that has developed and a degree of mythology surround-ing the partisanship of Westminster committees. The focus of these studies is almost exclusively focused on the Scottish Parliament and a comparative dimension is lack-ing. More comparative and qualitative empirical work on the intricate detail, manoeuvring and politics surrounding the legislative process is necessary before any definitive conclusions regarding the existence of 'new politics' can be drawn. Generally, it would be fair to say that the committees have, to date, not impacted on the policy process to the degree that the CSG had hoped for. Nevertheless, with a minority administration the committees of the Parliament are now likely to become more serious players in the Scottish policy-making process.

Overall there has been much scepticism about the notion of 'new politics'. Mitchell notes that new politics discussion of access and transparency has tended to empha-sise the legislative rather than the executive branch of government (2000: 607), despite the fact that the latter remains the key arena of policy-making. The implicit pluralist assumption that more representation, participation and deliberation will deliver better public policy outputs is also raised. Mitchell points to the Clause 28 debate on information on homosexuality in schools as highlighting some of the diffi-culties of a more open policy-making process in Scotland (2000: 616). Scotland's civil society may not be quite as mature and attuned to the civil rights part of liberal democracy as some home-rule campaigners may have thought. Mitchell has also suggested that 'new politics' tend to be vague and undefined and 'being fine as polemic but of dubious value as a serious effort to understand contemporary Scottish politics' (2001: 222). Mitchell criticises the advocates of new politics as adopting a very crude view of the relationship between institutions, processes and political culture and notes 'a growing realisation has emerged in Scottish politics that much remains the same as ever' (2000: 620).

Mitchell is not alone in his scepticism regarding new politics. Keating identifies a possible source of the naivety of some of its exponents. Civil society during the Conservative years was united in lobbying for Scottish interests, and this:

> ... allowed Scots to sustain the idea of being in a common cause, bound by shared values and a broad social consensus (and) this experience probably underlay some of the more naïve ideas floating around before 1999 that the Scottish Parliament could operate on the basis of consensus, banishing partisanship, conflict and lobbying.
>
> (2001: 7)

Overall, there appears to have been at least an initial exaggeration of the political differences engendered by the new devolved arrangements and a lack of acknowledgement of the continuing influence of the learned political culture of UK politics. The enduring influence of the UK's political parties (Labour, Liberal Democrat and Conservative) and the UK Home civil service ensure that certain 'features' of UK politics (e.g. a strong political executive) continue to have resonance in Scotland. As Winetrobe noted, there remained an attitude in the mindset of the executive that Parliament existed 'to facilitate the executive's agenda' (2001: 179). The election of an SNP minority administration in 2007 is likely to mark a significant turning point in this regard.

The Parliament was given significant powers over local government. Scottish local government has always been different in degree from its English counterpart in structure, policy agenda, process and output although the similarities still outweighed the differences (see McGarvey 2005). However, since devolution the differences have been accentuated. Various committee recommendations (Scottish Office 1999; Kerley Report 2000; McNish 2001) have fed directly into policy-making processes resulting in a different local government agenda. Similar-named policy initiatives exist (e.g. best value, community planning/leadership) but different approaches have been taken North and South of the border. The English agenda on such initiatives as elected mayors and beacon councils simply did not register in Scotland. The internal decision-making structures of the majority of Scottish local councils are marked by continuity, in contrast to England where an executive model of internal governance has become dominant. Local government scholars in England acknowledge that, 'Wales and Scotland may offer a different story' (Stoker and Wilson 2005: 250) to the one they outline. In 2007 the single transferable vote method was introduced for the local government elections in Scotland.

Table 2.4 Local Election Results 1974–2007

Year	Labour % vote (seats)	SNP % (seats)	Con % (seats)	Lib Dem % (seats)
2007 (Unitary)*	29 (348)	30 (363)	12 (143)	14 (166)
2003 (Unitary)	33 (509)	24 (181)	15 (123)	15 (175)
1999 (Unitary)	36 (551)	29 (204)	14 (109)	13 (161)
1995 (Unitary)	44 (613)	26 (181)	12 (82)	10 (121)
1992 (District)	34 (468)	24 (150)	23 (204)	10 (94)
1988 (District)	43 (553)	21 (113)	19 (162)	8 (84)
1984 (District)	46 (545)	12 (59)	21 (189)	13 (178)
1980 (District)	45 (494)	16 (54)	24 (229)	6 (40)
1977 (District)	32 (299)	24 (170)	27 (277)	4 (31)
1974 (District)	38 (428)	12 (62)	27 (241)	5 (17)

*Note: 2007 vote share figures relate to first preference votes.

Multi-member wards altered the party political complexion of councils even more than interim projections (see Curtice and Herbert 2005). Table 2.4 illustrates the scale of the change. Of Scotland's 32 councils only two (Glasgow and North Lanarkshire) had a party majority (both Labour). It was the Labour Party who were the big losers – losing over 161 councillors and control of 13 councils (compared to the post-2003 election position). The SNP were the big gainers – 'winning' the elections (in terms of elected representatives) as they did at the parliamentary election.

The introduction of STV for local elections also means that there are four different voting systems for Scottish council, Parliament, Westminster and European elections. This led the Secretary of State for Scotland to establish a Commission on Boundary Differences and Voting Systems chaired by Sir John Arbuthnott. In its final report key recommendations were the retention of the mixed member electoral system but with the introduction of open lists for regional MSPs for the Scottish Parliament elections and the introduction of STV for elections in Scotland to the European Parliament (as already occurs in Northern Ireland). It also suggested reviews of local government and Scottish Parliament boundaries to be concurrent, holding local and Parliament elections on separate days and a 'rapid move' towards the introduction of electronic voting and counting (Arbuthnott 2006). However, the recommendation to de-couple the parliamentary and local elections, because of the different voting systems being used, was not heeded. The May 2007 Parliament election resulted in record numbers of spoilt ballot papers – with confusion between ballots for the Parliament and local elections being cited as one of the reasons.

Devolution has also accelerated the divergence of the Scottish party system. Scotland, like Britain as a whole, had a classic two-party system until the 1970s. The key UK national parties - the Conservatives (called Unionists in Scotland until 1965) and Labour - were electorally dominant with the Liberals on the fringes and the SNP virtually non-existent. However, as in England, the two-party system came under increasing strain with the support of the two major parties declining on both sides of the border. The rise of the SNP and its dramatic impact at both of the 1974 General Elections changed the face of Scottish party politics (see Table 2.1). Nevertheless, prior to devolution, the mainstream UK political parties still managed Scotland by channelling demands to the UK level and reinforced the 'centralist bias' of government in the UK. For the Labour and Conservative Parties territorial objectives were subordinate to the goal of securing a parliamentary majority at the UK level (Midwinter *et al.* 1991: 76).

It was an illusion of continuity. Hassan suggests that although Scottish Labour continued to win elections in the 1980s and 90s it did so 'with a sense of complacency and, without the rethinking the party south of the border undertook' (Hassan 2004: 14). As Harvie argues, up against the Conservatives in the 1980s a party 'programmed for self-destruction, Labour did not really have to do very much' (Harvie 2004: 61). Equally, the distinctiveness of parties in Scotland was becoming more apparent. As Brown *et al.* argued in 1996:

> party labels (North and South of the border) may be similar but their histories and agendas are quite different, and increasingly so. . the political parties in Scotland cannot be taken as British Parties writ small.
>
> (1996: 117)

In the context of the Scottish Parliament the party system in Scotland is now clearly different from England. Devolution and the new electoral system initially resulted in an expanded party system in Scotland with both the Scottish Socialists and the Scottish Green Party gaining significant representation (six and seven MSPs respectively) in the Parliament at the 2003 election. After the 2003 election there were 17 MSPs (out of 129) from non-mainstream parties. The 2003 Scottish election also led to a loss of six seats for the Scottish Labour Party and an effective coalition majority reduced from 17 to five. This position was reversed in 2007 with the four major parties (SNP, Labour Conservatives and Liberal Democrats) again becoming dominant and the 'others' being reduced to just three (two Greens and one independent). Yet, this was still highly significant as it witnessed the SNP's breakthrough as the largest party.

Indeed, the 2007 election marked a major electoral turning point – it was the end of Labour's dominance of Scottish electoral politics. Prior to 2007, the Scottish Labour Party had not lost (in terms of winning the most seats) a Scottish General or Parliamentary election since 1959. Numerous commentators had referred to Labour as an establishment party (Hassan 2002; Irvine 2004; Saren and McCormick 2004). Paterson notes how, 'Labour people (or, more accurately Labour sympathisers) are everywhere – in the voluntary organisations, in local government, in the civil service, in government, even in business' (Paterson 2002: 59). Though 'everywhere' may be an exaggeration, the Scottish Labour Party's tentacles did stretch long and deep into Scottish institutions and civil society. The dominance of the Labour Party in Scotland started to raise questions about the closeness of the party's relationship with the state bureaucracy (both central and local) and organisations in wider civil society. A series of post-devolution political scandals highlighted the manifestation of this relationship: 'Lobbygate' (the party's close relations with political lobbyists), 'Officegate' (the party's close relations with trade unions and the legal profession),

'Wishawgate' (the party's close relations with trade unions), and 'Warkgate' (the party's close relation with the media). At the local government level the party faced scandals in Monklands, Glasgow, North Lanarkshire, Fife and Renfrewshire councils. Partly as a result of such problems Labour's status as Scotland's dominant party was weakening prior to 2007. The boundary changes at the 2005 Westminster elections resulted in a drop in Labour MPs returned to Westminster from 55 to 41. Following the 2007 Parliament and local elections the party's control of Scotland's governing institutions extended to only two councils in its heartlands - Glasgow and North Lanarkshire.

Another key institutional feature of Scottish politics is the continuing reliance on fiscal transfers (i.e. the block grant) from the Treasury. This undermines the autonomy of the Scottish Parliament as the allocation of funding is tied to patterns of English expenditure. Fiscal autonomy, whilst not a prerequisite for policy autonomy, is undoubtedly an important variable. The Scottish Government's macro-aggregates for increases in expenditure are dependent on the negotiations between the UK Treasury and the relevant spending ministers in Whitehall. This leads to an inevitable sense of 'lock in' to the UK agenda with spending ministers in Edinburgh naturally anticipating similar settlements to their counterparts in Whitehall. Health has been an expenditure priority of both London and Edinburgh, meaning that there are inevitable questions asked if the Scottish Minister is not pursuing a policy initiative the UK Ministry has labelled 'innovative, necessary, visionary'.

Heald *et al.* (1998) also suggested that the longer the facility to recalibrate Scotland's taxes lay dormant the less likely it was that anyone would use it. This may have been true when the political context was stable with Labour-led administrations north and south of the border, but at the 2007 election the SNP and the Liberal Democrats campaigned on a platform which would utilise the 3p tax facility in order to abolish council tax. The parliamentary arithmetic is such that the utilisation of this power (in the form of an introduction of a 'local' income tax) may well become a reality.

Overall, the institutional architecture of Scottish politics has witnessed the introduction of a shiny new Parliament, but much of the old buildings and infrastructure remain. The spotlight of the media in Scotland is fixed on Edinburgh now, with backbench MPs in the UK House of Commons barely registering any interest. The bodies responsible for public service delivery remain as before – NHS boards, local councils, non-departmental public bodies and agencies. Nevertheless, the pre-devolution suggestions of 'new politics' in Scotland were hopelessly exaggerated. During the first two terms, aspects of political party, media, civil service and parliamentary behaviour still reflect the old culture and practices of Westminster and Whitehall. Politics in Scotland has not been transformed overnight from being tribal, exclusive and partisan to inclusive and consensual. However, Cairney does note that while the processing of legislation remains partisan at the plenary stage the Government has been willing 'to remove the most controversial decisions from this arena and into a relatively businesslike and less partisan committee arena' (2006: 205) in the Scottish Parliament. There are mechanisms for cross-party working within the Parliament – the extent of their impact is still open to debate. Of course, following the 2007 election 'all bets are off' and henceforth we are likely to witness more changes in both the internal and external intergovernmental dynamics of Scottish politics.

Public policy

Devolution was, of course, not designed to simply result in institutional change; a key part of the argument for home rule was the notion that the previous Westminster and Whitehall dominance had led to public policies out of touch with public opinion. In other words, devolution was a way of ensuring that the agenda of change in England was not simply imposed on Scotland. It is, of course, not unrelated, that the campaign for home rule in Scotland gained momentum during the post-1987 period of the radical Thatcherite public sector reform agenda.

Prior to devolution the picture painted of public policy processes in Scotland was one of domination by administrative policy-makers. Midwinter *et al.* outline a well-ordered, rationally organised but strangely 'depoliticised' picture where 'the executive is more powerful in relation to Parliament than in England while within the executive the civil service holds great influence' (Midwinter *et al.* 1991: 92). Post-devolution, this 'unchallenged ability of civil servants and ministers to dominate policy has gone' (Lynch 2001: 2). Although the pre-devolution role of pressure groups tends to be underplayed, there is undoubtedly increased emphasis on democratisaton with parliamentarians and interest groups accorded a more significant role. Paterson, in an optimistic evaluation, suggests 'the Scottish Parliament is recovering the best of Scottish unionist policy-making' which was characterised by 'independent and innovative policy' (2000: 8) until the 1960s: Roberts, in a similar vein, suggests that Scotland is:

> both the standard bearer for devolved government and provides a 'laboratory' for further experimentation with regard to both the technical-administrative and political aspects of territorial planning, development and management.
>
> (2000: 250)

There is little doubt that public policy processes have changed, but the evidence on the outputs of these processes is more mixed.

In some policy areas the Scottish Government appears in tune with the UK Treasury's agenda. For example, the public sector in Scotland until 2007 pursued Private Finance Initiative (PFI)/Public Private Partnership (PPP) schemes with as much vigour. Private finance has played a significant part in the modernisation of Scotland's schools, hospitals and other public buildings. Some local authorities, most notably Glasgow (with Scottish Government encouragement), have also embraced Large Scale Voluntary Transfer (LSVT) in housing with ownership passing from council to housing association. Both these areas probably reflect the continuing policy reach and leverage of the UK Treasury in Scottish politics.

At the same time, according to social survey research, the top three policy priorities for the public in Scotland have been health, crime and education (Bromley and

Given 2005). It is largely on this public service and law and order agenda that the Dewar, McLeish and McConnell administrations focused. Again this domestic policy agenda bears more than a passing resemblance to that of the Blair administration in London. Equally, the use of Sewel motions by the Government should also be noted. These motions are passed by the Scottish Parliament to give Westminster the authority to legislate on devolved matters – in the first full parliamentary session 41 were passed (see Cairney and Keating 2004). Indeed journalists often commented that the Scottish Government would have been well advised to utilise a Sewel motion in 1999 rather than introduce new legislation on Section 2a if it had wanted to achieve its aims. This was the section in the 1988 Local Government Act which effectively prevented teachers from discussing gay sex education. The 1999 debate over Section 2a (28 in England and Wales) highlighted how susceptible the political process in a small polity can be to a coalition of religious leaders, tabloid media editors and a millionaire businessman. The 'Keep the Clause' group tapped into fairly conservative moral attitudes in Scotland (see Paterson 2000: 9) and succeeded in influencing its re-draft with 'the value of stable family life in a child's development' being emphasised.

Meanwhile the state in Scotland has remained more dominant in other policy areas compared to England according to key indicators such as expenditure, employment and housing. Equally, the impact of commercialism on the provision of public services such as education and health is less well-developed than south of the border. Fewer state activities have tended to be outsourced to the private sector. The 'in-house' culture of many Scottish local authorities meant that the vast majority of tendering contracts awarded under the Conservative Government's Compulsory Competitive Tendering (CCT) legislation were won by direct labour and service organisations of councils. A survey by the Convention of Scottish Local Authorities in 1991 established that only 24 (i.e. 8.4 per cent) of 286 council contracts were won by the private sector and that this represented only 2.7 per cent of the total value of the work (McConnell 2004: 158).

Consequently, it is perhaps not surprising to find that key aspects of the Blairite modernisation agenda were ignored, or deemed not suitable for implementation by the Scottish Government, e.g. foundation hospitals, beacon councils, elite universities and selective schools. The first represented a major difference with potentially significant repercussions for health care funding fiscal transfers in the future. The latter three reflected an inherited Scottish Office tradition of autonomy in local government and education policy. Fault lines between Scottish and English opinion have also become apparent over reserved policy matters such as immigration. The UK Home Office treatment of asylum seekers' 'dawn raids' and the Dungavel detention centre (all reserved matters) caused much political controversy in 2005. Opposition parties in Scotland used them to highlight the weakness of the Scottish Government's policy capability on these reserved matters.

However, one could argue that most of the 'devolution differentiation' in public policy has stemmed not from Scotland doing things differently since 1999, but from it staying the same while ministers in Whitehall pursued new policy trajectories. The most commonly cited policy differences stemming from Edinburgh are tuition fees, care for the elderly and STV for local elections. The introduction of all of these policies had more to do with the intricacies of managing a coalition administration from 1999 to 2007 than conscious decisions 'to be different'. All three policies emerged after much deliberation by commissions, and committees. In Scotland there are no 'up-front' tuition fees; instead students are asked to pay a graduate endowment after university when they are earning a salary. This policy emerged from the Cubie Committee's recommendations. The care for the elderly policy emerged from one of the UK Sutherland Committee's recommendations which, although rejected by the Blair Government, were accepted by the Scottish Government. The more proportional STV electoral system being used for the 2007 local elections stemmed from the deliberations of the Kerley Committee.

Keating (2005) suggests that the Scottish Government has simply adopted a more traditional social democratic model of public service delivery than England that emphasises professionalism and uniformity over choice and diversity. There appears to be a higher trust in the public sector professional in Scotland. As Loughlin notes, 'while the English approach has emphasised management, regulation and differentiation, the Scottish approach has stressed professional autonomy, consensus, egalitarianism and policy learning' (Loughlin 2005). The new public management agenda did not take root in Scotland. It has not penetrated organisation and management in the public sector in Scotland to the same degree as in England. This could be due to the differences in the powers of established interest groups in the public services fields. Civil society elites, because of Scotland's smallness, have tended to have deep and dense interconnections, with the village nature of Edinburgh making interpersonal connections common across important policy fields such as law, education, social services, housing, economic development and planning. Professional associations in these areas remain strong while institutions that may advocate market based solutions such as management consultancies and think tanks, as well as right-leaning media commentators, are all weaker in Edinburgh than London.

Overall, it is undoubtedly true that the Scottish Government has had greater latitude in framing its own policies than the old Scottish Office. A combination of factors account for this: the Parliament, the increase in political influence due to the higher preponderance of ministers, an enhancement of research and policy development capacity in the civil service, pressure group expectations and influence. However, the broad parameters of the Labour Party's UK policy agenda still provided the context and framework for the Labour–Liberal Democrat Scottish policy agenda between 1999 and 2007. Even at the level of rhetoric the agenda of the McConnell administration was not unlike that of the Blair Government. When it is considered that political rhetoric may tend to accentuate rather than dilute differences, the actual substance of policy outputs may have been even more similar. In that sense the difference from the previous Westminster–Scottish Office model is not so apparent. To the extent that policy differences have occured it has tended to be over implementation detail and adaptation.

Devolution is a necessary condition for policy autonomy; it is not, however, sufficient. There is no denying that the political environment of Scottish policy-making has changed. Nevertheless, there has been an unwillingness by successive

Labour First Ministers to rock the boat in relations with London. From a UK Labour Party perspective, substantial policy divergence tends to be viewed as a recipe for friction, confrontation and conflict. The election of the Alex Salmond-led minority SNP administration has of course changed the dynamic of Scottish-UK intergovernmental relations. Equally, devolution has, undoubtedly, enhanced the scrutiny and accountability of the public sector in Scotland in scope, quality and quantity. However, the evidence to date of undoubted changes in policy processes translating into substantial devolved policy differences is limited.

Conclusion

Constitutionally perhaps the most important question to be asked of devolution is does it make the break-up of Britain more or less likely? Pre-devolution, the constitutional conservatives suggested it would make it more likely, with UK doomsday scenarios. For veteran Labour MP Tam Dalyell it was a 'motorway with no exits' and ex-Conservative Secretary of State, Ian Lang, viewed the creation of a Scottish Parliament 'to be a halfway house, and one built on a slippery slope' (Lang 2002: 168). Many of the Liberal Democrat and Labour pro-devolution campaigners, on the other hand, tended to sell devolution as necessary to preserve the integrity of the union by closing the 'democratic deficit' that had emerged within it. From the vantage point of 2007 the political tide appears to be moving in favour of the former view. However, if independence is to happen it still faces significant obstacles.

Historically the fundamentalist wing of the SNP tended to be sceptical of the devolutionary incrementalist route to independence. But today the incrementalist approach dominates SNP thinking – it is the route to increased self-government. The SNP have deliberately placed some distance (in the minds of the electorate) between voting SNP and supporting Scottish independance. While the SNP has established itself as the alternative (to Labour) party of government the electorate is aware that before independence can happen a few other hurdles would have to be overcome, most notably a majority in the Parliament in favour of a referendum *and* a majority of the Scottish electorate voting in favour of it in a referendum.

Table 2.5 suggests stability in pre- and post-devolution Scottish constitutional preferences. Since 1997 public opinion on each constitutional option has remained fairly stable and between 1999 and 2007 the constitutional issue was on the back-burner of Scottish politics. It was always simmering though – the SNP, Liberal Democrats, Conservatives and Greens all advocated a greater degree of fiscal autonomy for the Scottish Parliament. Both the SNP and Greens are committed to independence. The new 'constitutional conservatives' are the Labour Party (Mitchell and Bradbury 2004: 334).

The 2007 election result and the establishment of Scotland's first SNP administration have brought the constitutional issue back to the forefront of Scottish politics. The campaign highlighted continuing unionist opposition in the form of the Conservative, Liberal Democrat and Labour Parties as well as the media. However, one notable feature was that it was only the Labour Party – in a highly negative campaign – which repeatedly questioned the economic and fiscal viability of the

Table 2.5 Trends in constitutional preference in Scotland, 1997–2004

	1997 Gen El	1997 Ref	1999	2000	2001	2002	2003	2004
Independence in or out the EU	26	37	28	30	27	30	26	32
Stay in UK with Parliament	51	41	59	55	60	52	55	45
Stay in UK with no Parliament	17	17	10	12	9	12	13	17

Source: Adapted from Curtice, J. (2004) and Curtice, J. (2006) Figure 9.8.

independence option. The other two were, in the main, happy to accept the notion that independence *was* a viable option. Nevertheless, the SNP will struggle to gain a majority in the Parliament to vote in favour of its stated manifesto preference of holding a referendum on the constitutional question in 2010.

The post-devolution literature in looking at institutions has still tended to focus on change and differences with the UK. Factors highlighting similarity and continued assimilation have, in comparison, been neglected. There is no doubt devolution has created a state of flux. However, the policy-making process remains incremental – the weight of institutional legacies and existing commitments limits the scope for change. Grand ideas in terms of a radical new post-devolution narrative in Scottish politics have been absent. The Scottish policy trajectory, although showing signs of branching off on a different path, is still not that different from that of Westminster and Whitehall. There are numerous factors limiting such change and promoting conformity. Not least is the fact that between 1999 and 2007 UK remained a relatively integrated polity, society and economy.

Devolution was the 'solution' to the excesses of British centralism and poor territorial management in the 1980s and 90s. To an extent it has solved the problem. The parts of the Blairite modernisation agenda deemed unsuitable for Scottish tastes have largely been ignored by the Scottish Government. The allegedly more egalitarian social democratic tastes have been catered for in terms of policies such as care for the elderly. However, whether the current settlement has truly realised the potential capacity for self-government is a more vexed question. The Scottish Government between 1999 and 2007 showed no inclination to test the parameters of the present 'settlement', indeed it adopted a very conservative approach. As Mooney and Poole have argued, the notion of a *New* Scotland in social policy terms is largely mythical (2004: 478 – original emphasis). The assumptions regarding social citizenship underpinning the UK Welfare State remain and act as a major constraint to any significant policy divergence in the UK today (Keating 2002: 11–14).

Changes have undoubtedly taken place – the new Parliament and the democratic procedures associated with it have injected a greater degree of pluralism in political processes, and the establishment of a minority SNP administration will surely accentuate this. Agendas in Scotland in different policy areas have changed. However, without some objective criteria for measurement (which is difficult to find other than through comparative analysis) it is hard to say by how much and to what extent devolution has been the causal factor. It is more the case that while change has taken place in England, the social democratic agenda of Scottish politics has proved far more durable and deep rooted. The Blairite modernisation agenda has not penetrated the professional base of universalistic directly provided services in Scotland. There is evidence of change but in many ways this has simply built on pre-devolution trends in divergence, though the politics of coalition management has had effects. Devolution was built on the existing system of government in Scotland, yet in many ways it has merely added a thick layer of democratic gloss to those institutions. A neglect of devolution's institutional inheritance could lead to an exaggeration of its impact on policy outputs.

References

Arbuthnott, J. (2006) *Putting Citizens First: Boundaries Voting and Representation in Scotland – the Arbuthnott Report* http://www. arbuthnottcommission. gov. uk

Arter, D. (2002) 'On assessing strength and weakness in parliamentary committee systems: some preliminary observations on the new Scottish Parliament', *The Journal of Legislative Studies*, 8(2): 93–117.

Arter, D. (2004) 'The Scottish Committees and the goal of a "New Politics": a verdict on the first four years of the devolved Scottish Parliament', *Journal of Contemporary European Studies*, April 2004, 12(1): 71–91.

Arter, D. (2002) 'On assessing strength and weakness in parliamentary committee systems: some preliminary observations on the new Scottish Parliament', *Journal of Legislative Studies*, 8(2): 93–117.

Bradbury, J. and Mitchell, J. (2001) 'Devolution: new politics for old?' *Parliamentary Affairs* 54(2): 257–75

Bromley, C. and Given, L. (2005) *Public Perceptions of Scotland after Devolution* http://www. scotland. gov. uk/Publications/2005/08/18151621/16231

Brown, A., McCrone, D. and Paterson, L. (1st edn) (1996) *Politics and Society in Scotland*, Basingstoke: Macmillan.

Brown, A., McCrone, D. and Paterson, L. (2nd edn) (1998) *Politics and Society in Scotland*, Basingstoke: Macmillan.

Brown, A. (2000) 'Designing the new Scottish Parliament', *Parliamentary Affairs*, 53(3).

Cairney, P. (2006) 'The analysis of Scottish Parliament committee influence: beyond capacity and structure in comparing West European legislatures', *European Journal of Political Research*, 45: 181–208.

Cairney, P. and Keating, M. (2004) 'Sewel motions in the Scottish Parliament', *Scottish Affairs*, 47: 115–34.

Curtice, J. (2004) 'Restoring confidence and legitimacy', in A. Trench (ed.) *Has Devolution Made a Difference?* Exeter: Imprint Academic.

Curtice, J. (2005) *The Implications and Consequences of Introducing STV for the Scottish Parliament Elections*, Edinburgh: Centre for Scottish Public Policy.

Curtice, J. (2006) 'Public attitudes and elections', in P. Jones (ed.) Scotland Devolution Monitoring Report January 2006 http://www. ucl. ac. uk/constitution-unit

Curtice, J. and Herbert, S. (2005) 'STV in local government elections: modelling the 2003 results', SPICE Briefing 05/31, Edinburgh: Scottish Parliament Information Centre.

Garret, J. (1992) *Westminster: Does Parliament Work?* London: Victor Gallancz.

Harvie, C. (2004) 'The economic and social context of Scottish Labour', in G. Hassan (ed.) *The Scottish Labour Party: History, Institutions and Ideas*, Edinburgh: Edinburgh University Press.

Hassan, G. (2002) 'The paradoxes of Scottish Labour: devolution, change and conservatism', in G. Hassan and C. Warhurst (eds) *Tomorrow's Scotland*, London: Lawrence & Wishart.

Hassan, G. (2004) 'The People's Party, still?' in G. Hassan (ed.) *The Scottish Labour Party: History, Institutions and Ideas*, Edinburgh: Edinburgh University Press.

Hassan, G. and Warhurst, C. (eds) (2002) *Tomorrow's Scotland*, London: Lawrence & Wishart.

Heald, D., Geghan, N. and Robb, C. (1998) 'Financial arrangements for UK devolution', in H. Elcock and M. Keating. (eds) *Remaking the Union*, Frank Cass: London.

Irvine, M. (2004) 'Scotland, Labour and the trade union movement: partners in change or uneasy bedfellows?' in G. Hassan (ed.) *The Scottish Labour Party: History, Institutions and Ideas*, Edinburgh: Edinburgh University Press.

Keating, M. (2001) 'Devolution and public policy convergence in the United Kingdom. divergence or convergence?' Seminar on Devolution in Practice 31.10.01, Institute of Public Policy Research.

Keating, M. (2002) 'Devolution and public policy in the UK: divergence or convergence?' in J. Adams and P. Robinson (eds) *Devolution in Practice*, London: IPPR.

Keating, M. (2005) *The Government of Scotland: Public Policy-making after Devolution*, Edinburgh: Edinburgh University Press.

Kellas, J. (1989) *The Scottish Political System* (4th edn), Cambridge; Cambridge University Press.

Kerley Report (2000) Report of the Renewing Local Democracy Working Group http//www.scotland.gov.uk/library2/doc16/rldw.pdf

Lang, I. (2002) *Blue Remembered Years*, London: Politicos.

Loughlin, M. (2005) 'Devolution has meant growing policy differences between Scotland, Wales and England – study' *ESRC Society Today* http://www.esrcsocietytoday.ac.uk/ESRCInfoCentre/PO/releases/2005/march/index8.aspx?ComponentId=8183&SourcePageId=6482

Lynch, P. (2001) *Scottish Government and Politics*, Edinburgh: Edinburgh University Press.

Macwhirter, I. (2002) 'The new Scottish political classes', in G. Hassan and C. Warhurst (2002) *Anatomy of the New Scotland*, Edinburgh: Mainstream.

McConnell, A. (2004) *Scottish Local Government*, Edinburgh: Edinburgh University Press.

McCrone, D. (1992) *Understanding Scotland: The Sociology of a Stateless Nation* (1st edn), London: Routledge.

McGarvey, N. (2005) 'Local government north and south of the border', *Public Policy and Administration*, 20(4): 90–9.

McNish, A. (Chair) (2001) *Scottish Local Government's Self-Review of its Political Management Structures: Report of the Leadership Advisory Panel*, Edinburgh: The Stationery Office.

Midwinter, A., Keating, M. and Mitchell, J. (1991) *Politics and Public Policy in Scotland*, Basingstoke: Macmillan.

Miller, W. L. (1981) *The End of British Politics?* Oxford: Clarendon.

Mitchell, J. (2000) 'New parliament, new politics', *Parliamentary Affairs*, 53(3).

Mitchell, J. (2001) 'The study of Scottish politics post-devolution: new evidence, new analysis and new methods?', *West European Politics*, Vol. 24, 216–223.

Mitchell, J. (2004) *Governing Scotland*, Basingstoke: Palgrave.

Mitchell, J. and Bradbury, J. (2004) 'Devolution: comparative development and policy roles', *Parliamentary Affairs*, 57(2): 329–46.

Mitchell, J. (2006) 'Re-inventing the Union', in W. Miller, (ed.), *Anglo-Scottish Relations Since 1900*, British Academy/Oxford University Press.

Mooney, G. and Poole, L. (2004) 'A land of milk and honey? Social policy in Scotland after devolution', *Critical Social Policy* Vol. 24(4): 458–83.

Nelson, F. (2001) 'Is this devolution or just duplication?' *The Times*, 26.7.01.

Parry, R. (2004) 'The civil service and intergovernmental relations', *Public Policy and Administration*, 19(2): 50–63.

Parry, R. and Jones, A. (2000) 'The transition from the Scottish Office to the Scottish Executive', *Public Policy and Administration*, 15(2): 53–66.

Paterson, L. (2000) 'Civil society and democratic renewal', in S. Baron, J. Field and T. Schuller (eds) *Social Capital: Critical Perspectives*, Oxford: Oxford University Press.

Paterson, L. (2002) 'Civic democracy', in G. Hassan and C. Warhurst (2002) *Anatomy of the New Scotland*, Edinburgh: Mainstream.

Roberts, P. (2000) 'Setting the pace: Scotland and the UK devolution project', in A. Wright (ed.) *Scotland: The Challenge of Devolution*, Aldershot; Ashgate.

Saren, J. and McCormick, J. (2004) 'The politics of Scottish Labour's heartlands', in G. Hassan (ed.) *The Scottish Labour Party: History, Institutions and Ideas*, Edinburgh: Edinburgh University Press.

Scottish Constitutional Convention (1995) *Scotland's Parliament: Scotland's Right*, Edinburgh: Convention of Scottish Local Authorities.

Scottish Office (1999) *Report of the Commission on Local Government and the Scottish Parliament*, McIntosh Report, Edinburgh: Scottish Office.

Shephard, M. and Cairney, P. (2004) 'Consensual or dominant relationships with Parliament? A comparison of administrations and ministers in Scotland', *Public Administration*, 82(4): 831–55.

Shephard, M. and Cairney, P. (2005) 'Does the Scottish Parliament matter? The use of legislative impact to explore the new politics', *Political Studies*, 53(2): 303–19.

Steel, D. (2001) 'A dozen differences of devolution', Speech to the Oxford Union – Monday 4 June, 2001, http://www.scottish.parliament.uk/nmCentre/news/news-01/pa01-031.htm

Stoker, G. and Wilson, D. (eds) (2005) *British Local Government into the 21st Century*, Basingstoke: Palgrave.

Winetrobe, B. K. (2001) *Realising The Vision: A Parliament with a Purpose, An Audit of the Scottish Parliament*, Constitution Unit: London.

3 Devolution in Wales

An unfolding process

Jonathan Bradbury

In contrast to Scotland, devolution in Wales in the late 1990s was some way from representing the settled will of the people. It received affirmation in the 1997 referendum by the tiny majority of just 0.6 per cent. There was also a problematic background to devolution in that distinct governmental capacity had generally developed slowly. There was not much cohesion even among elites who generally supported devolution. There had been nothing like the Scottish Constitutional Convention; the Labour Party, which had long been the dominant party, stayed aloof from other parties and was cautious. It offered proposals for a National Assembly with only secondary legislative powers, funded entirely by central government block grant, which were duly enacted in the 1998 Government of Wales Act. Supporters of devolution, nevertheless, took an optimistic line. The 1997 'yes' vote was a 30 per cent increase on the 'yes' vote in the 1979 referendum and the 'yes' campaign had promised much. Pro-devolutionists generally looked forward to more accountable governance and pluralist politics. They envisaged autonomy in a wide range of policy areas. Ron Davies, Labour's Secretary of State for Wales, 1997–1998, referred to devolution as 'a process rather than an event' (Davies 1999); it was expected that the Assembly's powers would evolve over time.

From these relatively constrained origins, this chapter considers the development of devolution in Wales in the years between 1999 and 2007. The first section clarifies the pre-devolution context and the expectations of what devolution might achieve. The second and third sections address developments in governance and politics, and public policy. The final section then explores political debates over further constitutional change. The analysis emphasises the pivotal role played by the Labour Party both in the government of the National Assembly and in developing the debate over the Assembly's future. Against their expectations Labour did not win a majority after the first elections in 1999, had a majority of just one after the 2003 elections (due to the presiding officer and his deputy being from other parties), which it subsequently lost, and returned again to simply being the largest party in 2007. Nevertheless, Labour was continuously in power from 1999, experiencing periods of minority government (1999–2000), coalition with the Liberal Democrats (2000–2003), majority government (2003–2005) minority government from 2005 to 2007 and then coalition with Plaid Cymru in 2007. Different Labour Party leaders – Alun Michael (1999–2000) and Rhodri Morgan (2000 onwards) – also marked distinct phases of Assembly development. Consequently, Labour broadly sustained the leadership of devolution in Wales and largely determined its development. This comprised a significant record of political change, but one which overall was characterised by gradualism, and the merits of which were contested both by advocates of greater political autonomy and by Labour's political opponents.

Contexts and expectations

Analysis of the pre-devolution context suggests both the potential for Welsh assertion but also its considerable limitations. Welsh history had bestowed a sense of national identity, the survival of the Welsh language, and distinct sentiments and affiliations. During the nineteenth and twentieth centuries Wales developed a radical heritage, which valued community and social justice. This was reflected first in the Liberal Party hegemony in Wales before the First World War, and then the growing Labour Party ascendancy during the twentieth century. Following the channelling of some radical sentiments into nationalism, the 1960s and 1970s saw the emergence of Plaid Cymru. Equally, with the growth of government there emerged institutions with a distinct remit for Wales in areas of policy such as health and education. Measures of broader administrative devolution led to the creation of the Welsh Office with a Cabinet post of secretary of state in 1964. The case for devolution was humiliatingly defeated in 1979 but the momentum for a renewed case from the late 1980s appeared much greater. Following the 1987 General Election Labour MPs were stung by the contrast between a predominantly Labour voting Wales and a Conservative Government still with unchecked power. Thereafter, the perceived quasi-colonialism of English Conservative MPs being appointed as Secretaries of State for Wales, and the imposition of Conservative state reforms created a Conservative British/English 'other' against which Wales could coalesce (Morgan 1982; Mungham and Morgan 2000; Jones and Balsom 2000).

Nevertheless, the case of devolution in Wales could not be described as entirely robust. First, Wales had never been a unified polity even prior to union and therefore had little clear sense of pre-union rights and inherited institutional infrastructures upon which to base precise claims for a measure of national autonomy within the UK. The Union of Wales with England in 1536 determined that Wales should be treated as part of a common political, administrative and legal system with England. Welshness remained an identity felt only by two-thirds of the population. Even then there was division between those who closely identified Welshness with speaking the language and those who did not. Such divisions were still linked in the popular imagination, if not as precisely in geographical terms, to the three Wales model, defined from the 1979 election survey as: British East Wales; Welsh South Wales; and Welsh speaking West and North West Wales (Balsom 1983). Institutional infrastructures developed in an *ad hoc* manner and were often contingent upon broader developments within the UK state. Overall, there was a high level of integration of Wales with England, economically, culturally and politically. In the sense that Wales viewed itself as a political nation and the UK was viewed from Wales as a union rather than unitary state, such sentiments were relatively limited and ungrounded (Bradbury 1998: 123–5).

Second, whilst the creation of the Welsh Office in 1964 was an important landmark in modern Welsh political history its responsibilities were more limited than
those of the Scottish Office; the post of Secretary of State for Wales was considered
of low Cabinet rank; and the policy capacity of the civil service was relatively low.
It is obviously a caricature to suggest that all civil servants did was to receive policy
papers from Whitehall and make the wording appropriate to Wales, but that is the
Welsh Office's principal inherited reputation. Griffiths' (1996) analysis of Welsh
Office policy in the 1980s and 1990s suggests that whilst ministers were able to
pursue a style of government that was considerably different from that of Mrs
Thatcher the substance of policy diverged much less. Equally, the policy-making
process was characterised by the perceived remoteness of the Welsh Office civil service and a highly under-developed notion of government by policy network. In many
ways the plethora of groups articulating the interests of society which is usually
understood to exist between government and the governed was not there. As
Paterson and Wyn Jones (1999) concluded, it was likely that while civil society
helped to bring devolution into being in Scotland, the reverse would be the case
in Wales.

Third, elite advocates remained strongly aware of the problems of group attitudes and public opinion. Although the politicisation of Welsh identity was
undoubtedly assisted by the experience of Thatcherism and there were growing
arguments that an assembly would be helpful in promoting Wales in a more
competitive and Europeanised market economy, these pressures remained limited.
Both public and private sector linkages with the rest of the British economy were
still very strong, and there were marked regional economic divisions across Wales.
As a result, much changed during the 1980s and 1990s, including greater support
for devolution from local government, trade union and business leaders. Yet, business hardly led the clamour for an elected assembly. Opinion in the Labour Party
became more pro-devolution but not conclusively so. There remained a sizeable
number of party members who were opposed or sceptical about the extent of
planned transfers of powers. Finally, the public opinion polls that were episodically
conducted revealed a great many 'don't knows'.

Overall, therefore, the backdrop to devolution in Wales was one of limited distinct
national identity and institutional development, and a devolution campaign that strug-
gled to command wide or deep support. The year 1997 was not a year zero but it was
closer to being one than in Scotland. In these circumstances the strategies adopted by
political elites in 1997 appear to have been critical to a case for political change. These
included a decision to hold the referendum as soon as possible after Labour's General
Election victory in 1997 to keep Conservative Government fresh in the memories.
There was a concerted effort to play down the potential divisions over Welsh identity
by stressing a civic Welsh identity that was more inclusive. The 'yes' campaign then
focused on functional arguments for devolution; foremost were economic development, improved public services, arresting the democratic deficit, and a voice in
Europe. The referendum was also held a week after Scotland's to get the momentum
from a Scottish 'yes' vote. In the event, devolution was still only passed in 1997 with
a 50.3 per cent 'yes' vote on a turn-out of only 50.1 per cent of the electorate. For
some this was a staggering rise in support, given the defeat in 1979 and the continued

problems of gaining support; but it remained a strong indicator of the work that lay ahead in consolidating devolution in Wales (see Bradbury 2003).

Against this context what hopes were raised by the 1998 Government of Wales Act and the debates about its implementation? The act was based on proposals developed in the Wales Labour Party between 1992 and 1997 under the stewardship of Ron Davies, Labour's then shadow Secretary of State for Wales. The National Assembly was composed of 60 members, elected by a mixed member proportional (MMP) electoral system. This provided for 40 members elected by simple plurality from single member constituencies and 20 members elected from party lists, four each from five electoral regions. The d'Hondt method was used in allocating regional list seats to make the results in each of the electoral regions more proportional. Candidates were allowed to stand both in constituency and list elections. Devolution did not provide the Assembly with primary legislative or tax raising powers. Instead it received the secondary and executive powers previously exercised by the Secretary of State and junior ministers at the Welsh Office. The bulk of the civil servants who had worked in the Welsh Office now transferred to working for the Assembly, albeit still as part of the UK civil service. The Wales Office remained as a rump department of central government to help manage relations with the new Assembly.

This was clearly a more limited settlement than provided for in Scotland both in terms of the extent of proportionality in the electoral system and the powers devolved. Even so, the settlement had considerable potential for changing politics in Wales. First, some recognition should be made of the innovation of an MMP electoral system in Wales at all. Until 1996 Labour's proposals still provided for a simple plurality first past the post electoral system, which would have guaranteed Labour majorities in the National Assembly. However, Ron Davies faced down potential scepticism or hostility within his own party. In revising plans ahead of the referendum in September 1997 it appears that part of the reason for deciding upon an MMP electoral system was to reach out to both Plaid Cymru and the Liberal Democrats in order to gain cross-party support for a 'yes' vote in the referendum as well as to provide viable numbers to create an effective opposition within the Assembly once it was established. Under the proposed system Labour still expected to gain a majority but it would at least guarantee greater representation for the other parties and help to legitimise the Assembly as a whole (see Andrews, 1999).

Second, the manner in which the Assembly was founded and powers devolved to it was innovative. Powers were delegated to the National Assembly as a corporate body rather than to ministers as representatives of the crown. The Assembly would delegate its powers to secretaries (later ministers) but the Assembly retained the legal responsibility for decisions carried out in its name. Subject committees for each area of policy would have both policy-making and scrutiny roles and Assembly secretaries would be members of the relevant committees. As the bill passed through Westminster it was recognised that any perception of a local government style of decision making would be damaging to the status of the Assembly so the bill was amended to include provision for a Cabinet composed of the Assembly secretaries to provide executive leadership. Nevertheless, the fusion of these two approaches still provided considerable potential for active committees in the development of policy-making. More generally, devolution was accompanied by the rhetoric of a 'new politics'. Within the Assembly this pointed towards greater cross-party working and indeed the possibility of coalition administrations. Outside the Assembly, it suggested more engagement with civil society, and a greater representation of a diverse Welsh society, in particular of women.

At the same time, the significance of the powers devolved to the National Assembly should not be underestimated. Secondary powers covered the NHS, education and lifelong learning, economic development, the road network, land use planning, environmental policy and agriculture, and a wide range of social justice and arts and culture responsibilities. The Assembly had powers of control and finance over local government and a wide range of quangos. The block grant for government expenditure in Wales came under an unprecedented system of scrutiny; and the National Assembly became the institution responsible for co-ordinating expenditure of EU structural funds aid. The Assembly would remain reliant on Westminster for the secondary powers to be given to the Assembly under primary legislation. Yet, the Assembly had the right to formulate Wales-only bills and bid for Westminster parliamentary time to have them enacted and thus empower the Assembly in specified areas. At the same time Davies' announcement that Welsh devolution would be 'a process rather than an event' suggested that these powers should be extended on the basis of experience.

The Welsh devolution settlement of 1997–1998 was clearly heavily managed by the Labour Party, but even within that context it offered scope for political change. If one takes into account Labour's perceived mismanagement of devolution between late 1998 and early 2000 it becomes apparent that incentives to develop the potential of devolution also rapidly became relevant. Unexpected pressures on the Labour Party emerged like a tragic comedy of errors from a single event. In November 1998 Ron Davies took a walk at night on Clapham Common in London, he got into the company of men who he said later robbed him, and subsequently he felt the need to resign to avoid causing the Government further embarrassment. He was subsequently pressed to step down also as Labour Assembly leader-elect. Immediately prior to this fiasco, the opinion polls suggest Labour would have won a majority in the Assembly, and it is reasonable to assume, other things being equal, that opinion would not have moved much by polling day. However, Tony Blair appointed a new Secretary of State, Alun Michael, who then decided to stand to become Labour's leader in the Assembly. He succeeded against the rank and file's favourite, Rhodri Morgan, only with the backing of the elected members/candidates and trade union sections of Labour's electoral college. As a result Michael was perceived as Tony Blair's New Labour 'poodle' in Wales. The subsequent strategy for the first elections in 1999 was also disastrous. Labour not only appeared to have a leader perceived to be denying the practical value of devolution; much worse, Labour ran largely an anti Plaid Cymru campaign that made Labour – the party that had introduced devolution – actually look anti-Welsh. Labour suffered their worst election result in Wales since 1983. Michael, nevertheless, decided to form a minority Labour Government subsequently perceived as continuing a Secretary of State style regime with little sympathy to the potential of the new Assembly (see Flynn 1999).

The Michael period was extremely important because it brought both Labour's electoral appeal and ownership of the process of devolution seriously into question. To regain its former position, Labour had to act radically. In January 2000 certain Labour Assembly members conspired with opposition members to engineer a vote of no confidence in Michael over a failure to gain assurances over UK Government match-funding for EU structural funds aid. Michael resigned, to be succeeded by Rhodri Morgan. In contrast, Morgan had a long association with both strong support for devolution and radical causes on the populist left of the party. Taking advantage of the British Labour Party's willingness to stand back he immediately set about re-establishing Labour's devolutionist and electoral credentials. Later in 2000 he engineered a coalition with the Liberal Democrats; re-branded the Labour Party in Wales as 'Welsh Labour' with policies that established 'clear red water' between Labour in Wales and New Labour at the UK level; and agreed readily to the Liberal Democrat request for a commission to look into the future powers and electoral arrangements of the Assembly. Lord Elis Thomas, the Assembly's presiding officer, went so far as to describe the day of Michael's resignation as 'the first day of devolution'. This captured the release of potential in the Assembly in acting against an unwanted first secretary; and recognised the incentives for Labour, given its self-inflicted wounds, to develop the potential of devolution even more than it might have done so as to re-establish the party's dominance.

Overall, while many were aware of the limited capacity in the 1998 Government of Wales Act there were still high expectations of change accompanying devolution. Even within the constraints of Labour dominance the Act released much potential for new approaches to governance and politics, autonomy in public policy and further constitutional development. The Michael episode then gave further impetus to Labour to fulfil this potential. Wales was set fair for being potentially unexpectedly interesting.

Politics and institutions

Devolution raised the possibility of considerable institutional and political change in Wales. This section looks at four key issues: voting behaviour and political parties, the adaptation of UK institutions; the operation of the new Assembly; and the Assembly's relations with other institutions of governance. Analysis conveys a mixed and contested picture of how expectations for devolution were met in practice, although few can doubt that overall the landscape of governance in Wales was changed considerably.

Devolution, combined with the operation of the MMP electoral system, offered the possibility of dynamic change in representation, voting behaviour and the party system in Wales. Key changes were indeed prominent. Internal candidate selection became a primary focus for the recruitment of more women elected representatives. Both Labour and Plaid Cymru used positive discrimination procedures in favour of women, leading to the achievement of an exactly gender balanced assembly after the 2003 elections, which with subsequent developments actually led to a female majority (Bradbury *et al.* 2000; Bradbury and Mitchell 2004). Labour also made efforts to positively discriminate in favour of BME candidates, but it was Plaid Cymru who in the end supplied the Assembly's first BME member in 2007.

Moreover, as has already been noted, the electorate voted in quite a distinct manner in 1999, and although Labour made a small recovery in 2003, the period 1999–2007 as a whole saw a pattern of distinctive multi-level voting. This is characterised by Labour appearing to do significantly worse in National Assembly elections compared to UK elections in Wales and Plaid Cymru significantly better, although its Assembly success gave Plaid Cymru a boost in its share of the vote for Westminster elections as well (see Tables 3.1 and 3.2). The Conservatives and Liberal Democrats' performances are broadly similar between the two levels. Whether such voting behaviour reflects the assertion of a distinct Welsh political arena and if so in what ways, is, nevertheless, a matter for debate. The low turn-outs – comparable to local council elections – the movement of support away from the party in government at the UK level, and a notable and rising vote for minor parties, including the Greens, the British National Party and UKIP, all suggested second order qualities to Assembly elections. Meanwhile, Trystan *et al.* (2003) correlated vote switching between Westminster and Assembly elections with voting 'on Welsh issues', although Curtice (2000) suggested that this should be more closely related to voting on 'standing up for Wales' in a UK setting.

Whatever the causes of trends in voting behaviour they engendered a greater degree of pluralism in the party system than Labour designers of devolution had envisaged. Elections created a multi-party system in which Labour was forced to

Table 3.1 Elections to the National Assembly for Wales 1999–2007

	Con	*Lab*	*Lib Dem*	*Plaid Cymru*	*Others*
1999					
Constit vote share	15.8%	37.6%	13.5%	28.4%	4.7%
Constit seats	1	27	3	9	0
Regional vote share	16.5%	35.4%	12.5%	30.5%	5.1%
List seats	8	1	3	8	0
Total	9	28	6	17	0
2003					
Constit vote share	19.9%	40.0%	14.1%	21.2%	4.7%
Constit seats	1	30	3	5	1
Regional vote share	19.2%	36.6%	12.7%	19.7%	11.9%
List seats	10	0	3	7	0
Total	11	30	6	12	1
2007					
Constit vote share	22.4%	32.2%	14.8%	22.4%	8.3%
Constit seats	5	24	3	7	1
Regional vote share	21.5%	29.6%	11.7%	21.0%	16.2%
List seats	7	2	3	8	0
Total	12	26	6	15	1

Turnout: 1999: 46.0%; 2003: 38.2%; 2007: 43.4%

Table 3.2 UK General Elections in Wales 1997–2005

	Con	Lab	Lib Dem	Plaid Cymru	Others
1997					
Vote share	19.6%	54.7%	12.4%	9.9%	3.4%
Seats	0	34	2	4	0
2001					
Vote share	21.0%	48.6%	13.8%	14.3%	2.3%
Seats	0	34	2	4	0
2005					
Vote share	21.4%	42.7%	18.4%	12.6%	4.9%
Seats	3	29	4	3	1

Turnout: 1997: 73.6%; 2001:60.6%; 2005: 62.4%

reach accommodations with other parties when working as a minority government and when it was in coalition with the Liberal Democrats between 2000 and 2003. In 2005 Labour showed further evidence of their vulnerability when Peter Law stood as an independent candidate at the UK General Election in protest at the use of an all-women shortlist to select Labour's candidate in Blaenau Gwent. This wiped out Labour's theoretical majority of one after the 2003 elections and reduced them to a minority administration again. Nevertheless, the changing political arithmetic did not lead to any conclusive changes in approaches to collaboration between parties. Although Labour worked with the other parties in periods of minority and coalition government it generally sought to assert its own policy priorities. Even after two terms of government in which Labour at best had a theoretical majority of one, the party's aim was still to govern alone on fairly traditional Westminster 'winner takes all lines'.

Ahead of the 2007 Assembly elections there was much talk about the possibility of a non-Labour all-party administration, covering Plaid Cymru, the Conservatives and the Liberal Democrats. Cross-party co-operation to thwart Labour policies in 2005–2006, including concerted opposition to Labour's 2006 budget, indicated its potential. In the wake of the 2007 elections, both Plaid Cymru and the Liberal Democrats broke off negotiations with Labour over coalition and confidence and supply arrangements, and joined with the Conservatives in proposing a so-called 'rainbow coalition' based on a shared policy agreement. Such a coalition seemed fraught with the problems of inter-party rivalry, and internal dissent in the Liberal Democrats in the short term prevented agreement. Nevertheless, the development of the 'rainbow coalition' idea pressed Labour to reach out again to other parties, leading ultimately to the Labour–Plaid Cymru coalition in July 2007. More change in inter-party relations was expected after 2007 than before.

Developments in key UK government institutions in Wales were also charac-terised by both continuity and change. Pre-eminent was the civil service. On the one hand, the civil servants working for the National Assembly remained part of the UK home civil service, headed by a permanent secretary and organised on a depart-mental footing very reminiscent of a Whitehall department divided into functional sections. Civil servants also continued to see their relationships with Whitehall departments as key reference points, not least because primary legislative powers still remained at the UK level. That said, the exact form of departmental organisation now followed a design led by the Assembly; it was the Assembly that decided which issues had synergies and should be coupled in ministerial portfolios. To give one example, transport was originally tied in with the environment, land planning and local government portfolio before later being merged with economic development. Such a choice did not follow Whitehall practice.

It took some time for civil servants used to the old Welsh Office ways of working to adapt to working with an Assembly Cabinet and Assembly committees. Similarly, the first two years of devolution were marked by turf wars between Whitehall departments and Assembly departments as well as unthinking ignorance in Whitehall of factoring devolution into various policy debates (Laffin and Thomas 2001). Nevertheless, the frameworks provided by formal memorandums of understanding and concordats and informal mediation by officials of the Wales Office helped to bed civil servants into the new machinery. Research appears to indicate that after two terms adjustments both to the more direct accountability required under devolution and the new intergovernmental relations had been made (Cole 2006).

Of equal importance as a UK 'institution' was central government finance, which came in the form of an annual block grant and upon which the Assembly was entirely dependent. This resulted from negotiations between the Treasury and Whitehall spending departments to determine a level of spending per head in England and then the operation of the Barnett formula to determine what then Wales would receive as a result. At the same time, the make-up of UK public expenditure estimates also created expectations for how spending of the Welsh block grant would be allocated. These dependencies raised some criticisms. For example, a broad body of opinion formed in favour of a needs-based rather than an expenditure based formula. Whilst this would have reduced the block grant for Scotland it was expected that it would increase it for Wales. Equally, after the 2003 elections the Labour Welsh Assembly government decided upon a policy of having their own comprehensive spending reviews to decide how the expenditure of the Welsh block grant would be broken up according to Welsh rather than English based priorities. However, neither of these issues was progressed very far. Labour refused to join the cause for a reform of the Barnett formula; and the comprehensive spending reviews failed to achieve notable changes in emphasis in expenditure by 2005, revealing the intrinsic political difficulties of changing gradually built up expenditure commitments rapidly. In this context continuities were more apparent than change.

The development of the Assembly as a debating institution itself also offered a potentially fertile area for innovation. One ought to dismiss the more extreme expectations of 'new politics'. There was no significant evidence of unusual cross-party working or suspension of party competition. Indeed, there was considerable tension over perceived competition between constituency members (usually Labour) and list members (almost entirely non-Labour 1999–2003 and entirely non-Labour 2003–2007) to provide local constituency representation. Some constituency AMs accused List AMs of abusing their positions to target representation on a more coveted constituency seat ahead of the next elections; resentments which often surfaced in Assembly debates (Bradbury and Mitchell 2007).

Equally, it was fairly rapidly agreed across all parties that the conceptualisation of the Assembly as a corporate body and the closely collaborative role this was intended to give committees was flawed. An Assembly review of internal procedures recommended in February 2002 that as far as the Assembly was legally allowed it should operate on the basis of a clear separation between executive and legislature. There was all-party agreement on this approach and in March 2002 there was a formal division between the Assembly and what was now termed the Welsh Assembly Government, with civil service staff equally separated between those under the charge of the presiding officer and those working for the Government. This clarified the conceptualisation of the assembly as a parliamentary style body in which committees could be active and influence policy but primarily have a review and scrutiny role. Secretaries, re-termed ministers, were no longer to be members of Assembly committees. Implicitly, this re-introduced House of Commons habits into the new Assembly setting.

Nevertheless, there was considerable take-up of the innovative ideas of the 1998 National Assembly Advisory Group report. In particular, the Assembly adopted family friendly hours both in terms of the phasing of Assembly sessions with school terms and 9–5 daily hours. All members continued to adopt a standard procedure of calling each other by their first name in the chamber. Subject committees, both before and after the *de facto* abandonment of the corporate body principle, delivered a number of influential reports. For example, the Education Committee was particularly respected during the 1999–2003 session for its innovative thinking. The Business Committee, chaired by the deputy presiding officer, created a more formal and open approach to the management of the Assembly business than seen in the secretive process of the 'usual channels' at Westminster (see Jones and Osmond 2000; Jones and Osmond 2002; McAllister 2000).

In 2006 the new building housing the Assembly plenary debating chamber, committee, meeting rooms and open access foyer, was opened in Cardiff Bay. It appeared to reflect the continued aspirations for the Assembly to make the political process more accessible. Members of the public could stand in the corridors of the Assembly and peer through sheet glass sides into rooms hosting even apparently private party meetings.

Finally, an important focus in considering institutional capacity lay in the Assembly relations with other institutions of governance in Wales. Key among these was elected councils, upon which the Assembly relied for the delivery of many public services. Local Government structure had been reformed as recently as 1994 and instead of instigating further reform the Assembly focused on developing an effective partnership with local councils (Laffin *et al.* 2002). Indeed, much was made of the Labour led Assembly Government's generally 'localist' policy style that privileged the role of councils. More generally, the Assembly Government developed consistent approaches to consultation over major policy reviews that helped to create policy networks where there had effectively been none before. Assembly committees became a byword for consulting groups representing civil society. Management of EU assistance included unprecedented consultation with civil society groups.

Nevertheless, there were critiques of the broader structures of Assembly governance. First, it was possible to allege an over-cosy relationship between the Assembly Government and local councils, many of which were Labour run. In sharp contrast to Labour group meetings at Westminster Labour local government representatives were routinely invited to Assembly Labour group meetings. The Welsh Labour spring conference in 2002 decisively opposed the Sunderland Commission's recommendation of introducing STV for local government elections, a proposal greeted with horror by Labour local government leaders. Only in the second term, 2003–2007, did the Assembly Government start to directly challenge local councils amid frustrations over competency in policy delivery. Second, it was possible to perceive a selective rather than pluralist flavour to the network relationships that ministers and Assembly departments developed in policy-making. For example, a notable criticism was that public and voluntary sector interests gained access to policy discussions much more easily than private sector interests. Equally, analysis of a number of areas of policy in Wales suggested the privileging of larger group interests and exclusion of or indifference towards more diverse civil society interests (Chaney *et al.* 2001; Royles 2004).

Finally, it was also possible to allege a trend in Assembly Government that was characterised more by centralism than 'new politics'. This focused on the 'bonfire of the quangos', announced in July 2004 and heralded as the unfinished business of devolution. The abolition of such quangos as the Welsh Development Agency, the Education and Learning Wales Agency and the Arts Council was followed by the incorporation of their functions into expanded Assembly Government departments under more direct managerial guidance of ministers and senior civil servants. Whilst the Assembly Government sought to portray this as a reform to make the delivery of government more accountable, critics characterised it as unwarranted centralisation and politicisation of functions best conducted by experts away from the direct control of ministers.

Consequently, the implications of institutional and political developments were mixed and contested. To this may be added two other fundamental issues that the political class barely even started to address. First, both the supply of and demand for the 'political' media in Wales remained weak, whether through television, radio or print outlets. Members of the National Assembly had major problems communicating their ambitions, policy discussions and achievements to Welsh society at any level. Second, the private sector in Wales remained relatively inchoate because of the lack either of large company players or large representative organisations. This made an engagement between governance and the private sector both fragmented and disjointed.

Overall, one may focus too much on the problems. Undoubtedly these existed; the development of new politics was patchy. Understanding of the character of change would profit from more investigation. Yet, for a comparatively short time period it remains the case that there were some significant changes right across the board relating to voting habits and the party system, the conduct of political business and styles of policy-making. Of course, this was a record of adaptation that occurred under a largely Labour-run Assembly government; it remained to be seen whether there might be more significant political and institutional changes in the context of a Labour–Plaid Cymru coalition administration.

Public policy

Whether the expectations of public policy autonomy were realised is also open to question and debate. On the one hand a plausible case could be made that the Welsh Assembly Government demonstrated the utility of the powers granted to the Assembly in a number of significant ways. First, the early years were characterised by review and the development of strategic plans. Second, the Assembly received the boost of significant increases in real terms of block grant funding, following successive UK Government comprehensive spending reviews, as well as EU structural funds aid of £1.2 billion between 2001 and 2006. From 2001 the Assembly Government emerged as a more active administration, armed both with the benefits of policy development and improved spending capacity. Third, as a fundamental expression of the political rhetoric of 'Welsh Labour' and 'Clear Red Water' there was increased spending on publicly run public services. Significantly, the administration played down any great usage of the UK Government's policy of investing in public services through the private finance initiative. Major efforts were made to address problems of economic and social renewal, notably through schemes to regenerate the South Wales Valleys.

The Assembly Government found that it could make significant policy developments through using the facility to lobby UK Government on legislative plans at Westminster. In particular, following a report on abuses in children's homes, the Assembly successfully lobbied the UK Government to pass the Children's commissioner for Wales Act in 2001. Of perhaps even greater broader significance was the passage of legislation in 2002 allowing the Assembly to reform the National Health Service in Wales. This reformed the structure to one led by 22 local health boards as the pre-eminent 'purchasing' health authorities. These had coterminous boundaries with local government to make the NHS more locally oriented, led by primary care concerns and capable of liaison with local social care agencies (Sullivan 2002; Greer 2005). Finally, as a result of clauses in the 2005 Railways Act and the 2006 Wales-only Transport Act the Assembly became a major strategic transport authority.

The Assembly found that there was also often significant scope for autonomy in how new primary legislation made at Westminster could be implemented in Wales. A key case where this facilitated policy divergence was in education. The first indication of a different approach in Wales to UK policy was the scrapping in July 2001 of the league tables of exam performance by which schools could be evaluated by parents. Subsequently, in contrast to the implementation of the 2002 Education Act in England, the Assembly scrapped the testing of seven year olds, did not utilise the private sector in the building of new state schools, did not encourage faith or specialist schools, and resisted the by-passing of local education authorities by allocating 90 per cent of resources directly to schools. Instead the Assembly followed a more public sector oriented agenda compared to the more marketised approach followed in England (see National Assembly for Wales 2001). A distinctive approach was also followed in respect of paying for higher education. Tuition fees and subsequently variable top-up fees were introduced for university students in England. In Wales tuition fees were accepted as a financial necessity, but to combat the possible inequalities of access the Assembly introduced means tested learning grants worth up to £1,500 per year for students in both higher and further education. In 2005 it was decided not to charge students variable top-up fees, but instead to compensate Welsh universities directly for any lost income compared to English universities.

A lot of these policies were of Welsh Labour design but there were also significant policy consequences from the coalition with the Liberal Democrats between 2000 and 2003. In particular, the Liberal Democrats were the source of policies to provide free school milk and to abolish prescription and dental charges for the under 25s and over 60s. It was in this context that a policy of free bus passes for the elderly was also introduced. Indeed there were Liberal Democrat claims that they in practice made Labour pay the heavy price of taking on board all of their main policies in return for their support in government. This in turn created some internal dissent in the Labour Party against Morgan's leadership. Peter Law, who was dropped from the Cabinet to make room for a Liberal Democrat minister in 2000, went as far as offering himself as a leadership candidate against Morgan in 2002.

Undoubtedly coalition created strains for the Labour Party. Yet Morgan generally calculated that by going into coalition and sticking with it Labour would gain the electorate's respect for doing what was necessary to bring stable government to Wales. It was in effect part of the long game played from 2000 to 2003 to win the much prized party majority at the 2003 elections. In winning a working majority of one this paid off and Labour came out with a significantly Welsh Labour manifesto endorsed. Cloaking it in the memory of Aneurin Bevan's famous Labour Cabinet resignation cause in 1950 Labour led on a policy of abolishing all prescription charges in the NHS. This was accompanied by a range of Labour 'popular' policies including free school breakfasts, free swimming for the elderly and free home care for the disabled. The period after the 2003 elections was marked by the gradual rolling out of most of these policies.

Yet to say that policy development was pursued without problems would be misleading. First, the constraints of the devolution settlement in 1998 have to be acknowledged. The types of policy capacity available to the Assembly were distributive and regulatory and not to any significant extent redistributive. There were numerous issues upon which the Assembly found its powers to be fragmentary or unclear. Equally, as new primary laws were passed at Westminster the listed secondary legislative and executive powers at the disposal of the National Assembly were inevitably also changed. This led to potential problems of unevenness, irrationality and fragmentation in the development of the Assembly's powers. Indeed there was a concern that over time the Assembly would find that its powers were being reduced by Westminster Acts for England and Wales that took no account of devolution.

A symptom of these problems was that Assembly members often simply became confused as to what were their powers.

There were numerous specific occasions when the Assembly found itself constrained in its policy options by UK Government policy. A notable case was social housing, where the Assembly set ambitious targets for improvement but was constrained by Treasury rules from enhanced public sector intervention, specifically through local council funding. Instead, despite ideas of creating co-operative tenant run organisations, the Assembly found stock transfer out of the public sector into existing housing associations the only really viable means of reaching its improvement targets. In other instances, the Assembly developed a settled view on an issue only to find it compromised. For example, despite declaring Wales a GM-free zone the Assembly found that it did not have the powers to stop companies conducting GM crops trials in Wales. In 2005 despite the Assembly's policy that Wales should be a nuclear free zone the UK Government's preference for renewing nuclear energy threatened to compromise any such autonomy. While the Scottish Parliament introduced a smoking ban, the Assembly was incapable of introducing its own desired ban until vested with powers from Westminster. The Assembly also found itself limited in its powers even when expected by UK Government to act. During the 2001 crisis of foot and mouth disease in the livestock industry, the UK Government expected the Assembly Government to take responsibility and yet the Assembly Government found that it did not have the necessary powers. Comparisons with the Scottish Parliament emphasised what the Assembly could not do legislatively without primary powers (see Rawlings 2003).

Equally, there was substantial criticism of what Labour had done with the powers they did have at their disposal. An early focus was the apparent timidity of its economic development policy. Even from within party ranks Ron Davies, the former Secretary of State, suggested that policy showed little difference from former Welsh Office thinking. Responses to events such as the closure of the Corus steel plant drew little admiration. In 2005 Peter Hain, then Secretary of State for Wales, criticised the decision to abolish the Welsh Development Agency, given what he described as its proven track record in fostering economic development. There was also criticism of inadequacies in both the spending of EU money and monitoring of funded projects. A constant source of embarrassment was the long delays and escalating costs of building the new Assembly building. Against this, Labour claimed it had done much to achieve the lowest levels of unemployment in Wales in a generation. The winning of high profile contracts, such as the defence training academy proposal for St Athan in South Wales, suggested competence in dealing with economic opportunities. The incorporation of the WDA into the Assembly Government's new department of enterprise, innovation and networks actually occurred with very few tears, and arguably represented a reorganisation of an agency that had lost its way. Even the new Assembly building received considerable praise when it was finally opened.

Perhaps most dramatically the administration received heavy criticism over its health policies. Even Welsh Labour MPs criticised the failure to bring down either hospital waiting lists or times at the same rate as had been achieved in England.

At the 2002 party conference Labour MPs suggested that Labour Assembly members were putting too much blind faith in long-term structure reform and publicly funded health care; it was ducking the tough decisions to utilise private finance to meet health needs more quickly. This issue was still raw in the run-up to the 2005 election, as Welsh Labour MPs were concerned that the lagging performance of the Welsh NHS would cost them their seats. Despite calls for her removal as early as 2002 Jane Hutt had remained the Assembly's Minister for Health since being appointed by Alun Michael in 1999. Although a link was denied she was finally reshuffled in early 2005 and her successor, Brain Gibbons, sought to present a health policy better balanced between long and short-term commitments.

On the issue of public spending the Assembly Government avoided certain problematic commitments. For example, it did not pursue a policy of free long-term care for the elderly. This was judged to be a potentially expensive commitment that the Assembly in the long term could not afford. However, in the post-2003 session an unexpectedly high number of claimants meant that Labour was not actually able to honour its manifesto pledge to provide free home care for the disabled. More significantly, the decision to not charge variable top-up fees to Welsh university students landed the Assembly with a bill for compensating the universities that in the long term was potentially unsustainable. As of April 2006 the period of real terms growth in the block grant and EU funding both came to an end at the same time. In a context of tougher budgets all of the Assembly's spending commitments were threatened with future retrenchment.

Overall, there remained many apparently intractable problems of public policy, notably the high levels of social deprivation and low levels of employability in a number of areas of the country, not just the South Wales Valleys. There was also undoubted unevenness in approaches to policy and dispute over its wisdom. Nevertheless, the early years of devolution were still marked in public policy terms by the Assembly being seen to push the limits of its powers and be distinctive from UK policy in a manner that had a substantive as well as rhetorical significance. The Labour administration developed increasing confidence in its broad ideological commitment to utilising the community rather than the competitive ethic, which Rhodri Morgan considered more appropriate to politics in a small country like Wales, where there was a consensus around progressive ideas. The appearance of energy and divergence may have been all the greater because of the Welsh Labour rhetoric. But despite its constraints, the 1999 devolution settlement had provided significant policy autonomy, and for a variety of reasons, including the added pressures on Labour after the debacle of the 1999 elections as well as the significantly less distinctive policy development from before devolution compared to Scotland, that autonomy was put to significant use. It is notable that the opposition parties focused less on what they would do that Labour had not, than that they should have the right to try and do it better.

Constitutional development

That there would have been renewed debate of Wales' constitutional position fairly quickly is beyond question. It was promised as much by the former Labour

Secretary of State, Ron Davies. Yet the emergence of renewed debate over the Assembly's powers arose perhaps more quickly because of the specific political circumstances of the post-1999 period. The Labour Party, weakened by the 1999 election result, faced pressure from Plaid Cymru and the Liberal Democrats, both over the holding of a debate and over who would lead it. Arguably, as a result Labour agreed to a formal constitutional review earlier than it might otherwise have done; in the process they also largely determined its outcome. Views of Labour's approach again differ but likewise ultimately the debates over constitutional development led to significant changes.

Desires to re-open the original devolution settlement were specifically given impetus by the Labour–Liberal Democrat coalition deal in September 2000. One of the results of the partnership agreement was the creation of a commission, chaired by Labour peer, Lord Richard. It began its deliberations in 2002 and after lengthy evidence-taking sessions it issued its report in March 2004 (National Assembly for Wales 2004). The report made three key recommendations. First, it confirmed the consensus on the desire to end the legal conceptualisation of the Assembly as a corporate body and to provide a statutory basis for the separation of executive and assembly. Second, it commented favourably on the Assembly's usage of its powers so far and concluded on the problems associated with pushing at the limits of its existing powers. The report advocated the enhancement of secondary legislative powers as an interim measure but also recommended a move towards the Assembly receiving primary legislative powers. The timetable for this was not immediate but it was nevertheless a clear stated goal. The report rehearsed the arguments over the Assembly having fiscal powers but concluded with no clear view. It was left open as to whether the move to primary powers should require the holding of a further referendum. Finally, the Richard Report concluded that not only would the number of Assembly members have to rise to 80 to take account of the Assembly's enhanced responsibilities, but also they should be elected on the basis of the single transferable vote method. On all fronts the Richard Report provided for a radical revision of the 1998 Government of Wales Act which nevertheless would be phased in gradually. The overhaul was to be expected to be completed between 2010 and 2013.

There was strong support in elite circles for the adoption of the Richard Report, led by the pressure group *Tomorrow's Wales*, as well as from the Liberal Democrats and Plaid Cymru. Nobody questioned the proposals relating to the legal status of the Assembly. There were differences of views, however, on the other two sets of proposals. Whilst many opposition voices advocated the full implementation of the Richard Report the Labour Party voiced different opinions. Labour First Minister, Rhodri Morgan, was a clear supporter of moving towards primary powers though not of STV. A majority of Labour MPs in Wales were sceptical of supporting a new settlement. A majority of Labour party members supported the development of devolution but they did not wish to be seen to be following a nationalist timetable. Ted Rowlands, the former MP and Labour member of the Richard Commission, had provided the one note of minority dissent in the Richard Report in saying that whilst he did not disagree with the arguments in the report he saw no cause for the report's immediate implementation. Both Labour AMs and members were deeply sceptical of the introduction of STV. Instead they wanted protection from what they saw as the unfairness of defeated opposition constituency candidates still getting elected as list members and then behaving as though they were constituency members ahead of future elections.

The constitutional question potentially raised significant problems for Labour in the run-up to the 2005 General Election. However, the Morgan administration and Peter Hain as Labour's Secretary of State for Wales appeared to broker a workable approach to developing the assembly which finessed reformist aspirations with Labour scepticism. In autumn 2004 Labour's policy response, *Better Governance for Wales*, confirmed that there was a consensus on the proposal to change the legal status of the assembly. However it dissented from the clarity of Richard's commitment to primary powers. Instead, it proposed that Westminster henceforth apply a convention to grant maximum discretion to the Assembly in implementing England and Wales laws and that the Government would prepare a White Paper on options for future change including that of primary legislative powers. It further stated that if this latter option were ever considered it would be subject to a fresh referendum. Finally, on electoral reform it ignored Richard altogether, arguing that the 60 member MMP system should remain, with the revision that candidates should not be allowed to stand for both constituency and list seats. This was an attempt to remove the incentives for list members to target their work in competing for future constituency seats (Wales Labour Party 2004).

On the central issue of powers *Better Governance for Wales* was essentially an attempt at providing an interim Richard Report for the real world. Whilst playing to gradualist and sceptical opinion on the pace of change and in turning down the STV proposal, Hain and Morgan sought to gain both Labour Party and public support for a policy, the underlying logic of which was still profoundly devolutionist. In the immediate pre-election period Morgan and Hain were attacked by Plaid Cymru for failing to provide leadership and face down devo-sceptics. Nevertheless, whilst Welsh Labour MPs and broad Labour member opinion were pleased by its gradualism, and specifically the promise of a further referendum on primary powers, leading Labour pro-devolutionists both at Westminster and Cardiff Bay publicly acknowledged its general intentions to take devolution forward. The constitutional issue was thus effectively neutralised as an election issue in 2005.

Following the election the Wales Office published a White Paper, also called *Better Governance for Wales* (Wales Office 2005). This confirmed much of Labour's pre-election policy, the key additions being on the issue of the Assembly's powers. The convention of Westminster legislation granting the Assembly maximum discretion could be given immediate effect. To this was to be added a procedure by which the National Assembly could request Parliament to pass orders in council allowing the Assembly to modify any past primary legislation as it applied to Wales as well. In addition, a mechanism for triggering a referendum on primary powers was proposed by which a two-thirds majority of Assembly members was required to initiate it, although it would need the support of Westminster as well. For these proposals, as well as the change of legal status and electoral reform proposals, a new government of Wales act was required. The bill was published in December 2005 and received royal assent in July 2006.

Criticism that Labour's proposals were half-baked and left the Assembly's powers vulnerable to the whims of central government remained (see Osmond 2005). However, the legislation introduced much of what the Richard Report had asked for in principle: it provided in an interim period for a significant broadening of secondary legislative powers; and provided a specific mechanism for the move to primary powers. Although Morgan said he did not believe a referendum would be won then, implicitly the prospect of primary powers was being laid down as not a case of if but when. Campaigners for further devolution simply switched to strategies for triggering a referendum. In this context the principal focus for dispute became the proposed reform of the electoral system. Labour were accused of leaving themselves open to the perception of partisanship in abolishing dual candidacy. The merits of this reform are open to debate. Nevertheless, it was the only issue upon which members of the Welsh Affairs Committee divided on strictly party lines (House of Commons 2005) and led to House of Lords amendments that threatened to derail the bill altogether before the Lords backed down against the Government's determination to retain this part of the package.

Consequently, the 2006 Government of Wales Act provided for the statutory confirmation of the working conventions of the separation of executive and Assembly, mechanisms for the enhancement of the secondary powers of the Assembly combined with a mechanism for moving towards primary powers, and a revision of the mixed member electoral system to take away the right to dual candidacy. It is not quite what the Richard Report advocated but it was still a significant development from the 1998 Government of Wales Act. A plausible claim could be made that it was in step with public opinion. Back in 1997 public opinion had appeared roughly split down the middle between those either favouring independence, a devolved Parliament or a devolved assembly on one side and those opposing devolution altogether on the other. Thereafter public opinion surveys appeared to show a country still roughly split down the middle, but now over what kind of devolution, rather than whether to have it at all. Within a few years of the referendum, just slightly more than half of survey respondents with stated opinions favoured either the devolved Parliament or independence, while the rest favoured either the *status quo* or abolition (see Table 3.3). Of course, the development of powers continued to move more slowly than elite pro-devolution opinion would generally have wished. On this issue the Labour Party, if not the constitutional conservatives as in Scotland, were clearly the arch constitutional gradualists, while Plaid Cymru ideally favoured independence, and the Liberal Democrats Scottish Parliament type-powers in a federal constitution. Even the Conservatives had moved to support the extension of powers. The question remained whether, as on other matters, Labour could continue to determine the constitutional agenda, against political opponents who might wish to quicken change. Of course, it remained uncertain how voters would respond when and if Wales' political leaders judged the mood to have become sufficiently robust to risk a referendum.

Table 3.3 Trends in Constitutional Preferences in Wales, 1997–2003

	1997	1999	2001	2003
Wales should be independent	13%	9%	12%	13%
Wales should remain part of UK but with own Parliament with some law making and tax powers	18%	35%	37%	36%
Wales should remain part of UK with its own Assembly that has only limited law making powers	25%	35%	25%	25%
Wales should remain part of the UK without an elected assembly	37%	18%	23%	20%

This is adapted from Curtice (2006) and based on data drawn from the Welsh Referendum Survey (1997), The Welsh Assembly Election study (1999), and Wales Life and Times Surveys (2001 and 2003). Figures do not add up to 100% as don't knows are not shown in the table.

Conclusion

This chapter has reviewed some of the main developments that occurred in the early years of devolution. On all issues developments were mixed and open to contested interpretation. Nevertheless, in going beyond the inevitable twists and turns of a political experiment enduring its growing pains one can discern clear changes on many fronts: dynamism in voting behaviour and party strategies; adaptation in the civil service; distinctive approaches to policy-making; distinctive substantive content to public policy; and a relatively swift review of the 1997–1999 settlement and move to a general (though not complete) agreement on the enhancement of that settlement. The general character of these achievements was that of a gradual process of change, in which as Cole (2006: 163) put it, 'on balance the scorecard is favourable to Welsh devolution. In spite of its lack of tax-varying or primary legislative powers, the Welsh Assembly Government can make a difference'.

In drawing overall conclusions one is drawn back to the fact that there remains much disagreement over the merits of this gradualism in the way that the Assembly made a difference. There are two principal competing narratives. The first stresses the idea that the hopes for real political autonomy were still to a considerable extent failed by the form of devolution introduced and by Labour's subsequent approaches to styles of governance, substance of public policy and development of the settlement. Labour, it could be argued, has always been behind the leading edge of thinking on both 'new politics' and constitutional reform; epitomised by Labour's response to the Richard Report. Labour has neither fully embraced political pluralism nor fully embraced the idea of Welsh political autonomy. Analysts within this line of thinking would stress the lost opportunity of devolution; but taking the long view suggest the capacity for the promise of 1997–1999 to come through with Labour interests being a major potential casualty along the way. This potential was highlighted by Labour's inability to gain a proper governing majority even in an MMP system with a relatively low proportion of list seats, the development of the potential in an alternative non-Labour coalition and ultimately in the advent of the previously unthinkable coalition of Labour with Plaid Cymru in 2007. Devolution may yet sow the seeds of decline in the old one partyist culture of Wales, and release the potential of both political pluralism and political decentralisation.

The alternative narrative is that the 'gradual' development of devolution could not have been otherwise. The public did not vote for the Assembly in mass numbers and after several years of its existence the chair of the 1997 'Yes for Wales' campaign put the situation fairly bluntly when he stated in 2001 that the Assembly was unloved and greeted by the public overwhelmingly with apathy and indifference (Morgan, 2001). Those who were genuinely sceptical of distinctive styles of policy-making, policy approaches and further constitutional powers may well have had fertile ground in which to drag their political heels. Instead, it may be argued that the Labour Party had been ready to clearly lead in developing a 'new politics' and distinctive policy under Ron Davies. In responding to the Alun Michael period, the Morgan leadership had then represented a strongly pro-devolution Labour elite faction, developing devolution in the only realistic manner possible without going dangerously ahead of public opinion. In the circumstances its achievements should not be under-appreciated.

Recognition of the existence of these two narratives is to assert that on one thing all are agreed; the reality of devolution in Wales in its early phase was strongly influenced by the pre-devolution limitations on Wales as a distinct political arena, the limitations of the 1998 settlement and the need to engage in polity building. Nevertheless, early development was also strongly characterised and affected by disagreement over how best to do that and significant party political battles over who should control its development and profit at the ballot box. This continues to be seen at work in Labour's efforts to remain the principal party of government in Wales, as well as the other three main parties' desires to get a grip on party government to take at least some ownership of the process of devolution, whilst wresting more electoral gains from Labour's increasingly vulnerable political base. The low politics of party competition have never been far away, and doubtless they will continue to be a major influence on the development of devolution in Wales.

References

Andrews, L. (1999) *Wales Says Yes*, Bridgend: Seren.

Balsom, D. (1983) 'Public opinion and Welsh devolution', in D. Foulkes, J. B. Jones and R. Wilford (eds), *The Welsh Veto*, Cardiff: University of Wales Press.

Bradbury, J. (1998) 'The devolution debate in Wales: the politics of a developing union state?' *Regional and Federal Studies*, 8: 120–39.

Bradbury, J. (2003) 'The political dynamics of sub-state regionalism: a neo-functionalist perspective and the case of devolution in the United Kingdom, *British Journal of Politics and International Relations*, 5,4: 543–75.

Bradbury, J. and Mitchell, J. (2004) 'Political recruitment and the 2003 Scottish and Welsh elections: candidate selection, positive discrimination and party adaptation', *Representation*, 40: 289–302.

Bradbury, J. and Mitchell, J. (2007) 'The constituency work of members of the Scottish Parliament and National Assembly for Wales: approaches, relationships and rules', *Regional and Federal Studies*, 17, 1: 117–46.

Bradbury, J., Denver, D., Mitchell, J. and Bennie, L. (2000) 'Devolution and party change: Candidate selection for the 1999 Scottish Parliament and Welsh Assembly elections', *Journal of Legislative Studies*, 6: 51–72.

Chaney, P., Hall, T. and Pithouse, A. (2001) (eds) *Post-Devolution Wales: New Governance – new democracy?*, Cardiff: University of Wales Press.

Cole, A. (2006) *Beyond Devolution and Decentralisation: Building Regional Capacity in Wales and Brittany*, Manchester: Manchester University Press.

Curtice, J. (2000) 'Is devolution succouring nationalism', *Contemporary Wales*, 13.

Curtice, J. (2006) 'A stronger or weaker union? public reactions to asymmetric devolution in the United Kingdom', *Publius: The Journal of Federalism*, 36, 1: pp. 95–113.

Davies, R. (1999) *Devolution: A Process not an Event*, Cardiff: Institute of Welsh Affairs.

Flynn, P. (1999) *Dragons Led by Poodles: The Inside Story of a New Labour Stitch-Up*, London: Politicos.

Greer, S. (2005) *Territorial Politics and Health Policy: UK Health Policy in Comparative Perspective*, Manchester: Manchester University Press.

Griffiths, D. (1996) *Thatcherism and Territorial Politics: A Welsh Case Study*, Avebury: Ashgate.

House of Commons (2005) Welsh Affairs Committee, *Government White Paper: Better Governance for Wales*, First Report of Session 2005–06, HC 551.

Jones, J. B. and Balsom, D. (2000) (eds) *The Road to the National Assembly for Wales*, Cardiff: University of Wales Press.

Jones, J. B. and Osmond, J. (2000) (eds) *Inclusive Government and Party Management*, Cardiff: Institute of Welsh Affairs.

Jones, J. B. and Osmond, J. (2002) (eds) *Building a Civic Culture*, Cardiff: Institute of Welsh Affairs.

Laffin, M., Taylor, G. and Thomas, A. (2002) *A New Partnership? The National Assembly for Wales and Local Government*, York: Joseph Rowntree Foundation.

Laffin, M. and Thomas, A. (2001) 'New ways of working: political-official relations in the National Assembly for Wales', *Public Money and Management*, 21, 2: 45–51.

McAllister, L. (2000) 'The new politics in Wales: rhetoric or reality?' *Parliamentary Affairs*, 53, 3: 591–604.

Morgan, K. O. (1982) *A History of Modern Wales*, Cardiff: University of Wales Press.

Morgan, K. (2001), 'Over-worked, under-resourced and unloved', *Agenda, Journal of the Institute of Welsh Affairs*, Autumn, 38–40.

Morgan, R. (2000) *Variable Geometry UK*, Discussion paper 13, Cardiff: Institute of Welsh Affairs.

Mungham, G. and Morgan, K. (2000) *Redesigning Democracy: The Making of the National Assembly for Wales*, Bridgend: Seren.

National Assembly for Wales (2001) *The Learning Country: A Comprehensive Education and Lifelong Learning Programme to 2010 in Wales*, Cardiff: National Assembly for Wales.

National Assembly for Wales (2004) *Report of the Richard Commission on the Powers and Electoral Arrangements of the National Assembly for Wales*, Cardiff: National Assembly for Wales.

Osmond, J. (2005) (ed.) *Welsh Politics Comes of Age, Responses to the Richard Commission*, Cardiff: Institute of Welsh Affairs.

Paterson, L. and Wyn Jones, R. (1999) 'Does civil society drive constitutional change?' in B. Taylor, and K. Thomson (1999) (eds), *Scotland and Wales: Nations Again?*, Cardiff: University of Wales Press.

Rawlings, R. (2003) *Delineating Wales, Constitutional, Legal and Administrative Aspects of National Devolution*, Cardiff: University of Wales Press.

Royles, E. (2004) 'Civil society and objective 1' *Contemporary Wales*, 16: 101–21.

Sullivan, M. (2002) 'Health policy: differentiation and devolution', in J. Adams and P. Robinson (eds) *Devolution in Practice: Public Policy Differences in the UK*, London: Institute of Public Policy Research, pp. 60–8.

Trystan, D., Scully, R., and Wyn Jones, R. (2003) 'Explaining the quiet earthquake: voting behaviour in the first election to the National Assembly for Wales', *Electoral Studies*, 22: 635–50.

Wales Labour Party (2004) *Better Governance for Wales*, Cardiff: Wales Labour Party.

Wales Office (2005) *Better Governance for Wales*, Cm 6582.

4 Northern Ireland

St Andrews – the long Good Friday Agreement

Rick Wilford

The protracted and interrupted process of securing a durable, if interim, political accord in Northern Ireland seems, finally, to have been secured by means of the 2006 St Andrews Agreement.[1] Following the acceptance of its requirements, all of Northern Ireland's parties agreed to give power-sharing devolved governance another try. On 8 May 2007 Dr Ian Paisley, the Leader of the Democratic Unionist Party (DUP), accepted the nomination as First Minister in the reconvened Northern Ireland Assembly, and Martin McGuinness, the deputy leader of Sinn Féin (SF), accepted the nomination as Deputy First Minister. The modern process of seeking an accord dates back to the 1998 Belfast Agreement, by which a devolved power-sharing assembly, accompanied by a North–South Ireland Ministerial Council and an East–West British–Irish Council, was established. Given the history of Northern Ireland, and the continuing divisions between unionist and nationalist-republican communities and politicians, one might have expected the very establishment of stable devolved governance to be a major achievement in itself. So it has proved, marking out Northern Ireland as entirely distinctive in the politics of devolution in the UK.

We cannot, of course, be sure, but the St Andrews Agreement appears to have marked a historic departure. Unlike the 1998 Belfast (or Good Friday) Agreement[2] St Andrews was not an agreement reached, signed, sealed and delivered by (most of) the parties, but rather represented the best estimates of the UK and Irish Governments of the terms upon which Northern Ireland's political and constitutional future could evolve. Nor was it an entirely novel deal: rather, it is better understood as an incremental reform of its 1998 predecessor, which remains the essential template for the governance of the region. However, the negotiations at St Andrews and those that occurred in its wake, including after the third Assembly election on 7 March 2007, did engineer some key changes in the operating procedures of the devolved institutions, most notably within the Executive Committee. These changes are designed to promote consensus over decision and policy-making and to manufacture the convention of collective responsibility among its ministers – a feature that was wanting during the first stuttering experience of devolution between December 1999 and October 2002. Important though these reforms are, the achievement of the Belfast Agreement remains undiminished: namely, that of reconciling the conflicting desires to, on the one hand, maintain the Union and the aspiration to unify Ireland on the other. In that sense the St Andrews Agreement is, like its predecessor, a contingent arrangement rather than a final settlement: it supplies a means of managing these mutually exclusive constitutional projects within a consociational framework.

The restoration of a devolved, inclusive, power-sharing administration in 2007 did not, however, just turn on inter-party, especially DUP-SF, agreement about procedural reforms: it also required significant policy shifts on the part of both the DUP and mainstream republicanism. This focused in the former's case on, the (reluctant) acceptance of sharing power with Sinn Féin (SF) and to agree a date for the devolution of policing and criminal justice;[3] and in the latter's, not only the decommissioning of the IRA's arsenal and its abandonment of criminality, but the endorsement of both Northern Ireland's police service and its criminal justice system.[4] In effect, the reciprocal demands made of both the DUP and SF were preconditions that had to be met in order to restore a fully inclusive, four-party government.

With those preconditions met, as they were, the DUP's readiness to swallow the power-sharing pill also required amendments to the operating procedures of the prospectively devolved institutions, particularly those relating to the four-party Executive Committee. At St Andrews, these changes were crafted in a way that dovetailed reforms sought by the DUP and others required by SF: there was, then, a certain symmetry to the statecraft involved in devising the St Andrews Agreement. This enabled both the DUP to claim that St Andrews was a *new* agreement and SF to state that it represented the *implementation in full* of the 1998 model: there is some truth in the former claim and rather more in the latter. As one might put it – and not without some justification – 'St Andrews is the Good Friday Agreement in a kilt'.

The central purpose of the chapter is to place the origins and future prospects of the St Andrews Agreement into context. The first section considers the 1998 Belfast Agreement's original consociational design. Four sections then consider in turn executive formation, intra-executive accommodation, executive action and the operation of the Assembly in the first period of the Assembly's halting existence up to October 2002. This is warranted because lessons, both positive and negative, can be drawn from that experience. The sixth section then considers the period of debate that followed the suspension of the Assembly up to its restoration in 2007. This relates the contents of the St Andrews Agreement to earlier attempts in 2003 and 2004 to broker agreement. The concluding section reflects on the immediate political pressures that pressed the parties to finally reach agreement, as well as the potential for the future.

The design of the 1998 Belfast Agreement

The characterisation of the 1998 Agreement as a 'bespoke'[5] (McGarry and O'Leary 2004: 24*fn*) form of consociational democracy with added confederal (and potentially federalising) structures is well documented (O'Leary 1998, 1999; Wilford 1999, 2001, 2004). The key criteria of a consociation (Lijphart 1968, 1969, 1977) were met by the Agreement: namely, executive power sharing founded on a cross-community basis; segmental autonomy or community self-government and equality in cultural life; the application of proportionality rules in both the government and public sectors; and the application of the unanimity rule enabling political leaders, especially but not exclusively from within the minority community, to defend their rights and interests within an executive context.

This consociational design was complemented by confederal dimensions: that is, the provision for both cross-border institutions between Northern Ireland and the Republic of Ireland and institutional linkages between the island of Ireland and the now devolved Britain. These constituted the three 'strands' of the institutional weave: within Northern Ireland, including a newly elected 108 member Assembly and, eventually, a 12-strong Executive Committee; between North and South via the North–South Ministerial Council (NSMC), underpinned by a set of new, institutionalised cross-border relationships; and East–West, by means of both the British–Irish Council (BIC) embracing the London and Dublin governments, the three devolved administrations, the Isle of Man and the Channel Islands, and the British–Irish Intergovernmental Conference (BIIG).[6]

The three-stranded design was a complex and much more sophisticated set of institutional arrangements than had hitherto been either proposed – or attempted – as a means of governing a devolved Northern Ireland. Moreover, the institutions were intended to interweave rather than stand alone – pull at one institutional thread and the whole would unravel – although that feature of the original pattern was subsequently abandoned, albeit on a temporary basis.[7]

In addition to the governing institutions, new human rights and equality regimes were instituted and there was provision for the independent review and reform of both policing and criminal justice matters within Northern Ireland. The British Government also undertook to normalise security arrangements, including the reduction of troop levels, to provide for the accelerated release on licence of qualifying prisoners, and made provision for the victims of the 'troubles'. Finally, a new space for the voluntary and other sectors – the consultative Civic Forum – was created with a brief to advise the Assembly on policy matters.

The Agreement did not foreclose the constitutional future of Northern Ireland but rather subjected it to the 'consent principle' (MacGinty *et al.* 2001). That is, *change* in its constitutional status would henceforth be determined through the exercise of popular sovereignty by its electorate (and, concurrently, by the electorate in the Republic of Ireland) through a referendum.[8] This open-ended future was enabled by the UK Government's repeal of the Government of Ireland Act (1920) which established partition, and the Irish Government's agreement to amend its Constitution (subject to endorsement in a referendum) such that its irredentist claim to the six counties would be replaced by an aspiration for unity. As Coakley (2001: 236) states, the subsequent reform of Articles 2 and 3.1 and 3.2 of the Irish Constitution 'gave explicit constitutional recognition to the right of Northern Ireland to opt out of a united Ireland'. In effect, under the terms of the Agreement unionists (and the minority of nationalists who are pro-Union) could not, against their expressed will, be 'trundled' into a united Ireland.

The open-endedness of the constitutional future had a dual appeal that contributed to its terrible beauty. Namely, it encouraged nationalists and, significantly, the SF leadership to claim that the Agreement was a staging post towards unification (an interpretation shared by anti-Agreement unionists). At the same time it reassured a sufficient majority of unionists and many loyalists: short of a significant reversal in Northern Ireland's demographic balance, accompanied by a corresponding growth in support for unification, unionists effectively hold the constitutional future in their numerically greater hands.

The Agreement was endorsed by concurrent referendums in both parts of the island of Ireland, duly held in May 1998. A key feature of the referendum campaign in Northern Ireland was the sharp division between pro- and anti-Agreement unionists. Three wicked issues incensed the latter (and troubled the former): the early release on licence of paramilitary prisoners, both republican and loyalist (also troubling for many nationalist voters); the reform of the Royal Ulster Constabulary; and the prospective inclusion of Sinn Féin in a devolved administration prior to the decommissioning of the IRA's arsenal. It was less the architecture of the Agreement and certainly not the principle of devolution that was at issue, but the presence in government of those regarded by many unionists as 'unreconstructed terrorists'. Hence, it was a matter of modest surprise that when the first Assembly election was held in 1998, overtly anti-Agreement unionist candidates secured marginally more first preference votes than their pro Agreement counterparts (Mitchell 2001).

The election proved to be the UUP's worst-ever electoral performance – until 2007, that is – and left the balance of pro- and anti-Agreement unionist Members of the Legislative Assembly (MLAs) delicately poised at, respectively, 30:28. This further complicated an already difficult situation for the UUP in general and, in particular, for its leader David Trimble, already beset by mounting disquiet within the wider unionist community over the wicked issues.

Executive formation

Though space precludes a careful plotting of the serpentine course of the unfolding political process, one can note some of its landmarks. In the difficult post-election context the Assembly met in shadow mode, initially on 1 July 1998 to elect David Trimble (UUP) and Seamus Mallon (SDLP) as, respectively, the First and Deputy First Ministers (Designate) on a joint ticket by way of cross-community support.[9] Their election epitomised the power-sharing character of the planned devolved administration. Under the terms of the Agreement they constituted a formally co-equal dyarchy, legitimised by a majority of both nationalist and unionist MLAs. In Mr Trimble's mind the UUP and the SDLP would constitute the still, small centre of a four-party Executive coalition in anticipating that the two major parties – the 'centre of gravity in Northern Ireland' – would constitute 'a voluntary coalition within the compulsory coalition' (Millar 2004: 57).

The composition of the Executive was to be determined by means of the d'Hondt mechanism that had been agreed by the parties as the proportional means of allocating departments among the major parties (Wilford 1999: 314; O'Leary 2004: 292). However, whilst the adoption of d'Hondt was consistent with consociationalism's proportionality principle, the precise size and hence balance of political forces within the prospective coalition was, at this stage, unresolved. The Agreement provided for a period of six months during which the proto-Executive parties were to agree the number and nature of both the devolved departments and cross-border bodies. However, none had engaged in any considered forethought about the structure of the Executive, much less about how they might seek consciously to achieve 'joined-up' government.[10] Moreover, there were no concerted inter-party negotiations about the division of the ministerial spoils once their number was agreed.

The size of the Executive was limited by the Agreement: in addition to the First and Deputy First Ministers, there would be a minimum of six and a maximum of ten departmental ministers. The negotiations, held between July and December 1998, over the number of departments and cross-border bodies were steered by the two largest parties, the UUP and the SDLP (see Godson 2004). The UUP accepted, in addition to the Office of First and Deputy First Minister (OFMDFM), that there would be ten departments (the SDLP's preferred figure) in exchange for 12 cross-border bodies (the UUP's acceptable maximum). According to one of its chief negotiators, the SDLP's justification for proposing ten departments was two-fold.[11] First, it ensured via d'Hondt that each of the four eligible parties would secure at least two ministries, thereby avoiding the risk of marginalising a single minister at the 'Cabinet' table. Secondly, the total of 12 ministers ensured parity of numbers, if not esteem, within the Executive since it would comprise six unionists (four UUP and two DUP) and six nationalists (four SDLP and two SF).

The adoption of the d'Hondt rule precluded the exercise of patronage (save for junior ministerial posts and special advisers in their own department) outwith their own parties by the First and Deputy First Ministers since it gave each of the four largest parties, which collectively took 90 of the 108 seats, the right to nominate ministers according to their respective strength in seats in the Assembly.[12] In effect, each of the devolved departments became the exclusive property of the relevant party for the duration of the Assembly unless that party was excluded from the Executive by way of a cross-community vote in the chamber.[13]

This provision leant the Executive the appearance of, in David Trimble's words, a 'compulsory coalition' (see above): but, in fact, participation in the Executive was (and remains) entirely voluntary. None of the four major parties was compelled to exercise its entitlement to a ministerial portfolio and, if one or more chose to do so, could have relinquished that opportunity and sat on what would have in effect been the 'Opposition' bench(es). Given that each of the major parties did nominate ministers, there were – as within any 'grand coalition' – significant centrifugal forces in the Executive, strengthened by the DUP's decision to take its two ministerial seats but to boycott all meetings of both the 'Cabinet' and the NSMC.

Intra-executive accommodation

When devolution got underway on 2 December 1999, the DUP sought to exploit its semi-detached position by acting as both a governing and an opposition party as and when it chose. For instance, although the Executive's draft budget proposals and its 'Programmes for Government' (PfG) required ministerial unanimity in order to be tabled within the Assembly, DUP ministers and MLAs tried to amend either or both when they were debated on the floor of the chamber.[14]

The DUP's ambivalent stance did complicate the operation of the Executive – as did its decision to rotate its ministers – but not to the point of immobilism.[15] Nor did it affect adversely the policy sectors most directly involved with the two departments or, indeed, the wider community. In effect, the DUP was in a 'win-win' situation. The other Executive parties – particularly, for electoral reasons, the UUP – could not be perceived or portrayed as penalising the interests served by the DUP's departments, whilst the party itself could ostensibly maintain its aloofness, the Assembly aside, from the Agreement's institutional nexus in the hope of reaping an electoral reward – which it duly did.

The Agreement did supply some 'glue' to the Executive, notably the Ministerial Code and the Ministerial 'Pledge of Office', together with the requirement to achieve agreement on draft budget proposals and the PfGs. However, as already noted, the requirement in respect of the latter two matters was breached, while the Code was not placed on a statutory basis.[16] The Pledge was also intended to lend some cohesiveness to the Executive by requiring ministers to 'participate with colleagues in the preparation of a programme for government' and 'to operate within the framework of that programme when agreed within the Executive Committee and endorsed by the Assembly'. Furthermore, it required them 'to discharge in good faith all the duties of the office' which included attendance at and participation in the NSMC, which was an 'essential responsibility' for ministers. Yet, the DUP boycotted the Council and, by way of retaliation, was blocked by the other Executive parties from attending meetings of the British–Irish Council.

At first sight, the DUP's absence from the NSMC seemed to be a breach of the Pledge. However, there was a saving provision in the Agreement enabling the First and Deputy First Ministers to make proxy arrangements so that the Council's relevant sectoral business could function notwithstanding the DUP's boycott. (In addition, OFMDFM represented the interests of the DUP's departments at the BIC.) Whilst expedient, this provision seemed both to invest the concept of 'essential responsibility' with a novel meaning and underlined the absence of the convention of collective responsibility within the Executive. Indeed, the Agreement vested authority in each of the individual departments rather than within the Executive as a whole thereby enabling ministers, all other things being equal, to act autonomously if they so chose – and some did.[17] There was, then, a textual warrant for the immanent centrifugalism within the 'Cabinet' that was accentuated by the DUP's boycott.

Yet the politics of accommodation intrinsic to consociational democracy found novel expressions in the, albeit constrained, adaptation to the DUP's tactics by the three other Executive-forming parties. Allowing officials from the DUP's departments to brief the Executive at 'Cabinet' meetings, routinising contacts between civil servants from Regional Development and Social Development with their counterparts in the two departments (Health, Social Services and Public Safety and Education) headed by SF ministers, bi- or trilateral meetings with UUP and/or SDLP ministers, and the practice of what the SDLP's first Finance Minister (Mark Durkan) termed 'government by correspondence course', each helped to oil the wheels of the administration.[18]

Such improvised measures enabled the (strained) business of government to proceed, aided by the need to 'agree' both the annual PfGs and budget proposals. Furthermore, there was a conscious attempt to lend some 'joined-upness' to the Executive through the introduction of the 'Executive Programme Funds' to the budgetary and policy-making process (EPF). Designed to dovetail with the strategic and thematic priorities of the PfGs, the five major policy areas covered by the EPFs were intended to encourage cross-cutting, joined-up work between and among the departments.[19] The Funds were withheld from the normal round of draft budget allocations and departments were invited to bid for them preferably, though not exclusively, on a cross-departmental basis, with final decisions on their allocation taken within the Executive Committee.

This was a hefty nudge towards collectivism but met with only partial success. According to Mark Durkan,[20] the majority of bids had a 'mono-departmental focus', rather belying the purpose of the EPFs. However, they did stimulate considerable interest. A total of £372m was set aside over a three-year period but in the first round of bidding there was a total of 139 calls on the EPFs totalling in excess of £581m, 62 of which were resourced at a cost of £146m, although all bar four of those bids came from single departments (Wilson and Wilford 2001: 98).

These attempts to counter the centrifugal dynamic within the Executive did not, however, prevent it from appearing as a chopped-up rather than a joined-up institution. Besides the operational difficulties caused by the DUP's tactics, there was a progressively deteriorating relationship between David Trimble and Seamus Mallon. In Mr Trimble's view this was caused to no small extent by Mr Mallon's tendency to manoeuvre for party advantage in order 'to promote themselves [the SDLP] as being more effective nationalists [than SF] at the business of beating unionists' (Millar 2004: 120–1). However, the First Minister's threat of resignation in February 2000 which ushered in the first suspension, his refusal to authorise the attendance of SF ministers at NSMC meetings, his actual resignation on 1 July 2001 occasioning two further suspensions, together did little to endear the UUP leader to Mr Mallon.[21] Indeed, Mr Trimble's resignation forced his co-equal Deputy First Minister also to resign. In September 2001 Mr Mallon announced that he would not seek re-election as Deputy First Minister should devolution be resumed, thereby paving the way for Mark Durkan[22] to run on a joint ticket with the former First Minister.[23]

The eventual election of Messrs Trimble and Durkan in early November 2001 enabled, for the first time since October 2000, all three institutional strands of the Agreement (given the DUP's semi-detachedness) to operate concurrently – which in total they did for just 20 of the 30 months of devolution. But against the backdrop of declining support of the Agreement within the unionist community, underlined by the DUP's electoral successes at the 2001 local and General Elections (and the corresponding advances made by SF), the first devolved mandate was living on borrowed time and was to survive for just 11 more months.[24]

Executive action

The fitful progress of devolution clearly constrained its potential. The neuralgic issue of decommissioning, far from being resolved within two years of the Agreement which many nationalists as well as unionists anticipated would be the case, created a debilitating political environment within which mistrust and suspicion thrived. Yet, whilst hobbled by this context, the devolved administration did work, at least up to a point. It did not, though, unlike in Wales and Scotland, develop an infrastructure of ministerial committees as a means of taking policy discussions forward. Apart from the issue of mistrust, and the difficulties caused by the DUP's absence from Executive meetings, the proportionality principle made it operationally difficult to establish an underpinning committee system.

The lack of a Cabinet system meant that business was conducted in Executive meetings which became rather cluttered occasions as a result. There were, however, just 58 meetings during the two and a half years of devolution, five of which concentrated exclusively on the foot and mouth crisis. Though an unimpressive work rate, it was not the case that it was a 'do-nothing' government but rather one that accomplished perhaps as much as could be expected in difficult circumstances.

The Executive's substantive policy achievements included the creation of a Children's Commissioner (modelled on the Welsh initiative), the development of new strategies for public health, regional development, transport and agriculture, the introduction of free public transport for pensioners, free nursing, though not (as in Scotland) personal care for the elderly, and a reformed scheme of student finance (albeit not as generous as that implemented in Scotland). In addition, the Executive set in train a fundamental review of Northern Ireland's system of public administration (excluding the devolved institutions), and it negotiated a new loan facility with the Treasury. Termed the 'Reinvestment and Reform' Initiative (RRI), this was designed to release monies expressly designed to tackle Northern Ireland's neglected infrastructure.

According to David Trimble, the RRI was the only significant achievement of the devolved government.[25] Though that is, perhaps, something of an overstatement – or at least undervalues some of the other advances made – its long-run financial implications are undeniable. Money borrowed will have to be repaid, even if at preferential rates. Here the Executive ran headlong into the financial realities of its near total reliance on the Barnett formula as the means of calculating its block grant. The only major revenue stream within Northern Ireland available to the Executive derives from the rates which, since they were last reviewed in the mid-1970s, have been based on the rental values of domestic and commercial property. The *quid pro quo* for the loan facility was, it transpired, Treasury insistence on a fundamental review of the rating system, which will henceforth be based on market values, and a review of the options for introducing water service charges. The latter was necessary because, since their privatisation in Britain, water services have not been factored into the Barnett formula so that the resources had to be found from within Northern Ireland to maintain and improve them.

Both issues were (and remain) highly contentious but final decisions were avoided because of the suspension in October 2002. This relieved the Executive (and the Assembly) from taking unpopular measures and thereby removed the risk of further straining its cohesion. The new rates and water charging regimes therefore became matters for the renewed direct rule team of ministers who did not shy away from taking controversial decisions.

The Assembly

Whilst the Executive lacked a stable, centripetal dynamic it was counter-balanced to some extent by inter-party linkages within the Assembly. This may seem an odd claim given that at times the chamber resembled a bear-pit, especially when the chronic condition of the wider 'peace process' became acute and/or crises erupted at communal interfaces. In addition, the divided nature of unionism, besides the acid state of relations that existed between the anti-Agreement parties and both the UUP and SF, suggests that the prospect of achieving inter-party co-operation within the Assembly was illusory. Yet, while not diminishing these obvious difficulties, at an institutional level the Assembly not only functioned, it did so on an increasingly systematic basis.

The absence of an official Opposition within the Assembly lent particular significance to its committees, especially the ten statutory committees.[26] Their chairs and deputy chairs were, like the ministers, nominated via the d'Hondt procedure save that neither could be drawn from the same party as that of the relevant minister whose department the committee shadowed (hence, another expression of power sharing). Each 11-strong statutory committee, one for each of the devolved departments, reflected in broad terms the respective strengths of the parties in the chamber so that the Executive-forming parties constituted their (nominal) numerical majorities.

The nexus between the statutory committees and their associated departments was dense and complex and arose from the expansive repertoire of roles allocated to the former. Like Westminster's select committees they scrutinised the policies, administration and expenditure of the departments and were free to pursue inquiries relating to departmental policies. That role was enhanced by their capacity to 'advise and assist' the departments 'in the formulation of policy' and was further strengthened by being invested with the power to *initiate* legislation. In addition, and like Parliament's standing committees, they took the committee stage of the legislative process.

This was a considerable and significant role set, the extent of which threatened to overload the committees especially since they proved reluctant to delegate to sub-committees as a means of spreading the workload and managing their agendas.[27]

Those agendas were constrained by their role in the legislative process; the obligation to undertake the committee stage of all primary legislation (and to scrutinise secondary legislation) meant that their relative autonomy was bridled by the varying weights of departmental legislative activism.

In addition to this structural constraint the committees were also hampered by a problem singular to Northern Ireland within the devolved UK, namely that of the dual and, in a very few cases, triple mandate. Sixty of the 108 MLAs were district councillors, a dozen were MPs, one of whom was also an MEP, and there were two peers in the chamber, including its Speaker. Such 'double-jobbing' meant that most members had to spread their energies across at least two spheres of elected representation rather than exerting a single-minded focus on the Assembly.

There were some advantages to the preponderance of councillors. It meant, for instance, that they brought both local knowledge and committee experience to the Assembly. However, operating within council chambers did not equip them with the necessary parliamentary skills. Such a dearth of expertise and legislative experience was, of course, unavoidable because of the long period of direct rule and its attendant democratic deficit which, *inter alia*, meant that none who were nominated to the Executive Committee had cut their ministerial teeth. But there was an operational disadvantage arising from the high proportion of councillors in the chamber: namely, there were occasional clashes between Assembly committee business and local council meetings such that statutory committees could be left inquorate as MLAs left to attend to business in the relevant district councils.[28]

To some extent, the dual mandate helps in explaining the operating style of the committees. Unlike in Scotland and Wales where committees tended to develop a more peripatetic character, those in the Assembly led a largely sedentary existence and seldom practised outreach by taking evidence outside Parliament Buildings at Stormont.[29] The sheer number of committees and the pool of available members also hampered their efficiency. Excluding the Speaker (Lord Alderdice), the ministers and junior ministers, the one-man UK Unionist Party, three of the NI Unionist Party's four MLAs, and both Lord Kilclooney (John Taylor) of the UUP, and Gerry Adams (SF), each of whom declined committee places, there were 87 members available to serve on the ten statutory, six standing and nine *ad hoc* committees, and the Assembly Commission. The effect was that 20 MLAs sat on just one committee while 67 served on two or more.

Taken together the mesh of constraints operating on the committees would suggest, wrongly, that they achieved little. For instance, between 2 December 1999 and the final suspension of the Assembly, 27 Executive Bills had been considered by them and a further 22 were at various stages of the legislative process. In addition, more than 600 statutory rules had been scrutinised and 43 inquiries had been initiated or completed. They had scrutinised 123 policy development matters on their own initiative, supplementing those referred to them by their associated departments, and considered 214 public consultations undertaken by the departments and their associated bodies.

Equally impressive was the evolution of joined-up working between and among the committees. For instance, committees from early on adopted the practice of seeking inputs from one another where a bill or public policy crossed departmental boundaries in order to take a more joined-up approach to its scrutiny and, for the same purpose, occasionally held joint evidence-taking sessions in relation to cross-cutting inquiries. In addition, the Finance and Personnel Committee collated and summarised the responses of all statutory committees to the draft spending plans of the departments and in so doing was enabled to propose a number of agreed changes designed to improve the scrutiny of the budgetary process. The development of such inter-committee co-operation also led to the creation of a non-statutory 'liaison' committee, consisting of the chairs or deputy chairs of the committees – except for those from the DUP[30] – designed to improve their standard operating procedures and achieve greater efficiencies in their work.

With a few exceptions, intra-committee relations were constructive, enabling them to operate within a not always entirely cordial, but at least a business-like atmosphere. The committees recognised that if they were to exert influence upon the relevant minister they needed to operate on a consensual basis rather than adopting inflexibly partisan, if not sectarian, positions. This *modus operandi*, albeit part of the folk wisdom practised by parliamentary committees, was also assisted to some extent by the nature of the inquiries they initially embarked upon. Two examples may suffice to make the point.

The Environment Committee, chaired by the DUP's William McCrea, chose quite consciously to inquire into the safety of school transport, precisely because it was unlikely to create inter-party or inter-communal strife.[31] Such conflict avoidance also led the Culture, Arts and Leisure Committee, chaired by Eamon O'Neill (SDLP), to steer away from contentious issues such as language policy as the topic for its first inquiry and into the safer waters of inland fisheries policy.[32] Although contrived, such choices did assist in promoting a certain *esprit de corps* within the committees, which was helpful in exerting a productive influence on their associated departments.

By the same token, the relationships struck between the chairs of the statutory committees and the relevant ministers were also instrumental in effecting stable intra-committee relations. One example was the solid working relationship achieved between the Chair of the Agriculture and Rural Development Committee, Dr Ian Paisley, the leader of the DUP, and the Minister, Brid Rodgers (SDLP), an Irish-speaking, no-nonsense nationalist. It evolved into a virtual partnership in part as the result of the successful preventive action taken by Ms Rodgers during the foot-and-mouth crisis. So impressed was the Committee that she was serially commended by its members for the decisive measures taken by her department.

Similarly, the Chair of the Education Committee, Danny Kennedy (UUP) and the Education Minister, Martin McGuinness (SF) achieved a 'formal and civilised working relationship' despite the fact that their parties were at odds over a number of educational policy issues.[33] Indeed, Mr Kennedy quite self-consciously sought to manufacture a consensus within the Committee by 'not presenting myself as the

Unionist alternative to the Minister'.[34] However, the relationship deteriorated because of the Minister's unilateral decision on the ending of the '11+' and the summary abolition of school performance tables. This was less because the UUP and SF had diametrically opposed positions on both issues and more because it stimulated a widespread perception, especially within the wider unionist community, that the Committee was powerless to exert restraint over the Minister. In Mr Kennedy's view, Mr McGuinness' decisions diminished the credibility of all statutory committees.

Relatively frequent informal meetings between Committee Chairs and ministers became established as devolution unfolded, but not to the point where the chairs over-identified with their associated departments. A healthy critical distance between the incumbents was the norm, forged by the common recognition among chairs that their task was to hold both the devolved administration to account and the committees together in order to perform small 'o' opposition roles.

The consensual style also extended to the standing Business Committee (akin to the Scottish Parliament's Business Bureau), chaired by the Speaker and comprising the party whips. It met weekly, with Assembly officials in attendance, in order to plan the order of business during the Assembly's plenary sessions. This worked successfully to the extent that recourse to voting on plenary business within the Committee was rare.[35]

In sum, not only was there a discernible committee *system* within the Assembly, the committees also developed as great, if not greater, a degree of joined-up scrutiny than there was joined-up government within the Executive. Moreover the procedure whereby all statutory committee reports were debated in the chamber ensured that the committees were integrated fully into the life of the Assembly, which itself assisted in joining up the business of the legislature. However, neither the committees nor ordinary members exploited their power to initiate legislation.[36] During the course of the first devolved mandate only one Committee Bill was enacted and just four Private Members Bills were tabled.[37]

While there were instances when MLAs emerged as party animals rather than as committee creatures, they were exceptions to this general rule. A mixture of conflict avoidance within the committees, together with a shared concern to achieve and maintain consensus, did enable them to achieve tangible outcomes. For instance, the committees were significantly more successful than individual MLAs in securing Assembly support for tabled amendments to Executive Bills: 76 per cent of committee amendments were agreed, compared to 25 per cent of those tabled by ordinary members (Northern Ireland Assembly 2004: 35).

Though many of the amendments were relatively minor, some were significant. Against robust opposition by the Health Minister, Bairbre de Brún (SF), the Health Committee secured the Assembly's agreement to an amendment that delayed the ending of GP fundholding for a year until an agreed replacement regime was achieved. Another example occurred over the Department of the Environment's Best Value Bill which the Environment Committee, against strong opposition from the Minister, almost wholly deconstructed and simplified.

Turning to the 24 inquiries conducted by the statutory committees and the standing Committee of the Centre which monitored OFMDFM, 62 per cent of their key recommendations were implemented by the relevant departments, albeit that the majority of them were process related (Northern Ireland Assembly 2004: 17). More substantively, the Committee of the Centre was successful in improving proposals from OFMDFM concerning the role and remit of the Children's Commissioner, including the Commissioner's investigative powers and his power to bring, intervene or assist in legal proceedings. Equally the Committee for Social Development secured major changes in policies to tackle homelessness, including the development of a preventative strategy and measures aimed at dealing with homelessness among under 18-year-olds.

The role of the Finance and Personnel Committee (FPC) in collating the scrutiny of departmental budgets by its sister committees led to marked improvements in the budgetary process. Its recommendation to provide more time for such scrutiny and consultation over budget proposals was successful, leading to the introduction of departmental 'position reports' furnished to each committee before they considered the draft budgets. Their provision extended the consultation period by a month, enabling the committees to engage with departmental stakeholders in the wider community, thereby lending more focus and transparency to the scrutiny process.

These improvements assisted in generating lobbies between the departments and the committees for Executive Programme Fund projects. For instance, the Health Committee joined in common cause with the Health Department in bidding successfully for EPF support for a new regional cancer centre in Belfast. Similarly, the Education Committee supported, equally successfully, the Department's EPF bid for funding to improve the fabric of rural schools.[38]

There were, however, procedural or structural weaknesses that compromised the Assembly's capacity to hold the Executive to account. In relation to the first set of budget proposals, for instance, two committees (Social Development and Health) were unable to respond to their Department's draft bids because insufficient time was available to them, a situation caused by the press of other business. In addition, the capacity of the Committee of the Centre to scrutinise OFMDFM was constrained. This situation arose because the First and Deputy First Ministers secured majority support within the Assembly via the votes of UUP and SDLP members for their proposal that the external (i.e. strands two and three) functions of the Office should be reported to the Assembly by way of statements and oral questions and answers, rather than be subject to committee scrutiny. Thus, cross-questioning in the more forensic context of a committee room was denied in relation to half of the Office's responsibilities. More generally, the statutory committees were severely hampered in their scrutiny of North–South matters. The procedure whereby the plenary and sectoral business of the NSMC was reported, after the event, to the Assembly by way of ministerial statements denied the committees the opportunity of cross-questioning ministers in advance about the agendas and options to be discussed at the meetings.

From suspension to restoration

Whilst the experience of devolution from 1999 to 2002 was fitful and, consequentially, its policy achievements were modest, this did little if anything to shake the confidence of key policy-makers in London, Dublin and Belfast in the potential of the original 1998 template. That is evident from the paper trail produced by the two Governments following the reintroduction of direct rule in October 2002. While key Anglo-Irish policy statements – from the Joint Declaration (NIO: 2003), via the Comprehensive Agreement (NIO: 2004) to, finally, the St Andrews Agreement (NIO: 2006) – contained both (important) differences of procedural detail and, necessarily, of timing, each nailed its 'consociational plus' colours to the Anglo-Irish mast.

The period from suspension to St Andrews has, of course, witnessed the emergence of a markedly different political environment, epitomised by the transformation in the electoral landscape. This was foreshadowed in 2001 when SF first overhauled its ethnic rival, the SDLP, establishing a lead that it has extended at all subsequent elections. Two years later at the second Assembly election, the DUP overtook the UUP and has since wholly eclipsed its major unionist competitor. To cut the electoral story short, Northern Ireland has become a dominant two-party system presided over by constitutionally implacable foes (see Table 4.1)

For many, the electoral dominance of the DUP and SF appeared to preclude any prospect of the restoration of a fully inclusive, power-sharing administration. However, the context was altered significantly with the announcement by the IRA in July 2005 that it had 'formally ordered an end to the armed campaign'. The landmark statement signalled, to all intents and purposes, that its long war was over.[39] Two months later, the Independent International Commission on Decommissioning[40] (IICD), the body charged to oversee the process of weapons disposal, reported that the fourth and final act(s) of decommissioning represented 'the totality of the IRA's arsenal' such that it 'has met its commitment to put all its arms beyond use'. In an attempt to copper-fasten the IICD's judgement, the act(s) were witnessed by two clerics, a Catholic and a Methodist, who concluded that 'beyond any shadow of doubt, the arms of the IRA have now been decommissioned'.[41]

As far as the IICD was concerned the matter of IRA decommissioning had been resolved, a conclusion shared by both the UK and Irish Governments. That left two further issues to be settled before the DUP could actively contemplate participation in an administration that included SF. The first was the issue of the IRA's alleged involvement in criminality, the monitoring of which falls to the Independent Monitoring Commission (IMC).[42] The second was the preparedness of the IRA, via SF, to endorse the new policing service and the reformed criminal justice system.

As was, and is, the case with the IICD, the significance of the IMC to the peace and political processes cannot be overstated, notwithstanding SF's trenchant opposition to it.[43] In the period since the completion of its decommissioning the IMC has confirmed in a succession of reports that the IRA has abandoned terrorism, violence and organised criminal activity and that its leadership is committed to the

Table 4.1 Elections in Northern Ireland, 1998–2007

Election	UUP		DUP		SDLP		SF	
	N	%	N	%	N	%	N	%
1998 Assembly	172225	21.3	145917	18.0	177963	21.9	142858	17.6
2001 Westminster	216839	26.8	181999	22.5	169865	20.9	175392	21.7
2001 Local Government	181336	22.9	169477	21.4	153424	19.4	163269	20.6
2003 Assembly	156931	22.7	177944	25.7	117547	16.9	162758	23.5
2005 Westminster	127314	17.7	241856	33.7	125626	17.5	174530	24.3
2005 Local Government	126317	18.0	208278	30.0	121991	17.0	163205	23.0
2007 Assembly	103145	14.9	207721	30.1	105164	15.2	180573	26.2

Votes (N) and Vote Shares (%)

Note: The Assembly and Local Government elections employ the STV method of proportional representation: the results are, therefore, the first preference votes cast for each of the four major parties. The Westminster elections employ the 'first past the post' or simple plurality method as in the rest of the UK.

use of exclusively peaceful and democratic means in pursuit of Irish unification. That left the vexed issue of support for policing and the criminal justice system to be resolved. That it bulked large in the calculations of not just the DUP but also the UK and Irish Governments was underlined by the inclusion in the St Andrews Agreement of the following:

> We believe that the essential elements of support for law and order include endorsing fully the Police Service of Northern Ireland and the criminal justice system, actively encouraging everyone in the community to co-operate fully with the PSNI in tackling crime in all areas and actively supporting all the policing and criminal justice institutions.[44]

The statement, authored by the two Governments, was also to be included in a revised Ministerial Pledge of Office set out at St Andrews. The Pledge imposed four new obligations on prospective ministers including 'to uphold the rule of law based as it is on the fundamental principles of fairness, impartiality and democratic accountability, including support for policing and the courts as set out in paragraph 6 of the St Andrews agreement' (see above). This placed enormous pressure on the SF leadership and its political strategy, and it worked. Following the recommendation of the party's Executive on 28 December 2006, a month later at a special party conference the delegates overwhelmingly supported a motion endorsing the PSNI and the criminal justice system.

That outcome radically altered the political context and paved the way for the restoration of devolution in the wake of the Assembly election scheduled by the Agreement for 7 March. However, although the election did take place on the appointed date, as has been the case throughout the peace process, other deadlines established at St Andrews were breached by the parties, including the creation of a new Executive by 26 March.[45] Nevertheless, despite the delay the consociational die was cast: no matter how reluctantly, the DUP had to accept that if devolution was to be restored the Executive would, of necessity, include the reconstructed republicans of Sinn Féin. The DUP had conceded as much in the build-up to the (abortive) Comprehensive Agreement of 2004. While in the best of all possible worlds it would prefer a voluntary coalition shorn of republicans, the DUP had then accepted SF's participation in a fully inclusive Executive provided there was a conclusive and transparent end to the decommissioning of the IRA's arsenal and the abandonment of its alleged criminal activities. At the same time SF had consistently reconciled itself to a set of, in its view, temporary partitionist institutions, thereby supplanting the 'long war' with a lengthy political haul towards unification.

Space precludes a systematic comparison of the Anglo-Irish proposals for restoration contained in the Joint Declaration, the Comprehensive Agreement and the St Andrews Agreement. There are continuities and discontinuities between and among the proposals, not least in relation to the standard operating procedures of the new Executive (see below) and, as in 2004, the Agreement brokered at St Andrews bears the impression of both DUP and SF demands, including the revisions to the Ministerial Pledge of Office. Thus, whilst the commitment to support policing and the courts met a DUP requirement, as did the obligation to 'promote the interests of the whole community . . . towards the goal of a shared future', the requirements to 'observe the joint nature of the Office of First and Deputy First Minister' and 'participate fully in the Executive Committee, North–South Ministerial Council and British–Irish Council' were inserted at the behest of SF.

Both a revised Pledge and a statutory Ministerial Code were prefigured in 2004, and each is revisited in the St Andrews Agreement. The Code is interesting for two reasons. First, because it is to be placed on a statutory basis and, secondly, because it included the matter of individual ministerial responsibility rather than being restricted to a declaration of ministerial interests and the commitment to the Nolan standards of public service. In effect, one purpose of the Code is to bridle the opportunity for ministers to embark on solo policy runs. In that sense, it and the Pledge can be understood as means of engineering collective ministerial responsibility, a behavioural norm that was not established in the first Executive.

This effort to manufacture ministerial collectivism is evident elsewhere in the St Andrews Agreement. For instance, it proposed that where no ministerial consensus can be reached over a decision and a vote is needed, any three ministers can require such a vote to be taken on a cross-community basis: i.e., it will require the support of both unionist and nationalist ministers to be carried. Similarly, decision making could be hindered by the provision enabling 30 MLAs to refer 'important ministerial decisions' back to the Executive, albeit only once rather than repeatedly. Given that the DUP was the only party to secure more than 30 MLAs at the election its Assembly bloc could be mustered to at least frustrate decisions almost at will. One can view these provisions in two ways. Either they could be used to create gridlock, and thereby strain the Executive's planned cohesion, or, alternatively, they could be perceived as a set of checks and balances that operate to produce a working (if coerced) form of consociational democracy within which the politics of accommodation may be practised.

Other changes included the procedure for filling the posts of First and Deputy First Ministers. In 1998 the incumbents were elected, by means of cross-community consent, on a joint ticket; the 2004 Comprehensive Agreement proposed that all 12 ministers would be nominated via the d'Hondt process and then be endorsed *tout court* by a cross-community vote (the 'Executive Declaration') in the Assembly; by contrast, the 2006 proposal does not require endorsement by the Assembly. Instead, the largest Assembly party (the DUP) would nominate the First Minister, and the second largest (SF) the Deputy First Minister: thereafter, the remaining ten ministers were to be nominated via d'Hondt.[46] In effect, it is a form of political anointment that spares both the DUP's and SF's MLAs from the discomfiture of endorsing the other's candidate, while denying the Assembly the opportunity to invest the nominees (and the other nominated ministers) with a legitimising vote.

Two other changes, each prefigured by the 2004 Comprehensive Agreement are, first, the repeal of the UK Government's suspensory power, demanded both by SF and the SDLP; and, secondly, the proposal preventing MLAs from changing their communal designation for an Assembly term unless associated with a change of membership of a political party. The latter will prevent the procedural 'inventiveness' that occurred in November 2001 enabling the election of Messrs Trimble and Durkan but, at the same time, copper-fastens communalism within the chamber (see note 23).

As in 2004, St Andrews also provides for an operational review and an efficiency review of the strand one institutions (matters high on the DUP's agenda), the latter to include in its brief the devolved departmental structure. There is something of a disposition towards a reduction in the number of departments among the parties which will likely mean the evolution of a smaller Executive in the foreseeable future. Moreover, the restated determination by the UK Government to transfer policing and criminal justice powers back to Northern Ireland (by May 2008), an objective shared by all parties, will itself force the issue of the number of departments. The 1998 Agreement provided for up to ten ministries, plus OFMDFM, so that institutional space for a new policing and criminal justice department would have to be found by merging at least two of the existing ministries.

The St Andrews Agreement also restated the intention to reduce the responsibilities of OFMDFM. By common ministerial consent,[47] the Office was overloaded with functions between 1998 and 2002 and a leaner, slimmer version will be welcomed. Elsewhere, St Andrews carried over commitments from the Comprehensive Agreement, including placing the Committee of the Centre on a statutory footing (previously it was a standing committee, created by means of an Assembly vote tabled by Messrs Trimble and Mallon); ensuring that, via the Ministerial Code, all NSMC and BIC papers will be circulated to the full Executive prior to a scheduled meeting of either body and that any minister has the right to seek Cabinet discussion on such papers (this would have the effect of bridling ministerial autonomy in relation to both North–South and East–West matters). Lead ministers will have a statutory right to attend meetings of both the NSMC and BIC where his/her interests are under consideration, thus preventing the First or Deputy First Minister from blocking a minister from attending either or both, as David Trimble had done in relation to the attendance of SF ministers at the NSMC. In addition, the Executive and the Irish Government will appoint a review group to examine *both* the efficiency and value for money of the existing cross-border implementation bodies *and* the case for additional bodies and areas of cross-border co-operation where mutual benefit would be derived.

Finally, St Andrews reiterated the earlier ambition of the UK and Irish Governments to encourage the creation of a new East–West inter-parliamentary framework embracing all three devolved Parliaments and the two sovereign governments; and to establish a standing secretariat for the BIC, likely to be based in Northern Ireland. It also proposed that the Northern Ireland Executive would encourage the Assembly parties to establish a North–South parliamentary forum and support the creation of an independent, representative North–South consultative forum appointed by the two administrations.

Conclusion

There is, in summary, a direct line of descent from the 1998 Agreement to that published at St Andrews. In its institutional essentials, the original template remains intact though one should not diminish the procedural amendments ushered in by the St Andrews Agreement. The key question is whether the revised model can work, especially given the unlikely DUP/SF relationship at the top of the administration (see Table 4.2).

Some commentators stress the coerced nature of the process. Had the efforts to revive devolution failed, both the UK and Irish Governments made it clear that it would not be a case of a reversion to orthodox direct rule. When Messrs Blair and Ahern visited Northern Ireland in April 2006 in order to try to kick-start the restoration of devolution they re-confirmed that the Belfast Agreement 'is the indispensable framework for relations on and between these islands'.[48] To that end, legislative provision was made for the convening of the (virtual) Assembly elected in November 2003 with its primary purpose the election, by means of parallel consent, of the First and Deputy First Ministers and, thereafter, the allocation of ministerial posts via the d'Hondt mechanism.

Anticipating that this was unlikely to occur immediately, the statement stipulated that the Assembly would meet for a maximum of three, six-week periods, one before and two after the summer recess, with a deadline of 24 November 2006 for these matters to be resolved. Should these efforts succeed, the third Assembly election scheduled for May 2007 would be postponed for one year to enable the new administration to bed-down. If, however, they failed, then the statement indicated

Table 4.2 Northern Ireland Assembly executive posts, 1999 and 2007

Party	1999	2007
UUP	First Minister; Enterprise, Trade and Investment; Environment; Culture, Arts and Leisure.	Health, Social Services and Public Safety; Employment and Learning.
DUP	Regional Development; Social Development.	First Minister; Finance and Personnel; Enterprise, Trade and Investment; Environment; Culture, Arts and Leisure.
SDLP	Deputy First Minister; Finance and Personnel; Employment and Learning;* Agriculture and Rural Development.	Social Development.
SF	Health, Social Services and Public Safety; Education.	Deputy First Minister; Education; Regional Development; Agriculture and Rural Development.

* The original title of the Department was Higher and Further Education, Training and Employment. Its title was changed by means of an Assembly Act in July 2001.

Notes: When the Executive was first established, it comprised six Unionists and six Nationalists. The Executive formed after the 2007 election comprises seven Unionists (five DUP, two UUP) and five Nationalists (four SF and one SDLP). No Executive was established following the second Assembly election in 2003. Had it been established, it too would have included seven Unionists and five Nationalists.

that it would not lead to the resumption of the *status quo ante* of unilateral direct rule from London. Instead, there would be a 'step-change in advancing North–South co-operation and action' via the 'joint stewardship' of London and Dublin. Although the nature of the change was undefined it was interpreted widely as involving a 'greener' form of direct rule. To underline the point, the statement made it clear that failure to restore the institutions would mean that the salaries and allowances payable to the MLAs would cease beyond the 24 November deadline.

Despite these beginnings, the process of reaching agreement in 2006–2007 could still be said to reveal developments in approach that make the durability of devolution a plausible prospect. Following the intervention of the UK and Irish Governments the Assembly was duly convened on 15 May 2006. It had an inauspicious start. The attempt a week later by Gerry Adams to secure cross-community support for his nomination of Ian Paisley as First Minister and Martin McGuinness as Deputy First Minister failed when Dr Paisley refused to be nominated. During the first six weeks of its reincarnation there were just six plenary sessions of the Assembly, the dates and the agendas for which were fixed by the Secretary of State, Peter Hain. Mr Hain also provided for the creation of a 14 MLA-strong 'Preparation for Government Committee' whose purpose was to 'identify key issues that have to be resolved and debated by the Assembly to prepare for Government'.[49] This foundered when its members failed to agree on the Chairmanship of the Committee, obliging Mr Hain to intervene to appoint two rotating chairs, Francie Molloy (SF) and Jim Wells (DUP) whom he had earlier appointed as Deputy Speakers of the Assembly.[50] Though the Committee met until the recess began on 7 July it made little headway.

However, progress was made in the run-up to St Andrews and, more particularly, in its wake. While the parties failed to establish an administration by the initial deadline of 24 November 2006, both Governments interpreted their collective mood, most significantly that of the DUP, to be in favour of the re-establishment of an inclusive administration. That interpretation enabled the creation of a further breathing space extending beyond the 24 November deadline. The Assembly, which met on six further occasions, became, by virtue of the Northern Ireland (St Andrews Agreement) Act 2006, the 'Transitional Assembly' with effect from 24 November for a period up to the end of January 2007 when it was to be dissolved in anticipation of the third Assembly election on 7 March.

During the brief tenure of the Transitional Assembly the Preparation for Government Committee was transformed, by direction of the Secretary of State, Peter Hain, into the 'Programme for Government' Committee with a brief to agree priorities for a restored Executive and to make preparations for restoration. It laid some of the groundwork for a new administration and created, via its six sub-committees, a positive working atmosphere between and among the parties.[51]

With the election over, the Transitional Assembly met on two further occasions in the run-up to the 26 March 'deadline' for the establishment of the new Executive. However, after a series of intensive negotiations between the DUP and SF that deadline was pushed back to 8 May, allowing the former to claim that it had secured a longer period to test the commitment of the mainstream republican movement to exclusively peaceful and democratic means and SF to secure a binding, public commitment from the DUP to enter an inclusive devolved administration. This, together with a statement from the SF President, Gerry Adams, was duly delivered in the form of a televised statement by Dr Paisley; with, remarkably, the two men sitting in close proximity at Parliament Buildings.

During the seven-week period leading up to devolution day on 8 May, the auguries for a functioning, stable government were promising. Unlike in 1998–1999, the parties embarked on a series of negotiations designed to secure agreement on the allocation, via d'Hondt, of the departments and to identify their respective ministers-in-waiting. By early April, both had been achieved. This meant that the shadow ministers could gain access to their departments in order to be briefed by officials and thereby hit the ground running when powers were transferred. In addition, the Executive parties met collectively with the then Chancellor Gordon Brown to try to extract additional public expenditure for Northern Ireland earmarked to tackle its infrastructural needs. They also secured the agreement of the Secretary of State to postpone the introduction of water service charges – due to be applied in early April – for one year, thereby enabling the Executive to revisit the issue.

Barring accidents, the renewal of devolution will progress in much more auspicious circumstances than was the case after December 1999. That is not to diminish the inherent difficulties of implementing and managing the terms of the St Andrews Agreement. As the 'midwife' of the Belfast Agreement acknowledged almost a year after it was reached, '[T]he implementation of agreements is as difficult and as important as reaching them . . . [A]s we are now seeing in Northern Ireland . . . getting it done is often harder than agreeing to do it' (Mitchell 2002: 89).[52] That the first attempt, headed by the more moderate UUP and SDLP, foundered implies that a union of constitutional extremes may not prosper. However, though it will be an uncomfortable form of political cohabitation, the DUP-SF led administration may yet confound us all and demonstrate that in consociational politics, as in love, opposites can attract.

Notes

1 The text of the *Agreement at St Andrews*, published on 13 October 2006 by the UK and Irish Governments, is available at www.nio.gov.uk

2 *The Agreement: Agreement reached in the multi-party negotiations*, Belfast, HMSO, nd.

3 The St Andrews Agreement specifies May 2008 as the scheduled date for the devolution of policing and criminal justice powers.

4 The Sinn Féin *ard fheis* endorsing the party Executive's motion recommending 'critical support' for the police and the criminal justice system (North and South) was held on 28 January 2007. The motion is available at www.sinnfeinonline.com/ news/319

5 I freely acknowledge the corrective drawn by these authors to my earlier (Wilford, 2001: 4) characterisation of the Agreement as an 'off the peg model'.

6 The BIIG, established under the terms of a new British–Irish Agreement which 'subsumed' the Anglo-Irish Agreement (AIA) of 1985, was designed to promote bilateral co-operation on as yet non-devolved issues of mutual interest between the two sovereign governments.

7 On 27 November 2002 a new Anglo-Irish Treaty provided for the continuation of the six North–South implementation bodies, administered under the aegis of the NSMC, on a care and maintenance basis. Though it would cease to have effect upon the resumption of devolution, the treaty seemed to breach the 'interlocking and interdependent' relationship between the NSMC and the Assembly set out in the 1998 Agreement.

8 The authority to take the decision to hold a referendum on the constitutional future of Northern Ireland rests with the Secretary of State alone. S/he would only do so if persuaded that there was a mood for change to, not for the maintenance of, the constitutional *status quo*.

9 They were elected by means of the 'parallel consent' test set out in the Agreement. This required an overall majority in the Assembly (n55), including a majority of both nationalist and unionist members. To enable this test to be applied, all MLAs had to register themselves as either 'nationalist', 'unionist' or 'other' when signing the members' register at the (shadow) Assembly's first plenary session. A second test of cross-community support for what the Agreement termed 'key decisions' was the 'weighted majority'. This required the support of at least 60 per cent of MLAs present and voting in the chamber, including at least 40 per cent of both nationalist and unionist members. In the case of the joint election of the First and Deputy First Ministers, only the parallel consent test was applied. Even though the SF MLAs abstained from the vote, there was a sufficient number of SDLP MLAs to meet the parallel consent test. The 'key decisions' subject to these tests were pre-determined by the Agreement and included, besides the election of the First and Deputy First Ministers, the election of the Assembly's Speaker, the Assembly's standing orders and budget allocations to the devolved departments. In addition, any 'petition of concern' supported by at least 30 MLAs was subject to the cross-community voting rules.

10 This was confirmed to me in a series of interviews held with party negotiators during 2005 and 2006.

11 Interview with Sean Farren, October 2005. David Trimble (interview with the author in October 2005) was reconciled to the existence of ten departments from the outset. See also Godson (2004).

12 David Trimble was the UUP's nominating officer for the UUP ministers, but it was John Hume, the party leader, not Seamus Mallon, who nominated the SDLP's ministers. Two junior ministerial posts, one each for the UUP and the SDLP, were created in OFMDFM in December 1999. The first incumbents were Dermot Nesbitt (UUP) and Denis Haughey (SDLP). Mr Nesbitt subsequently became Environment Minister (replacing party colleague Sam Foster who had resigned on health grounds), and was replaced by James Leslie (UUP). According to David Trimble (interview with the author, October 2005), the junior ministers were never integrated fully into the work of the Office. In his view, this situation arose in part because of the reluctance of senior civil servants to take their policy lead from them in lieu of the First and Deputy First Ministers. Additionally, it was, in Mr Trimble's view, because Seamus Mallon insisted that every statement or recommendation from the junior ministers had to be issued on a joint basis and that any decisions arising from their activities had to be referred to the First and Deputy First Ministers for action. Though Mr Mallon's insistence on this joint approach harmonised with the spirit and the letter of power sharing, it slowed decision processes and otherwise created inefficiencies and considerable ill-feeling within OFMDFM. Information derived from interviews with the former ministers and junior ministers.

13 Several attempts were made by anti-Agreement parties to exclude Sinn Féin from the Executive but each failed because the SDLP, wedded to the inclusiveness embodied in the Agreement, refused to support the exclusion motions.

14 The DUP was not unique in this respect: SF ministers and MLAs on occasion also sought to alter aspects of the budgets or the programmes that had previously been agreed within the Executive.

15 When devolution was restored at the end of May 2000 following the first period of suspension, the DUP announced that it would henceforth rotate its two ministerial positions among its MLAs. It did so on two occasions during the lifetime of the Assembly: first in July 2000 when Gregory Campbell and Maurice Morrow replaced Peter Robinson and Nigel Dodds at, respectively, Regional Development and Social Development and again in November 2001when the initial pairing resumed their ministerial roles.

16 During an interview with the author (October 2005), David Trimble disclosed that he had delayed signing-off on the Code because had he done so and it had been formally adopted, he would likely have been found to have breached its terms because of his refusal to authorise the attendance of the two SF ministers at sectoral and plenary meetings of the NSMC. SF sought a judicial review of Mr Trimble's action and won its case in the High Court.

17 The Education Minister, Martin McGuinness (SF) provided two of the clearest examples of a minister embarking on a solo-run. He announced the ending both of the publication of school league tables and the transfer test for primary school children (Northern Ireland's version of the 11+) without either the agreement of other ministers or the statutory Education Committee.

18 Such tolerance did have its limits. When the DUP re-joined the restored Executive in May 2000, it stated that its (soon to be rotated) ministers would not be bound by the ministerial code so that they could 'uncover and reveal what is going on in the heart of government'. The Executive retaliated by, among other things, ending the routine distribution of its papers to the DUP's ministers, other than those relating to its two departments, an action later upheld in the High Court (see Wilson and Wilford, 2001: 88.)

19 They were 'Social Inclusion/Community Regeneration'; 'Service Modernisation'; 'New Directions'; 'Infrastructure/Capital Renewal'; and 'Children'. See www.ofmdfmni. gov.uk The PfG's strategic priorities were: 'Growing as a Community'; 'Working for a Healthier People'; 'Investing in Education and Skills'; 'Securing a Competitive Economy'; and 'Developing North–South and International Relations'. See www.ofmdfmni.gov.uk

20 Interview with the author, November 2005.

21 Such disruption could have been exacerbated. For instance, had the First Minister's three ministerial colleagues also resigned on 1 July, so too would the DUP's two ministers (Wilson and Wilford 2001: 89). This would have collapsed the Executive since a standing order laid by the then Secretary of State, Dr Mo Mowlam, on 15 July 1999, required that it should contain at least three unionists and at least three nationalists (Wilford and Wilson 2000: 84*fn*). The fact that the UUP ministers did not resign was a signal of the party's (admittedly strained) desire to keep devolution ticking over. It did, however, mean that an acting First and Deputy First Minister, respectively Sir Reg Empey (UUP) – who also retained his portfolio as Enterprise, Trade and Investment Minister – and Seamus Mallon, had temporarily to be put in place. Mr Trimble's resignation also led the Secretary of State, Dr John Reid, to suspend the Assembly on two occasions, each for just 24 hours, in order to forestall calling a fresh election, which caused outrage among anti-Agreement unionists.

22 Mr Durkan also became the leader of the SDLP following John Hume's resignation in September 2001 and continued in the role of Finance Minister until his party colleague, Sean Farren, replaced him in December 2001: in turn, Dr Farren was replaced as Employment and Learning Minister by Carmel Hanna (SDLP).

23 The process of electing Messrs Trimble and Durkan proved a contentious and litigious affair. It was only achieved when three members of the Alliance Party and one Women's Coalition MLA re-designated themselves temporarily as 'unionists' in order to secure their election by means of the required parallel consent voting procedure. (The other Women's Coalition member re-designated herself as a 'nationalist'.) Following this inventive episode,

the DUP sought a judicial review of the election on the ground that it had occurred beyond the maximum period of six weeks that was allowed for a period of suspension (the six weeks had elapsed at midnight on 3 November) and, as such, the Secretary of State was obliged to dissolve the Assembly and call a fresh election. The case eventually reached the House of Lords on 25 July 2002 when the Law Lords upheld the Secretary of State's decision on the narrowest of margins (3:2).

24 Time series data of public opinion about the Agreement and the outworking of devolution can be found on the *Northern Ireland Life and Times Survey* site at www.ark.ac.uk

25 Interview with the author, October 2005.

26 There were also six standing committees and provision for consultative *ad hoc* committees to be created at the request of the Secretary of State in relation to reserved matters: there were nine *ad hoc* committees during the Assembly's mandate (see the committee page at www.niassembly.gov.uk). The standing committees – Audit, Procedure, Standards and Privileges, Public Accounts, Business and the Committee of the Centre – varied in size from five to, in the case of the Committee of the Centre, 17 members.

27 Only three committees, two standing and one statutory, created temporary sub-committees. These were the Committee of the Centre (EU affairs) and the Procedure Committee (Legislative Review and Parliamentary Questions); and the Enterprise, Trade and Investment Committee (on the Giant's Causeway as part of its major inquiry into tourism).

28 To remedy this operational problem the Procedure Committee proposed that the quorum for committee meetings should be reduced from five to three. See Procedure Committee *Minutes*, 27 February 2002.

29 Towards the latter part of the Assembly's first term, the Enterprise, Trade and Investment Committee experimented with 'conferencing' during its tourism inquiry, the only departure from the norm of oral evidence taking. Only 78 committee meetings or site visits were held outside the precincts of Parliament Buildings out of a total of more than 1,000 meetings.

30 The DUP refused to participate in the liaison committee because it had no statutory basis.

31 Interview with the author, December 2004.

32 Interview with the author, October 2005.

33 Interview with the author, November 2005.

34 Ibid.

35 A practice developed within the Committee whereby if three of the whips of the four Executive parties were able to agree on the ordering of business then their collective view tended to prevail. A similar pattern of co-operative behaviour characterised the Assembly Commission. Chaired by the Speaker, the six-strong Commission was charged to provide and maintain the property, services and staff required for the purposes of the Assembly. It held 47 meetings during the devolved period and held only one vote throughout, that on the highly controversial proposal to display lilies in the Great Hall of Parliament Buildings during the 2001 Easter period. The issue was so contentious that an emergency debate was arranged to debate the Commission's decision to permit the display. See the Assembly's *Official Report* (Hansard), 10 April 2001.

36 One statutory Committee Chair, Danny Kennedy (Education) claimed that there was 'a certain nervousness' about the prospect of introducing a Committee Bill on the part of the Committee's members, whilst among Assembly officials servicing it there was 'a certain reluctance to clash with the Department'. The net effect was that the Committee did not discuss the possibility of introducing a Bill. Interview with the author, November 2005.

37 The standing Standards and Privileges Committee introduced the Committee Bill providing for the creation of the Assembly Ombudsman for Northern Ireland. The first Private Member's Bill (PMB), introduced by the Women's Coalition, sought to create

the post of Children's Commissioner, but it was superseded by legislative proposals forwarded by OFMDFM. Billy Armstrong (UUP) tabled the second PMB, an Agriculture (Amendment) Bill. It, together with three further PMBs, lapsed with the final suspension. The major explanation for the absence of such legislation seems to have been a lack of maturity or understanding on the part of ordinary members that these opportunities were available to them. (On one occasion the author was telephoned by an MLA who enquired whether committees could initiate legislation.) In addition, the press of business, together with both scheduling problems and maintaining a quorum, tended to militate against the tabling of draft legislative proposals by the committees.

38 However, this meant that committees became cheerleaders for departmental bids rather than acting as a means of promoting interdepartmental, joined-up bids, which was the intended purpose of the EPFs.

39 On 28 October 2005, Gerry Adams, the Sinn Féin President, uttered the long sought after phrase on Ulster Television. Questioned about the IRA's stance following the September 2005 decommissioning act(s), he stated 'The war is obviously over'.

40 The IICD in October 2003 reported on the third and then largest act of IRA decommissioning – the first two occurring in October 2001 and April 2002 – but it proved insufficient to persuade the then leader of the UUP, David Trimble, to re-enter a devolved Executive.

41 Both the IICD's statement and that of the two witnesses, Revd. Harold Good and Father Alec Reid, are available on www.nio.gov.uk 26 September 2005.

42 The IMC was established formally in January 2004, and thereafter produced a series of reports documenting the activities of all paramilitary organisations, and the process of security normalisation ('demilitarisation' in republican terms) undertaken by the UK Government. It has four members: Lord (John) Alderdice, the former Speaker of the Assembly; John Grieve, former head of the Metropolitan Police's anti-terrorist squad; Richard Kerr, a former deputy director of the CIA; and a retired Irish civil servant, Joe Brosnan. The IMC's reports are available at www.nio.gov.uk

43 Sinn Féin has consistently characterised the IMC as the handmaiden of 'securocrats', that is the police and the intelligence community.

44 St Andrews Agreement, paragraph six.

45 For a contemporaneous account of the peace process, including the events leading up to and beyond the St Andrews Agreement, see the regular monitoring reports available at www.ucl.ac.uk/constitution-unit/research/devolution/MonReps/NI

46 In both 1998 and 2004, the largest party in the largest (Assembly) designation, i.e. 'unionist' or 'nationalist', would nominate the candidate for First Minister and the largest party in the second largest designation the Deputy First Minister. The change wrought at St Andrews thus turned the election into a *de facto* plebiscite for the post of First Minister. The prospect (or fear) that SF might emerge from the election as the largest party and that Martin McGuinness would become First Minister was seized upon by the DUP as a means of mobilising its electorate to ensure that such an outcome would not materialise.

47 This became apparent during interviews conducted by the author with former ministers during 2005 and 2006.

48 NIO press release, 6 April 2006.

49 NIO press release, 5 June 2006.

50 Mr Hain appointed Eileen Bell (Alliance Party) as Speaker of the Assembly.

51 The Official Reports and Committee Minutes and Reports of both the Assembly and the Transitional Assembly are available at www.niassembly.gov.uk

52 Senator George Mitchell, who chaired the talks leading to the Agreement, delivered the speech from which this extract is taken in February 1999.

References

Coakley, J. (2001) 'The Belfast Agreement and the Republic of Ireland', in R. Wilford (ed.) *Aspects of the Belfast Agreement*, Oxford: Oxford University Press.

Godson, D. (2004) *Himself Alone: David Trimble and the Ordeal of Unionism*, London: Harper and Collins.

Hadfield, B. (2001) 'Seeing it through? The multifaceted implementation of the Belfast Agreement', in R. Wilford (ed.) *Aspects of the Belfast Agreement*, Oxford: Oxford University Press.

Lijphart, A. (1968) *The Politics of Accommodation: Pluralism and Democracy in the Netherlands*, Berkeley / Los Angeles: University of California Press.

Lijphart, A. (1969) 'Consociational democracy', *World Politics* 21: 207–25.

Lijphart, A. (1977) *Democracy in Plural Societies: A Comparative Exploration*, New Haven, London: Yale University Press.

MacGinty, R. Wilford, R., Dowds, L. and Robinson, G. (2001) 'Consenting adults: the principle of consent and Northern Ireland's constitutional future', *Government and Opposition* 36, 4: 472–92.

McGarry, J. and O'Leary, B. (2004) *The Northern Ireland Conflict: Consociational Engagements*, Oxford: Oxford University Press.

Millar, F. (2004) *David Trimble: The Price of Peace*, Dublin: The Liffey Press.

Mitchell, G. (2002) 'Towards peace in Northern Ireland', in M. Elliott (ed.) *The Long Road to Peace in Northern Ireland*, Liverpool: University of Liverpool Press.

Mitchell, P. (1999) 'Futures', in P. Mitchell and R. Wilford (eds) *Politics in Northern Ireland*, Boulder: Westview Press.

Mitchell, P. (2001) 'Transcending an ethnic party system? The impact of consociational governance on electoral dynamics and the party system', in R. Wilford (ed.) *Aspects of the Belfast Agreement*, Oxford: Oxford University Press.

Northern Ireland Assembly (2004) *Report of the Working Group on the Review of the Effectiveness of Committees*, Belfast: Northern Ireland Assembly.

Northern Ireland Office (1998) *The Agreement: Agreement reached in the multi-party negotiations*, Belfast and London: Northern Ireland Office.

Northern Ireland Office (2003) *Joint Declaration by the British and Irish Governments*, Belfast: NIO.

Northern Ireland Office (2004) *Proposals by the British and Irish Governments for a Comprehensive Agreement*, Belfast: NIO.

Northern Ireland Office (2006) *Agreement at St Andrews*, Belfast: NIO.

O'Leary, B. (1998) 'The 1998 British–Irish agreement: power sharing plus', London: The Constitution Unit.

O'Leary, B. (1999) 'The 1998 British–Irish agreement: consociation plus', *Scottish Affairs* 26, Winter: 1–22.

O'Leary, B. (2004) 'The nature of the Agreement', in J. McGarry and B. O'Leary, *The Northern Ireland Conflict: Consociational Engagements*, Oxford: Oxford University Press.

Patten Report (The Independent Commission on Policing for Northern Ireland) (1999) *A New Beginning: Policing in Northern Ireland*, Belfast: Northern Ireland Office.

Walker, C. (2001) 'The Patten Report and post-sovereignty policing in Northern Ireland', in R. Wilford (ed.) *Aspects of the Belfast Agreement*, Oxford: Oxford University Press.

Wilford, R. (1999) 'Epilogue', in P. Mitchell and R. Wilford (eds.) *Politics in Northern Ireland*, Boulder: Westview Press.

Wilford, R. (2001) 'The Assembly and the Executive', in R. Wilford (ed.) *Aspects of the Belfast Agreement*, Oxford: Oxford University Press.

Wilford, R. (2004) 'Northern Ireland: resolving an ancient quarrel?' in M. O'Neill (ed.) *Devolution and British Politics*, Harlow: Pearson Longman.

Wilson, R. and Wilford, R. (2001) 'Northern Ireland: endgame' in A. Trench (ed.) *The State of the Nations 2001: The Second Year of Devolution in the United Kingdom*, Thorverton: Imprint Academic.

Wilson, R. and Wilford, R. (2004) 'The virtual election: the 2003 Northern Ireland Assembly Election', *Representation* 40, 4: 250–65.

Wilson, R. and Wilford, R. (2006) 'From the Belfast Agreement to stable power sharing', ESRC Devolution and Constitutional Change Programme.

Part II
Regionalism in England

5 Institutional capacity in the English regions

Graham Pearce

The UK has traditionally been viewed as a classic example of a unitary state. Nonetheless, while political power was centralised, by 1997 different arrangements had evolved to combine central control with decentralised decision-making through separate government departments for Northern Ireland, Scotland and Wales. These institutional structures eased New Labour's programme of political devolution in the Celtic nations (Jeffery 2007). There was no direct equivalent tradition of administrative devolution for England and, although central government had a long-established presence in the nine 'standard' regions, including Greater London, this was primarily focused on the delivery of government functions, rather than the management of territory. Despite these limitations, the Labour Government was able to build on an emerging form of 'technocratic' regionalism, which combined 'top-down' administrative decentralisation with 'bottom-up' co-ordinating initiatives, derived from individual regions and localities. The former was primarily enabled by individual government departments working through the 'integrated' Government Offices (GOs) – Whitehall's principal representatives in the regions – established by the Conservative Government in 1994; the latter through the activities of regional Local Government Associations (LGAs).

During New Labour's first term reforms were targeted in two areas. First, in response to long-standing concerns that the abolition of the Greater London Council in 1986 had left a vacuum which, over time, exposed the need for policy co-ordination, a Greater London Authority (GLA) was established in 2000 comprising an elected Assembly and Mayor with 'strategic' powers, including economic development, policing and emergency services and transport. Second, the formal structures of governance in the regions beyond the capital were strengthened. The roles of the GOs in administering and co-ordinating national policies at regional and local levels were extended to provide central government with a more coherent presence in the regions. Regional Development Agencies (RDAs) were also appointed to co-ordinate regional economic development and regeneration initiatives and improve the regions' competitiveness through the preparation and implementation of Regional Economic Strategies (RESs). In addition, as a step towards regional democracy, indirectly elected Regional Chambers (subsequently restyled 'Assemblies') comprising local authority councillors and representatives of regional business and community interests were established. They became responsible for championing regional interests, leading the preparation of Regional Housing, Spatial and Regional Sustainable Development Strategies (RHSs, RSSs and RSDFs), overseeing the RDAs and co-ordinating a range of regional strategies. This institutional 'troika' was expected to work together to interact with the bewildering collection of government 'quangos' (quasi-autonomous non-governmental organisations) and business and community bodies present in the regions and participate in the vertical networks that connect EU, national and sub-national government.

Further moves toward regionalisation in England were advanced in Labour's second term and were framed in the 2002 White Paper 'Your Region, Your Choice: Revitalising the English Regions'. It did not, however, offer the unequivocal commitment to regional government that some might have desired (Cabinet Office and DTLR 2002). A 'twin track' approach was proposed entailing firstly, enhanced powers for the troika and secondly, elected regional assemblies (ERAs), where there was evidence of public support expressed in regional referendums. It was also made a precondition that the creation of ERAs should be accompanied by a move to a pattern of unitary (single tier) local government in those areas served by both county and district councils.

Following a 'soundings' exercise to judge the level of interest in each region in having a referendum, in June 2003 John Prescott, the Deputy Prime Minister (DPM), announced that the three northern regions would be the first to hold referendums on establishing ERAs. In July 2004, however, the Office of the Deputy Prime Minister (ODPM) announced that, because of concerns over reports of irregularities in recent all-postal voting in local and European Parliament elections in the North West and Yorkshire and the Humber (the referendums were also to use all-postal voting), only the North East would move forward to a referendum. Opposition politicians, however, were swift to insist that the Government was responding to Labour backbenchers' reports that referendums in the North West or Yorkshire would be lost. The referendum in the North East proceeded as planned in November 2004; however, an overwhelming majority (78 per cent) voted against an elected regional assembly. As Rallings and Thrasher (2005) observe, the ERA as proposed struck few positive chords with a large majority of the North-East electorate and the referendum effectively ended any prospect of regional government in England, at least in the foreseeable future. Despite this setback to the democratisation of the regional tier, Whitehall has continued to decentralise powers to the regional bodies where it is judged to add value to service delivery, and regions have become the locus for the preparation of strategies covering a wide range of policy areas. Indeed, since the referendum a series of Treasury commissioned reviews have been published on land-use planning (Barker 2006), transport (Eddington 2006) and skills (Leitch 2006), which Burch *et al.* (2007: 6) perceive 'as mapping out the terrain on which future approaches to policy and governance between the national and local scales in England will be decided'.

Although falling short of reforms elsewhere in the UK, some observers see these developments as heralding a less hierarchical, more fluid, multi-level form of governance. They highlight the emerging regional institutions' potential to open up new spaces within which networks of regional elites and activists can achieve greater influence over decision making and secure a more consistent approach to the delivery of regional priorities (Healey 2006; Sandford 2006; Bogdanor 2005; Bache and Flinders 2004; Haughton and Counsell 2004). Others, however, assert that this account of evolving intra-state relations has been greatly overstated. They maintain that England is now the most centralised of all the large countries in Western Europe and central departments and their executive agencies continue to exert direct control or influence over more than 90 per cent of public expenditure in the regions. Indeed, the national state retains a pivotal role and, rather than providing regional actors with the freedoms to orchestrate policies, Whitehall departments are employing regional administration to deliver their own policies and programmes (Jeffery and Wincott 2006; Lodge and Mitchell 2006; Ayres and Pearce 2005; Jones *et al.* 2005; Adams *et al.* 2003; Brenner 2004).

A more considered view suggests, however, that rather than the outcome of a conscious strategy, New Labour's interest in regional governance has been the consequence of a complex bargaining process and *ad hoc* and largely unco-ordinated politically driven actions by separate Whitehall departments (Deas and Lord 2006; Mansfield 2005; Pearce and Ayres 2005; Sandford 2005). Moreover, because each region has its own unique socio-economic, political and institutional inheritances, the impacts of decentralisation may be more diverse than previously recognised (Hardill *et al.* 2006; Goodwin *et al.* 2005).

The purpose of this chapter is to explore these competing accounts through an examination of the evolving capacities of the key regional institutions. It seeks to:

- briefly examine New Labour's rationale for decentralising functions to the regions
- assess the contribution and the constraints on the activities of the three key regional institutions – Government Offices, Regional Development Agencies and Regional Assemblies
- explore the capacity of regional institutions to develop a more co-ordinated approach to the management of their territories
- reflect on future prospects for regional government in England.

New Labour's rationale for decentralisation

Reforms to English regional government since 1997 form part of a wider debate across Europe about the scope for 'rescaling' government by transferring political and administrative controls away from central government and creating new forms of regional and metropolitan governance (see for example, Ward and Jonas 2005; Keating 2004; Loughlin 2004; Brenner 2003; Herrschel and Newman 2002). In addition to potentially democratising the regional tier and giving England a more influential voice in a devolved UK, Labour's reform agenda was, therefore, motivated by a desire for gains in policy efficiency and effectivness and a belief that decentralising responsibilities for some policy areas to the regions could:

- bring together a range of expertise drawn from all levels and sectors within regions to better plan and integrate investment decisions and improve service delivery

- build on the productive capacity of underperforming regions and thereby contribute to national economic growth
- respond to interrelated issues such as economic development and regeneration, housing, spatial planning and transport that cross local authority boundaries.

Each of these requirements has shaped the roles, structures and resources of regional institutions, as well as approaches to decentralisation across Whitehall. Enhancing government's capacity at the regional level was conceived as contributing to the objectives of the White Paper 'Modernising Government', which set out to improve the integration, delivery and quality of services by directing responsibility for delivery downwards (Cabinet Office 1999). Furthermore, there had been long-standing concerns about the capacity of traditional Whitehall structures to deal with policy issues that reach across departmental boundaries. Consequently, measures were deemed necessary to better integrate central government policies with a regional dimension, ensure that service delivery matched local circumstances and improve understanding of local and regional issues in the design of national policy (Cabinet Office 2000a, 2000b).

In 2001 unease about growing regional economic differences also led the Treasury, the [then] ODPM and the Department for Trade and Industry (DTI) to adopt a shared target to make sustainable improvements in the economic performance of all English regions and, over the long term, reduce the persistent gap in growth rates between them. This was to be achieved by 'building on the indigenous strengths in each locality, region and country ... regionally balanced growth, led by the regions themselves, is not only desirable in its own right but also essential to deliver economic prosperity and employment for all' (HM Treasury and DTI 2001: iii).

Decentralisation was also underpinned by a growing recognition that, while appropriate for services where equity of distribution is required, uniform, national solutions cannot respond effectively to the diversity of policy issues facing different regions or localities. Territorial flexibility is viewed as essential in efforts to improve public services and economic performance, and increasingly regions have become regarded as convenient for the joining-up of policy areas – small enough to allow for face-to-face contact upon which trust and co-operation can be built – and large enough to permit economies of scale and scope (Cabinet Office and DTLR 2002; Amin and Thrift 1994).

The evolving roles of the 'troika'

Government Regional Offices

The creation of 'integrated' GOs in 1994 brought together regional officials from the Departments of Employment, Environment, Transport and Trade and Industry. The Offices were intended to bring greater consistency to the work of central departments and make Whitehall more responsive to the needs of individual regions. However, a Cabinet Office report, 'Reaching Out' (2000a) was highly critical of Whitehall's ability to present a coherent picture of central policies with a regional dimension, and of the absence of any single government official or body responsible for integrating those policies. Reforms to the GOs were seen as necessary to improve policy co-ordination and, because significant areas of public policy with a regional dimension lay outside the Offices' remit, domestic departments not already co-located in the GOs were urged to do so. In Whitehall cross-cutting measures and joint departmental Public Service Agreements (PSAs), including a regional dimension where appropriate, were adopted and departments were encouraged to create new, or expand existing, regional teams. An interdepartmental Regional Co-ordination Unit (RCU), now located in the DCLG (Department for Communities and Local Government), was also established to support the GOs, provide a channel of communication between the Offices and the centre, and facilitate a more corporate approach to regional issues across Whitehall.

Since 2002, seven additional Whitehall departments have established a presence in the GOs: the Departments for Culture Media and Sport (DCMS), Education and Skills (DfES), Food and Rural Affairs (DEFRA), Health (DoH), Work and Pensions (DWP) and the Cabinet and Home Offices, supported by a single administrative annual budget. Some 350–450 civil servants are integrated or co-located in each GO. These are now charged with administering and influencing central government programmes jointly worth £6.5 billion annually, contributing to the delivery of over 40 specific PSA targets, giving feedback on the effectiveness of departmental programmes, linking departmental policies and providing a regional input to policy formulation. They are also responsible for influencing the formulation of a wide range of regional strategies and negotiating and monitoring Local Area Agreements (LAAs) drawn up between central and local government. In addition, GOs work to improve underperforming local authorities and promote Local Strategic Partnerships (LSPs), comprising public, private and community sector stakeholders.

The Offices, therefore, perform a wide-ranging set of tasks and are responsible for significant resources. The reality, however, is that central departments retain control over frontline funds and the GOs' capacity to shift resources between budgets to meet regional priorities is constrained. Moreover, concerns remain about the degree to which central departments are genuinely integrated in the Offices, and expectations about the GOs' delivery capacities vary across Whitehall. In addition, there is unease that the GOs' human resources are being strained by constant demands to adapt to evolving Whitehall agendas, demonstrate their added value to sponsor departments and respond to reductions in administration budgets (Pearce *et al.* 2008).

GOs are primarily structured around functional directorates, although efforts have been made to establish a 'matrix' form of administration, in which functional teams take responsibility for GO activities relating to specific sub-regions. This is perceived as a way of breaking down departmental boundaries and responding more effectively to the needs of localities. Nonetheless, the proportion of GO staff working in 'place-based' teams was only 5 per cent in 2005 and efforts to increase GO links with regional and sub-regional bodies are often crowded out by the growth in programme administration (HM Treasury and ODPM 2006). Furthermore, despite an assurance that the Offices should lead in negotiating budgets and agreeing outcome targets, as part of the evolving system of LAAs, their freedom to do so without constant reference to Whitehall is constrained, raising questions about the extent of the GOs' devolved authority (ODPM 2005).

In addition to their presence in GOs, central departments are represented in the regions through a dense, but disjointed layer of quangos. Estimates of their number vary, from 174 in the North East, to 130 in the East of England and 169 in the South West and, given the scale of their operations, anxieties have been expressed not only about the accountability of these organisations to the regions, but also the potential for policy duplication or overlap (House of Commons Communities and Local Government Committee 2007). In response to such concerns the English Regions White Paper gave GO Regional Directors a fuller role in co-ordinating these bodies' activities through their chairmanship of newly created 'Regional Boards'. However, quangos work to separate parent departments with different timetables, funding regimes, targets and geographical boundaries, and the extent to which their activities can be co-ordinated is restricted. Furthermore, ambiguities have arisen in reconciling the GOs' role in chairing the Regional Boards with the Assemblies' function, also spelt out in the White Paper, to align the proliferation of regional strategies and influence quangos' activities.

The most recent Government statement on the GOs' roles was contained in a 'Review of Government Offices' (HM Treasury and ODPM 2006). It endorsed the added value that the Offices bring in helping departments to understand how best to apply national policies regionally and locally, assisting regional and local partners to maximise the effectiveness of policies and investment and exploit synergies, challenging partners to work together, removing obstacles to implementation, advising ministers and speaking for Whitehall in the regions. The Review also concluded, however, that rather than being based upon a well-structured template, designed to secure a more consistent approach to regional policy-making and delivery, the Offices' functions had evolved piecemeal. In future, rather than concentrating on programme administration, it recommended that GOs should have a more tightly focused, strategic and analytical role based around three core activities:

- working with regional and local partners, helping to set strategic objectives and priorities and monitoring performance against these
- playing a key role in advising departments on the opportunities and risks in taking forward the devolved decision-making agenda and, in return, being granted greater freedoms and flexibilities over national policies designed to impact on specific localities
- supporting and challenging those bodies responsible for developing regional strategies, helping to improve the quality and consistency of regional strategies and ensuring that departmental approaches take account of these strategies.

Taken together, it is asserted that these reforms should lead to increased efficiency. They are being accompanied by a reduction in GO staff numbers of a third by 2008 and a shift towards a higher proportion of staff with negotiating, networking and analytical skills, which is intended to facilitate further administrative decentralisation. Even so, the GOs' capacity to become genuinely regional strategic bodies continues to be hampered by their limited reach over the activities of regional quangos and tensions between the Offices' role as 'critical friend' to the regions and their quasi-judicial function in scrutinising regional strategies and challenging regional partners on behalf of central government. Furthermore, while the Regional Co-ordination Unit – the GOs Whitehall hub – is responsible for managing and representing the GOs, it has limited resources and faces considerable difficulties in combining these tasks with encouraging inter-departmental working around regional issues and assessing the potential impacts of government policy in the regions.

Regional Development Agencies

RDAs are non-departmental public bodies. Each possesses some 200–400 staff and is chaired by a 12–15 member board appointed by the Secretary of State for the DTI, comprising a majority of members with a private sector background. The Agencies have five statutory purposes:

- furthering economic development and regeneration
- promoting business efficiency, investment and competitiveness
- promoting employment
- enhancing the development and application of skills relevant to employment
- contributing to sustainable development.

Their creation signalled part of a shift away from reliance on national policies to divert mobile investment and resources for public infrastructure to less favoured areas and the assertion that regions should build on their indigenous productive capacities. Crucially, the Agencies' status as the focal point for the funding of regional economic development and regeneration initiatives, and their anticipated contribution to improving regional productivity and performance, has attracted growing Treasury interest. The outcome is that the Agencies have acquired increasing responsibilities, including socio-economic policies for rural areas, tourism and managing business support services in the regions.

RDA programme expenditure since 1999 amounts to £10.8 billion and annual expenditure has risen from £1.1 billion in 2000–2001 to a projected £2.3 billion in 2007–2008. Although formally accountable to the DTI, the DCLG funds nearly three-quarters of the eight RDAs' budgets, primarily to support the delivery of its neighbourhood renewal and housing markets/sustainable communities programmes. DTI funding, which accounts for a further fifth, is directed at raising business productivity, supporting small firms and export businesses and attaining greater Labour market capacity. Each RDA is expected to make progress on targets relating to a set of mandatory, core outputs within agreed ranges. These are intended to be clearly measurable and ascribed either directly to the RDA or to the activities of the Agency and its partners and focus on:

- job creation – number of jobs created or safeguarded
- employment support – number of people assisted to get a job

- business creation – number of new businesses created and demonstrating growth after 12 months and businesses attracted to the region
- business support – number of businesses assisted to improve their performance
- regeneration – public and private investment levered in support of RES infrastructure priorities
- skills – number of people assisted in their skills development.

The Agencies' main tasks are dominated, therefore, by the delivery of economic outputs. Indeed, in aggregate during 1999–2006, RDAs claim to have met or exceeded the gross output targets set by central government, recording over 771,000 jobs created and safeguarded, some 58,000 new businesses established, 12,000 hectares of brownfield land reclaimed and £8.2 billion private sector funding levered (England's Regional Development Agencies 2006).

Evidence of the RDAs' impact on productivity differentials, overall contribution to regional economic performance and their influence on the macro-economy has proved harder to verify. This can be attributed in part to inconsistencies in evaluation processes, but also reflects the fact that, although RDAs are expected to contribute to improving the performance of regional economies, their funding represents less than 2 per cent of regional public spending, which is not sufficient of itself to make a significant impact on regional economic disparities (Cochrane 2006; Morgan 2006; Fothergill 2005). Consequently, the Agencies have become increasingly aware of the need to influence the substantial levels of public expenditure managed by other bodies, which contribute, directly or indirectly, to economic development, including the budgets of the Learning and Skills Council (LSC), Communities England and the National Health Service. The stress on a more holistic assessment of funding sources is potentially significant, but its effectiveness depends upon the RDAs' capacity to persuade key stakeholders that, rather than being the sole preserve of the Agencies, responsibility for preparing and implementing regional economic and related strategies should be shared. It also implies that a degree of congruence should be sought between the overlapping priorities and targets of a complex array of agencies, and agreement be reached on which organisations should take the lead for different goals and tasks.

In addition to their economic focus RDAs have a statutory duty to contribute to sustainable development and recent guidance stresses that sustainable development should be at the heart of RESs (DTI *et al.* 2006). However, the Government's regional policy continues to emphasise economic development, and responsibility for sustainable development is dispersed across the regional troika and other bodies. Indeed, in contrast to the specific targets associated with the RDAs' economic remit, recent evidence presented to the House of Commons Communities and Local Government Committee indicated that there are no core targets attached to their contribution to sustainable development, making this 'requirement less effective and the performance of the RDAs in this regard impossible to measure' (2007: 23). Not unexpectedly, the Sustainable Development Commission (SDC) (2005) has also commented critically on the RDAs' capacities to deliver environmental and social inclusion objectives alongside economic outcomes, as well as the variable importance attached to environmental goals in different regions.

RDAs have a dual mandate to implement Government policy and develop economic strategies appropriate to their regions, which must be formally approved by the respective Regional Assemblies. During the early years RDAs were accountable to separate government departments for the funding of 'legacy programmes', each with separate monitoring and evaluation criteria. This constraint was eased in 2001 when the Agencies were granted discretion to switch resources within a Single Programme (or 'Single Pot'), which pooled sponsor departments' budgets in ways RDAs considered most effective in delivering integrated outcomes and exercising their strategic added value role. These financial 'freedoms' were accompanied, however, by stretching national outcome targets, leading to anxieties that the Agencies' strategies would continue to reflect national priorities rather than those collectively agreed with regional partners. The House of Commons Committee of Public Accounts (2004) confirmed, for example, that despite measures to streamline, RDAs operated with over 40 different Whitehall funding streams, each with separate monitoring and evaluation criteria.

Demands were made that a new balance be instituted between meeting central government targets and empowering the regions to develop their own objectives and priorities. In response, a new RDA Tasking Framework was adopted in April 2005 (DTI 2004a). It required the Agencies to show in their corporate plans how they would address the priorities identified in both their economic strategies and their new PSA targets on outcome indicators relating to regional economic performance, productivity, regeneration and sustainable development and, through these, to the delivery of other targets. At the same time the DTI took steps to embed regional issues more deeply within its own policies and processes, strengthen the engagement of RDAs in national policy-making and ensure that policy should be led at an appropriate territorial level of government and informed by national, regional and sub-regional needs (DTI 2004b). It is too early to assess the impacts of these measures, but they are a reminder of the tension between the requirement that RDAs should react flexibly to regional issues and Whitehall's demands that the Agencies should implement national policies.

Two further initiatives have recently been introduced to increase the RDAs' accountability: Impact Evaluation Frameworks (IEFs) and Independent Performance Assessments (IPAs). IEFs are at an early stage and involve each Agency assessing the overall impacts of their programmes on regional and national outcomes, including their contribution to drivers of productivity and key PSA targets, to assist in developing a better understanding of how resources have been used and which interventions have been most successful (DTI 2006). IPAs combine RDA self-assessments with evaluations by the National Audit Office based upon five criteria: ambition, prioritisation, capacity, achievement, and performance management (National Audit Office 2005). The Assessments currently completed confirm that overall RDAs are performing well, although variably, and that while strong on ambition, their capacity was judged less satisfactory. Given the complexity and breadth of their remit this is not unexpected and there are anxieties that the Agencies are overstretched. For example, reservations have been expressed about the RDAs' capacity to influence the plethora of sub-regional partnerships, which the Agencies are dependent upon to deliver their strategies. Both IEFs and IPAs, therefore, reflect recurrent concerns in Whitehall and RDAs that too few resources have been allocated to assess the Agencies' capacities and impacts and, more specifically, the need to improve the evidence base relating to RDAs in advance of the 2007 Comprehensive Spending Review (CSR) (HM Treasury 2006).

Regional Assemblies

The political origins of the 'voluntary' Assemblies lie in the Labour Party's commitment to regional government made during the mid-1990s. They were not, however, created in an institutional vacuum and, apart from the South East, all regions already possessed Local Government Associations (LGAs), which also acted as Regional Planning Bodies (RPBs). Nonetheless, the level of collaboration between local authorities varied and, alongside variations in socio-economic conditions and regional identity, these separate legacies have influenced the level of political support for Assemblies in different regions. Labour's traditional dominance in the North East assisted the transition process but in the West Midlands tensions about the respective responsibilities of the Assemblies and the region's LGA were only settled in 2005. By contrast, the East Midlands Assembly and regional LGA merged in 1999 but, four years later, formal links were broken. In the North West and Yorkshire and the Humber long-standing rivalries between local authorities have been diminished by building representation from the regions' sub-regions into the Assemblies' political structures. By contrast, the geography of the South West has inhibited regional working and, while London's growth is a powerful incentive for local authorities in the East and South East regions to collaborate on planning issues, there is limited regional cohesion.

Apart from scrutinising the work of the RDAs to inform and review progress on the delivery of policy, the Assemblies' roles were initially ill defined. Nonetheless, they have steadily acquired a number of statutory and other functions:

- they were designated in 2004 as Regional Planning Bodies (RPBs), responsible for preparing draft 15–20 year statutory Regional Spatial Strategies, which set out broad development goals, covering issues such as infrastructure and the distribution of housing and employment. They are intended to be integrated with other regional strategies
- in 2006 Assemblies assumed the role of Regional Housing Boards (RHBs), responsible for providing advice to ministers on regional housing investment priorities. The merger of housing and planning functions, linked to scrutiny of regional economic strategies, was conceived as a way of enabling Assemblies to better integrate these key strategies
- they took the lead with regional partners in drawing up Regional Sustainable Development Frameworks (RSDFs), launched in 2001

• assemblies contribute to the advice to ministers provided through the Regional Funding Allocations (RFA) exercise introduced by the Treasury in 2005, which seeks to inform regional spending priorities.

In addition, Assemblies are encouraged to engage in and contribute to other areas of policy work, collaborate with government bodies operating in the regions and promote regional priorities in Whitehall. Many Assemblies also have links with regions in other European states and all contribute to the funding of regional offices in Brussels.

In fulfilling these tasks Assemblies have adopted broadly similar structures. On average each has about 90 members, comprising 60 councillors, nominated by local authorities and 30 'social and economic partners' (SEPs), including representatives from business, environmental and social groups, faith communities and trades unions. The number of Assembly members is primarily determined by the need to ensure that all local authorities in a region are represented. Responsibility for overseeing the Assemblies' activities falls to Executive Committees or Boards, including Assembly chairs, vice chairs and a balance of representation from local government and SEPs. Beneath the executives are committees and advisory groups, covering issues such as spatial planning and transport, RDA scrutiny, social inclusion and EU policies. Committees are usually made up entirely of Assembly members, while advisory groups are partnership based, including local government officers, civil servants and representatives of private and community interests.

Regional Assemblies were initially largely dependent on local authority financial contributions and 'support in kind'. But, as their responsibilities have grown, they have become more reliant upon central government. The provision of resources dedicated to regional spatial planning has been especially significant because it has enabled Assemblies to expand their planning teams and promote a stronger perspective on regional priorities, reduced local government's control over the regional planning process and raised the Assemblies' regional profile. Some Assemblies also receive revenues from local government training services and contributions from other regional partners to support joint activities.

The outcome was that in 2004–2005 Assemblies had a joint income of some £28 million, about 60 per cent of which was provided by the DCLG, tiny in comparison to the funding available to the GOs and RDAs (Pearce and Ayres 2007). Each Assembly, therefore, has an average annual income of about £3.5 million, but there are significant variations, which reflect the variable populations of regions, levels of local authority funding and the ability of Assemblies to take on additional roles. A more accurate measure of their capacity can be gained from identifying the number of staff employed in the 'core' duties of regional planning, strategy co-ordination and RDA scrutiny. On average fewer than 30 staff are employed in such tasks in each Assembly and there is a strong impression that they face strategic overload, both in terms of professional and administrative staff resources and demands upon members' time.

Given the Assemblies' limited decision-making powers and funding their work is characterised as consensual. Nonetheless, suggestions that disagreements on party political, sectoral or territorial lines have been suspended would be misleading. There are clear differences between the political parties over the role of Assemblies, as well as distinct territorial differences of interest, especially among local authority representatives. The allocation of a proportion of seats to SEPs is innovative and is seen as an opportunity to add legitimacy to the Assemblies, harness the energies, skills and resources of individuals representing the different sectors of civil society and provide a channel of communication into the wider community (Sandford 2006). Indeed, the quality of their contribution has been praised by GO and RDA senior officials, who regard SEPs as less parochial and more visionary then their local authority counterparts. Furthermore, an important spin-off from their engagement in the Assemblies has been to encourage various groupings, especially from the business and voluntary sectors, to re-organise their representation to present a stronger and more cohesive regional voice. Some SEPs however, notably from the business community, have expressed impatience about what they perceive as the limited capacity of Assemblies, their bureaucratic modes of working, the inadequate level of staff support for members and the extent of their own influence compared with that of local authorities and other 'resource-rich' public bodies. In contrast, although relationships have improved, elected representatives have articulated mixed views about the inclusion of nominated, 'non-political' members on Assemblies.

All Assemblies have made progress in scrutinising the work of the RDAs, which must have regard to their views. However, there is no formal requirement that the Agencies should respond to or act upon those views. In some regions the scrutiny process initially prompted considerable hostility between Assemblies and RDAs and although tensions have diminished, there remain strains over the respective roles, status and the parity of esteem afforded to the 'economic' focus of the RESs and the environmental and social considerations in RSSs. Despite improvements, anxieties also remain about the Assemblies' effectiveness in challenging RDAs to account for the resources at their disposal for the organisation of budgets and for the Agencies' added value. Some Assemblies aspire to extend the scrutiny process beyond RDAs to make other NDPBs operating in the regions accountable to Assemblies to secure greater consistency between the activities of these multiple agencies.

Assemblies are expected to act as 'voices for their regions'. However, their activities and those of the English Regions Network (ERN), which acts as the Assemblies' umbrella body, have a low profile in Whitehall. The exceptions are the regular meetings between DCLG junior ministers and Assembly leaders and gatherings of DCLG and DfT civil servants and Assembly staff engaged in spatial planning. Responsibility for preparing the statutory RSSs rests with the Assemblies and government advice stresses that while the strategies should have regard to national policies, they should be region specific. Such an endorsement might be regarded as an opportunity for Assemblies to acquire greater discretion over both the process and content of RSSs and increased flexibility over the use of regional budgets to deliver the strategies. Indeed, following the Barker Review of housing supply (HM Treasury and ODPM 2005), Assemblies were required to prepare

'Implementation Frameworks' indicating both the mechanisms involved and the organisations responsible for implementing different aspects of the RSSs (ODPM 2004). Moreover, Assemblies are responsible for assessing the conformity of 'Local Development Frameworks', prepared by local authorities with RSSs, which is intended to further assist co-ordination. The stress on linking strategy, investment and implementation has the potential to improve the alignment of policies and resources, make funding allocations more transparent and better equip regional bodies to negotiate with Whitehall on the scale and distribution of regional funding. In practice, however, Assemblies have limited room to redirect resources to meet regional priorities; the Secretary of State for the DCLG remains formally responsible for approving and issuing RSSs and the key public bodies active in the regions are geared to delivering national targets (Pearce and Ayres 2006).

Co-ordinating mechanisms

As we have seen, regional government in England is shared between the troika of Government Offices, Regional Development Agencies and Regional Assemblies, which then has to work with a fragmented array of predominantly single purpose, quasi-autonomous bodies with overlapping responsibilities and strategies (Counsell *et al.* 2007; Pollitt and Talbot 2004; Skelcher 2000). As the Audit Commission (2007: 9) recently observed, although 'working relationships between the troika tend to be good, and there is evidence of them working together to set priorities and develop a shared agenda for the region, few working at the local or regional level feel that this equates to regional leadership in an overarching sense'. Moreover, reliance on multiple and complex networks, relationships and partnerships raises complex issues about inclusivity, transparency and accountability as well as more practical concerns about 'partnership overload' and the availability of staff with appropriate communication, negotiating and network skills.

Despite these limitations a variety of hybrid mechanisms have been adopted to secure greater consistency across the proliferation of mandatory and voluntary regional strategies – upwards of 30 in each region. The North West and West Midlands Assemblies have adopted 'Concordats', drawn up with the GOs, RDAs and other bodies, including the Environment Agency and Learning and Skills Council, setting out respective roles and responsibilities for collective decision making. To make decision making more streamlined and accountable in 2005 the North-West Assembly created an 18-strong 'North-West Board', comprising council leaders, representatives of business and wider civic society, the Chief Executive of the RDA and the Regional Director of the North-West GO. Similarly, in the Eastern region a 'Regional Partnership Group' has been established, combining Assembly and local authority leaders and representatives from other regional bodies, including the Environment Agency, GO, LSC and RDA. Its brief is to examine how regional and local government can work together more effectively, assess the support required from central government to ensure the region achieves its full potential in economic, social and environmental terms and advise Whitehall on regional funding priorities.

The growing awareness that economic and social progress is unattainable in the absence of environmental sustainability has resulted in increasing stress being placed upon 'Regional Sustainability Development Frameworks'. These are seen as providing a unifying approach to regional development, including a common set of objectives, targets and indicators against which regional strategies are prepared and monitored. A cursory inspection of recent regional strategies reveals the prominence now given to sustainable development issues. At the same time, the first round of RSDFs prepared in 2001 was widely censured for both their lack of analytical content and guidance and limited influence in 'mainstreaming' sustainable development principles into other regional strategies (Sustainable Development Commission 2005). In responding to these criticisms 'Securing the regions' futures' (DTI *et al*. 2006) stressed the importance of sustainable development as a key ingredient in the formulation of regional policies. Nonetheless, there is still confusion about how sustainable development should be defined and applied and, although Government guidance requires that Regional Economic and Spatial Strategies should be framed around sustainable development principles, the Government has baulked at making sustainable development the primary purpose of Assemblies, GOs or RDAs.

In responding to the aspiration that key public bodies operating in the regions work to a common template, Assemblies serving the East of England, East Midlands, North East, South East, South West and Yorkshire and the Humber have brought together regional stakeholders to prepare 'Integrated Regional Frameworks' (IRFs) or 'Integrated Regional Strategies' (IRSs). IRFs aim to provide a single strategic reference point, within which key regional strategies are nested. Integration focuses on the horizontal linkages between the key strategies, but there is no single action plan for delivery, which is principally the responsibility of the component regional strategies and their sponsoring organisations or partnerships. IRSs seek to extend the process by setting out a unified regional strategy which works across economic, social, spatial and environmental issues and an implementation plan. Both tools can be viewed as a shift towards a more corporate approach to regional policy-making and implementation. Doubts remain, however, about their capacity to reconcile underlying tensions and translate objectives into real world consequences. Indeed, no region has systematically assessed the opportunities for rationalising strategies and, because no single organisation is responsible for integration, a major challenge for Assemblies is to ensure that agreements on regional priorities between stakeholders are followed through (Snape *et al*. 2005). More fundamentally, concerns have been expressed about whether regional governance arrangements are sufficiently advanced to justify the costs and the complexities of integrating strategies, the limited incentives to secure 'buy in' from partners responsible for delivery and the potential rigidities arising from IRFs/IRSs.

The Treasury's growing interest in regional governance as a way of improving the use of resources was reflected in the publication in July 2005 of a framework of 'Regional Funding Allocations' for each region. Details were given for the period to 2007–2008 and projections for the period up to 2015–2016, covering economic development, housing and transport (HM Treasury *et al*. 2005). While housing and economic development figures had been published previously, the inclusion of regional transport allocations was new. Within these allocations Assemblies, GOs and RDAs were jointly invited to prepare advice to ministers on how resources should be spent in advance of the 2007 CSR. Ostensibly, the RFAs signal the Treasury's commitment to capture the benefits of longer-term regional investment strategies. Indeed, the English Regions Network (ERN) (2006) has suggested that, over time, they could lead to devolved budgets in other policy areas, accompanied by a commitment from Whitehall departments and regional stake-holders to a set of shared targets designed to meet individual regional needs. However, it would be misleading to overstate their significance; RFAs account for less than 1.5 per cent of total public expenditure in the regions, the freedom to transfer funding between policy areas is constrained by existing commitments and the choice of allocations is made in isolation from decisions on other potential funding sources. Moreover, although it is claimed that 'the eight English regions demonstrated the maturity to produce strategically coherent [RFA] submissions' (ERN 2006: 2), more prudent assessments of the process underline the limited capacities of England's regional institutions to set realistic and affordable regional priorities, plan and deliver investment programmes, identify infrastructure bottle-necks, lever private sector investment and evaluate programme priorities (Beswick, *et al.* 2006; Segal Quince Wicksteed 2006).

Conclusion

At the beginning of this chapter the question was posed as to whether the emerging regional institutional architecture can be seen as marking a shift in the territorial organisation of the state and the beginning of a more co-ordinated approach to regional policy-making. New Labour is outwardly committed to the decentralisation of a range of functions to enable stakeholders to identify and capitalise on their regions' strengths and provide greater coherence to regional policy-making. The most tangible outcome is the range of powers, resources and influence gathered by the core regional institutions. Regions have also become the focus for the preparation of economic, spatial and other strategies, which has been matched by a strengthening of technical capacity and an increasing stress on implementation. In addition, a dense set of policy networks has emerged, bringing together diverse national, regional and local interests, which is reflected both in the high levels of interaction between public agencies operating in the regions and the business and voluntary sectors' enhanced representation at the regional level.

Regionalism has also permeated Whitehall, especially in the form of the Treasury's growing interest in improving regional productivity and reducing regional economic disparities. Even so, the regional agenda is still not high on the list of the Labour Government's priorities. It has not pledged to reduce the absolute gap in regional prosperity between the South East and much of the rest of the country and England remains the only nation in Western Europe, including Scotland and Wales, without a national spatial framework setting out a coherent vision for the country as a whole. Indeed, despite Whitehall's professed commitment to pursue a more nuanced approach to meet individual region's needs, centrally prescribed structures reinforce the view that regions are predominantly uniform and regional bodies continue to operate in an institutional context that inhibits integrated approaches to policy-making. Joining up policies and public expenditure within regions, therefore, remains problematic and efforts to establish a clear mission and identify critical tasks are frustrated by an abundance of often unrelated priorities and actions. As the House of Commons Communities and Local Government Committee recently observed, 'Although the GOs themselves are expected to work across boundaries, departments within Whitehall have proved very reluctant to work in a similarly joined-up manner' (2007: 16).

Uncertainties have also arisen over the respective roles of the triumvirate of regional institutions, and GOs and RDAs struggle to combine their dual functions of responding to both national and regional priorities. While Assemblies can be considered genuinely 'regional' institutions, they lack political legitimacy, are largely invisible to the general public and, though charged with a co-ordinating role, are unable to forge policy or delivery mechanisms in an autonomous way. Indeed, rather than identifying the limitations of existing arrangements and co-ordinating those policies that need to be delivered regionally, Whitehall remains suspicious about the notion of devolved decision making and its approach to regionalisation has been the outcome of largely unco-ordinated actions.

Alongside reliance on partnership arrangements to assist in easing tensions between bodies taking forward related policies, several mechanisms have been adopted as means for securing greater consistency between regional strategies and the activities of stakeholders. These include Integrated Regional Frameworks and Strategies, Regional Sustainable Development Frameworks and, most recently, Regional Funding Allocations. Nonetheless, such informal co-ordination methods are not sufficient to resolve fundamental disagreements over policy or resources, are often perceived as bland and non-descript and lack precision in connecting policy objectives to methods of delivery. Indeed, decision making remains centralised in Whitehall, while responsibility and accountability for implementation are fragmented between national agencies and a multitude of local authorities and private and community interests, which limit the capacity of regional actors to shape policies and delivery to the needs of their territories.

As for the future, government arrangements in England remain unsettled. Following the North-East referendum there have been demands from some quarters for a shift towards 'city-regions' as an antidote to England's 'failed devolution' experiment and as a way of building on the economic potential of England's provincial cities (Harrison 2007). As yet, however, there is no consensus about how city-regions, involving collaboration between local authorities serving the major cities and their hinterlands, might be governed or how they should relate to the broader regions (DCLG 2006). Moreover, there are few signs that Whitehall is yet inclined to devolve wide-ranging powers and resources to local government.

It is far more likely that functions will continue to be transferred either downwards from Whitehall or upwards from local government to the regional tier. Over time, this accumulation of powers could conceivably lead the key regional institutions to acquire a tighter community of interests, extend their joint capacities, develop a more integrated approach to managing funding and reach a point where political regionalism replaces functional regionalism. But this process is by no means inevitable and, although the troika may gain additional discretion over institutional design, policy and delivery mechanisms, the key lesson from the past decade is that Whitehall's approach will remain uneven and 'deconcentration' will only be sanctioned in those areas where there will be the least challenge to central government. While ministers may endorse the need for a more orchestrated approach to regional development, as Sandford (2005) observes, the harsh reality is that regional 'co-ordination' is used mainly to provide a plausible justification for business as usual and sub-national partners are left to negotiate with a patchwork of public bodies with very different levels of commitment to the regional tier.

Note

This chapter draws together findings from research into emerging patterns of governance in the English regions, funded through the Economic and Social Research Council's Devolution and Constitutional Change Programme, Grant Number L21952113.

References

Adams, J., Robinson, P. and Vigor, A. (2003) *A New Regional Policy for the UK*, London: Institute for Public Policy Research.

Amin, A. and Thrift, N. (1994) 'Living in the global', in A. Amin and N. Thrift (eds), *Globalisation, Institutions and Regional Development in Europe,* Oxford: Oxford University Press, 39–74.

Audit Commission (2007) *Submission to the Sub-national Review of Economic Development and Regeneration*, London: Audit Commission.

Ayres, S. and Pearce, G. (2005) 'Building regional governance in England: the view from Whitehall', *Policy and Politics*, 33, 581–600.

Bache, I. and Flinders, M. (2004) 'Multi-level governance and British politics', in I. Bache, and M. Flinders (eds) *Multi-level Governance*, Oxford: Oxford University Press, 93–106.

Barker, K. (2006) *Barker Review of Land Use Planning: Final Report Recommendations*, London: Stationery Office.

Beswick, A., Denton, A. and Revill, M. (2006) *The Regional Funding Allocation Process: Practical Lessons and Implications for the Future*, Leeds: JMP Consulting.

Bognador, V. (ed.) (2005) *Joined-up Government,* Oxford: Oxford University Press.

Brenner, N. (2003) 'Metropolitan institutional reform and the rescaling of state space in contemporary Western Europe', *European Urban and Regional Studies*, 10, 297–324.

Brenner, N. (2004) *New state spaces: Urban Governance and the Rescaling of Statehood*, Oxford: Oxford University Press.

Burch, M., Harding, A. and Rees, J. (2007) *Neither Cities nor Regions: The Continuing Dilemma of English Regionalism,* English Regions Devolution Monitoring Report, Manchester: University of Manchester.

Cabinet Office and Department for Transport, Local Government and the Regions. (2002) *Your Region, Your Choice: Revitalising the English Regions*, London: Stationery Office.

Cabinet Office. (1999) *Modernising Government*, London: Stationery Office.

Cabinet Office. (2000a) *Reaching Out: The Role of Central Government at the Regional and Local Level,* Performance and Innovation Unit, London: Stationery Office.

Cabinet Office. (2000b) *Wiring it up: Whitehall's Management of Crosscutting Policies and Services,* Performance and Innovation Unit, London: Stationery Office.

Cochrane, A. (2006) 'Devolving the heartland: making up a new social policy for the South East', *Critical Social Policy,* 26, 685–96.

Counsell, D., Hart, T., Jonas, A. and Kettle, J. (2007) 'Fragmented regionalism? Delivering integrated regional strategies in Yorkshire and the Humber', *Regional Studies,* 41 (forthcoming).

Deas, I. and Lord, A. (2006) 'From a new regionalism to an unusual regionalism? The emergence of non-standard regional spaces and lessons for the territorial reorganisation of the state', *Urban Studies,* 43, 1847–77.

Department for Communities and Local Government. (2006) *Strong and Prosperous Communities: The Local Government White Paper,* London: Stationery Office.

Department of Trade and Industry. (2004a) *England's Regional Development Agencies, RDA Corporate Plans for 2005–8, Tasking Framework,* London: DTI.

Department of Trade and Industry (2004b) *Creating Wealth from Knowledge: Five Year Programme,* London: DTI.

Department of Trade and Industry. (2006) *Evaluating the Impact of England's Regional Development Agencies: Developing a Methodology and Evaluation Framework,* DTI Occasional Paper No. 2, PA Consulting SQW Ltd, London: DTI.

Department of Trade and Industry, Department for Environment, Food and Rural Affairs and Office of the Deputy Prime Minister (2006) *Securing the Regions' Futures,* London: DEFRA.

Eddington, R. (2006) *The Eddington Transport Study, The Case for Action: Sir Rod Eddington's Advice to Government,* London: Stationery Office.

England's Regional Development Agencies (2006) *Comprehensive Spending Review 07: RDA Impact Report for HM Government,* London: RDA National Secretariat.

English Regions Network (ERN) (2006) *Adding Value to the Regions: Report to the ERN,* Altrincham: Regeneris Consulting.

Fothergill, S. (2005) 'A new regional policy for Britain', *Regional Studies,* 39, 659–67.

Goodwin, M., Jones, M. and Jones, R. (2005) 'Devolution, constitutional change and economic development: explaining and understanding the new institutional geographies of the British state', *Regional Studies,* 39, 421–36.

Hardill, I., Benneworth, P., Baker, M. and Budd, L. (2006) *The Rise of the English regions?* London: Routledge.

Harrison, J. (2007) 'From competitive regions to competitive city-regions: a new orthodoxy, but some old mistakes', *Journal of Economic Geography,* 7, 311–32.

Haughton, G. and Counsell, D. (2004) *Regions, Spatial Strategies and Sustainable Development,* London: Routledge.

Hazell, R. (2006) 'The English Question', *Publius,* 36, 37–56.

Healey, J. (2006) *Speech by the Financial Secretary to the Treasury at the Core Cities Summit,* Bristol, 27 June, London: HM Treasury.

Herrschel, T. and Newman, P. (2002) *Governance of Europe's City-Regions: Planning, Policy and Politics,* London: Routledge.

HM Treasury (2006) *Terms of Reference for the Sub-National Economic Development and Regeneration Review,* London: HM Treasury.

HM Treasury and Department for Trade and Industry (2001) *Productivity in the UK: 3 – The Regional Dimension,* London: HM Treasury.

HM Treasury and Office of the Deputy Prime Minister (2005) *The Government's Response to Kate Barker's Review of Housing Supply,* London: Stationery Office.

HM Treasury and Office of the Deputy Prime Minister (2006) *Review of Government Offices*, London: Stationery Office.

HM Treasury, Department for Transport, Department for Trade and Industry and Office of the Deputy Prime Minister (2005) *Regional Funding Allocations: Guidance on Preparing Advice*, London: Stationery Office.

House of Commons Communities and Local Government Committee (2007) *Is There a Future for Regional Government?* Fourth Report (HC - 352-I), London: Stationery Office.

House of Commons Select Committee on Public Accounts (2004) *Success in the Regions*, Fifty-first Report (HC-592), London: Stationery Office.

Jeffery, C. (2007) 'The unfinished business of devolution: seven open questions', *Public Policy and Administration*, 22, 92–108.

Jeffery, C. and Wincott, D. (2006) 'Devolution in the United Kingdom: statehood and citizenship in transition', *Publius*, 36, 3–18.

Jones, M., Goodwin, M. and Jones, R. (2005) 'State modernisation, devolution and economic governance: an introduction and guide to debate', *Regional Studies*, 39, 397–403.

Keating, M. (2004) *Regions and Regionalism in Europe*, Cheltenham: Edward Elgar.

Leitch, S. (2006) *Leitch Review of Skills: Prosperity for all in the Global Economy – World Class Skills, Final Report*, London: Stationery Office.

Lodge, G. and Mitchell, J. (2006) 'Whitehall and the government of England', in R. Hazell (ed.) *The English Question*, Manchester: Manchester University Press, 96–118.

Loughlin, J. (2004) 'The transformation of governance: new directions in policy and politics', *Australian Journal of Politics and History*, 50, 8–22.

Mansfield, B. (2005) 'Beyond rescaling: reintegrating the national as a dimension of scalar relations', *Progress in Human Geography*, 29, 458–73.

Morgan, K. (2006) 'Devolution and development: territorial justice and the North–South divide', *Publius*, 36, 189–206.

National Audit Office (NAO). (2005) *Guidance on Independent Performance Assessment of the Regional Development Agencies*, London: NAO.

Office of the Deputy Prime Minister (2005) *A Process Evaluation of the Negotiation of Pilot Local Area Agreements: Final Report*, London: ODPM.

Office of the Deputy Prime Minister (2004) *Planning Policy Statement 11: Regional Spatial Strategies*, London: ODPM.

Pearce, G. and Ayres, S. (2005) *Decentralisation to the English Regions: Assessing the Implications for Rural and Transport Policies*, ESRC Devolution and Constitutional Change Programme, Briefing No 16, Edinburgh: University of Edinburgh.

Pearce, G. and Ayres, S. (2006) 'New patterns of governance in the English regions: assessing their implications for spatial planning', *Environment and Planning C*, 24, 909–27.

Pearce, G. and Ayres, S. (2007) 'Emerging patterns of governance in the English regions: the role of Regional Assemblies', *Regional Studies*, 41 (July).

Pearce, G., Mawson, J. and Ayres, S. (2008) 'Regional governance in England: a changing role for the Government's Regional Offices?' *Public Administration*, 86 (January).

Pollitt, C. and Talbot, C. (eds). (2004) *Unbundled Government: A Critical Analysis of the Global Trend to Agencies: Quangos and Contractualisation*, London: Routledge.

Rallings, C. and Thrasher, M. (2005) *Why the North East said 'No': The 2004 Referendum on an Elected Regional Assembly*, ESRC Devolution and Constitutional Change Programme, Briefing No. 19, Edinburgh: University of Edinburgh.

Sandford, M. (2005) *Devolution is a Process not a Policy: The new Governance of the English Regions: Briefing No. 18*, ESRC Devolution and Constitutional Change Programme, Edinburgh.

Sandford, M. (2006) 'Civic engagement in the English regions: neo-corporatism, networks, new forms of governance', *Regional and Federal Studies*, 16, 221–38.

Segal Quince Wicksteed (SQW) (2006) *Desktop Analysis of Regional Funding Allocation Advice to Government: Report to the English Regions Network*, Cambridge: SQW.

Skelcher, C. (2000) 'Changing images of the state: overloaded, hollowed-out and congested', *Public Policy and Administration*, 15, 3–19.

Snape, S., Aulakh, S. and Mawson, J. (2005) *Integration of Regional Strategies*, Report to the English Regions Network, Coventry: University of Warwick.

Sustainable Development Commission (SDC). (2005) *The Next Steps: An Independent Review of Sustainable Development in the English Regions*, London: SDC.

Ward, K. and Jonas, A. (2005) 'Competitive city-regionalism as a politics of space: a critical reinterpretation of the new regionalism', *Environment and Planning A*, 36, 2119–39.

6 Co-ordinating governance in the South-East mega-region

Towards joined-up thinking?

Peter John, Steven Musson and Adam Tickell

The reorganisation of sub-national governance in the United Kingdom has been an enduring theme of New Labour's political programme. Following the party's election to national government in 1997, elected governments in Scotland and Wales were soon established. A further round of regional restructuring followed with the creation of an assembly for Northern Ireland and in 2000 a city-wide mayor and assembly for London. But elsewhere in England, the process of decentralisation was more problematic. Although an extensive system of regional governance was created, attempts to create a democratically accountable form of regional government that would mirror the Greater London Assembly elsewhere in England failed. This culminated in a resounding Government defeat in a referendum on elected regional government in North-East England in November 2004 (Tickell *et al.* 2006).

Supporters of regional government in the UK have long argued that the reorganisation of sub-national governance would benefit the national economy. The creation of more autonomous regional institutions would bring an 'economic dividend', enabling locally led economic development strategies to be developed and through this overall national competitiveness could be improved at the same time (Morgan 2006). Such a view was also reflected in the urban politics of England, where cities began to organise to promote their own economic and political interests in relation to those of London. For example, the English Core Cities group was established in 1995 by local authorities in the eight largest cities outside London designed to reflect and enhance their shared national and regional roles. The importance of these core cities as a scale of sub-national governance was further enhanced by plans to connect them to their urban hinterlands through the creation of city-regions. These proposals drew on research that understood global city-regions, or large extended urban areas, to be an increasingly dominant form of spatial organisation in the global economy and as the main local drivers of national competitiveness. Beyond this economic role, city-regions were also seen as an important scale of government intervention, large enough to take on the strategic role of elected regional assemblies but small enough to be politically coherent and to deliver public services effectively.

This chapter begins by discussing recent developments in the urban governance of England, including the strengthening of regional government and the emergence of city-regions as spaces of governance. The implications of these changes for England's largest urban area, the London mega-region, are considered. Although there are many shared policy issues, the region is highly fragmented especially between London and the county councils that lie beyond the urban core. Central, rather than local government has played a major strategic role delivering key projects, leading to claims that central government is the *de facto* regional government of London and the South East (John *et al.* 2005).

Two case studies illustrate the process: the Thames Gateway regeneration area and the 2012 Olympic Games. The argument is that, if city-regions elsewhere in England are to emerge as new sub-national spaces of governance, the enduringly strong role of central government and the lack of co-ordination between urban core and hinterland that characterise London and the South East will need to be addressed.

Urban governance in England

The United Kingdom has long been described as a highly centralised state (Amin *et al.* 2003). Not only is London the largest urban area, but it also dominates national agendas in economic, political and cultural matters. One of the driving forces behind regional government in the UK for ten years or more has been the need to address such geographical imbalances and to create a more decentralised form of governance, albeit where central government retained control of key strategic and policy issues. Against this background of centralised power, from the mid-1990s onwards cities in England outside London began to organise to promote their own economic and political interests in relation to London. For example, the Core Cities Group, comprising Birmingham, Bristol, Leeds, Liverpool, Manchester, Newcastle, Nottingham and Sheffield, was established in 1995. As an association of urban local authorities, it aims to promote the competitiveness of cities and their regions, to regenerate their urban fabric and to strengthen their profile in the UK and Europe. From the outset, the Core Cities regarded themselves as being at the heart of wider regional economies. As such, the group stated that: 'our focus includes the economic relationship between our cities and their regions in the same way that the prosperity of the South East is fundamentally determined by London's success' (Core Cities Group 2001).

The case for strengthening urban authorities in the UK gained more widespread support following the establishment of the Core Cities Group, in particular from the role of cities as drivers of regional economic development. Sir Sandy Bruce Lockhart, Chairman of the Local Government Association and Leader of Kent County Council, argued that in other European cities such as Frankfurt and Madrid: 'With greater devolution of powers on taxation and clear powers over transport, infrastructure, planning, economic development and skills, they have managed to develop local economies with an inbuilt and self-generated dynamism that benefits not just the city, but pulls in the whole region' (LGA 2006). Such issues of competitiveness and local economic development have been the remit of regional government, in particular Regional Development Agencies, under

New Labour (Kitson *et al.* 2004). However, following the failure of elected regional assemblies in England, the focus of sub-national economic governance may have begun to switch away from regional government to new city-regions. For example, research commissioned by the former Office of the Deputy Prime Minister (ODPM, now CLG) recognised that the economic reach of core cities was becoming greatly expanded beyond their administrative boundaries and that: 'As a scale for policy intervention in England, the city-region has greater economic and cultural resonance than current administrative regions and local authority districts' (Marvin *et al.* 2006).

The development of city-regions in the UK is still at an early stage. However, the importance of cities as drivers of national and international economies has long been recognised. For Scott, global city-regions are increasingly important drivers of global economic growth and change, as places where advanced services and information-processing activities are centred (Scott 2001). Elsewhere, global city-regions are seen as emerging political spaces, increasingly capable of protecting their interests through autonomous political action on a national and world stage (Ward and Jonas 2004). Alternatively, mega-regions, more commonly referred to as mega-urban regions (MURs), or extended metropolitan regions etc. have been identified in South-East Asia (McGee 1991; McGee and Robinson 1995; McGee 1997). The conceptual importance of these large urban areas is gaining increasing currency within Europe, in particular in the European Spatial Development Perspective document (Jensen and Richardson 2001). A mega-region extends its influence into the surrounding rural areas, sometimes located up to 100 km from the urban core.

London and the South East share many characteristics with mega- and global-city-regions. Although larger than most South-East Asian mega-regions, with economic influence spreading up to 240 km from the urban core, London and its hinterland nevertheless constitute an extended metropolitan area (Buck *et al.* 2002). However, the region remains administratively and politically fragmented. Central government plays a key role in the strategic formulation and co-ordination of policy. This may reflect the importance of the region to the national economy and the frequent conflation of regional and national policy interests. As such, capacity for autonomous political action from within the region is limited. This runs counter to theoretical claims that this capacity is a defining characteristic of the global city-region. But whether or not it constitutes a true mega- or global city-region, London and the South East (or the South-East mega-region as it is called hereafter) is undoubtedly larger and more internationally connected than any other region in the UK. Although differences of scale make comparisons difficult, the experience of co-ordinating governance across the South-East mega-region speaks to the development of city-regions elsewhere in the UK. In particular, the dominance of the urban core over its hinterland and the role of central government in the strategic co-ordination of regional policy are highlighted. Drawing on the cases of the Thames Gateway regeneration area and the 2012 London Olympic Games, it is argued that projects deemed to be of national importance and those which cut across existing administrative boundaries pose particular challenges in this respect.

Governing the South-East mega-region

The South-East mega-region is the core of the UK economy. It is home to over a quarter of the national population and accounts for one-third of Gross Value Added (National Statistics 2004). London and its hinterland dominate national employment in key economic sectors such as financial services, ICT and scientific research and development. Accounts of this economic dominance have tended to portray London as a world or global city (for example Castells 1996), in particular focusing on the financial, legal and corporate networks of international power concentrated in the City of London (Gordon *et al.* 1992; Beaverstock *et al.* 2003). However, this fails to capture fully the nature of the regional economy, which is based on a metropolitan core but extends over a large, dense economic area. Furthermore, as Allen, Massey and Cochrane note, the economic geography of the regional economy is spatially discontinuous and some areas are excluded from the economic processes that dominate the region more generally (Allen *et al.* 1998).

A number of key intractable policy problems demand central government intervention in the mega-region. One is the housing market. In the first quarter of 2006, average house prices were £221,900 in the South East and £258,511 in London, compared with £173,000 for the UK as a whole (West *et al.* 2003; Sweeting 2003). There are knock-on implications for labour costs and for attracting skilled workers to the already stretched regional labour market; house prices also affect the quality of public services upon which business depends, such as health and education. The other is public and road transport. The South-East mega-region is heavily congested, with existing infrastructure operating at or close to its maximum capacity. As such, more effective and integrated planning has become a key issue across the mega-region: for the growth in housing demand, both social and private housing; for investment in public transport and roads, particularly links in and out of London; for improved public services to support the private sector economy; and for skills training and the labour force.

Since 2000, London has been granted a special spatial focus through the creation of the Mayor and the Greater London Authority (GLA). The Mayor of London has a general responsibility for economic and social development and environmental improvement and is also responsible for setting the budgets for the GLA, Metropolitan Police, London Fire Brigade and Transport for London. In July 2006, the Government extended the strategic powers of the Mayor to include adult skills, economic development, housing, planning and transport (DCLG 2006). The GLA, which has 25 elected members, scrutinises the Mayor's activities and makes proposals and recommendations in the light of its own research. However, the new London government does not have the power or inclination to give leadership to the mega-region. The spatial focus of the Mayor and the GLA is clearly on the capital (HBOS 2006). The London Plan, the Mayor's Spatial Development Strategy published in February 2004, concentrates on planning, housing, transport and economic development issues with respect to London and limits any discussion of the wider regional context in which the strategy must operate. Indeed, the Greater London Authority Act (1999), which specifies the powers of the Mayor and the

GLA, requires the London Plan to deal only with matters that are of strategic importance to Greater London. The plan incorporates central government's regional planning guidance for the South East and Mayor Ken Livingstone indicated that he would work with other local authorities. But in its response to the London Plan, the Association of London Government, which lobbies on behalf of the 32 London boroughs, indicated that any form of pan-regional thinking on the part of the GLA was limited (ALG 2002: para. 60–3).

While the spatial focus of the GLA is clearly bounded, an analysis of the London economy shows its interdependence with the economic space of the wider region. In 2000, 21 per cent of the London workforce commuted into the city (Buck *et al.* 2002). Furthermore, the population growth predictions for London have prompted a house-building programme that includes sites across the South East. As Travers writes: 'London as an urban economy is far larger than the London central business district, larger even than the administrative boundary of the GLA, and on some measures, larger than the South-East region' (Travers 2003: 138). The economy of London does not operate in isolation from that of the South East, nor does it simply pull in labour from a series of satellite commuter towns. Rather, London can be seen as the metropolitan core of a wider regional economy into which it is functionally but not politically embedded.

Central government is a key player in the city politics of London, to an extent that can scarcely be imagined elsewhere in the UK. Successful projects, like the Jubilee Line extension and the successful 2012 London Olympic Games bid, owe more to selective initiative and central government intervention than to the efforts of local and regional government (Travers 2001). To an extent these political relationships are structurally inscribed; the power of the Mayor is tightly constrained and a strong role is retained both by the London boroughs and central government (Sweeting 2002; Travers 2002). Such structural weakness may explain why the GLA has focused on London-wide issues, but it also emphasises the way in which the complex, fragmented urban space is not completely defined by the formal boundaries of the metropolis. The GLA must also work with a powerful and increasingly co-ordinated business lobby in London. On key political issues including the Crossrail rail development scheme and the creation of airport capacity in London and the South East, business interests have sought to engage directly in the policy development process (John *et al.* 2005). As such, the GLA is faced by a set of market and political pressures unique to any devolved regional authority in the UK. In some respects, given the local pressures that it faces, it is unsurprising that a wider and more complex set of mega-regional political issues have not been addressed.

Beyond Greater London, the boundaries of the mega-region become less clear. Allen *et al.* argued that the economic geography of South-East England is like a 'doily', with some parts of the region being closely interconnected while others, even though close to the metropolitan core of the region, are in fact excluded (Allen *et al.* 1998). A wave of prosperity has radiated out to the west of London, while some areas to the east, such as parts of Kent, have been left behind. This gives rise to distinctive local political interests that compete with each other to influence policy. Places like Milton Keynes are growth poles on their own, with very different opportunities and problems to the rest of the mega-region. Perhaps because of this diversity, business does not lobby hard for spatial concerns, which contrasts with longstanding attempts by sections of business in the North West and North East (Tickell and Peck 1996). In London business focuses on planning in London, the regulation of the financial sector or a range of national level issues. It tends not to look at the wider mega-region as a source of its prosperity. More fundamentally, the region is fragmented into sub-regions and tends to have weak contacts with the central regional actors. To regional political leaders, the South-East region seems to be like a 'doughnut', 'bolted' around London. The region also appears to be politically and economically fragmented (Musson *et al.* 2004), lacking a clear set of issues around which the new region could be constructed, without the internal cohesiveness that could bind the new institutions of regional government together (John 1997).

In spite of the fragmentation, it is natural that policy-makers from the relevant bodies in the South-East mega-region interact across a range of functional concerns. While it is unsurprising that such contacts have developed at some level, the more fundamental issue is whether this indicates a pattern of governance that addresses the wider strategic issues facing the mega-region. SERPLAN, the South-East Regional Planning Conference, and the Government's regional planning guidance document for the South East, RPG9, previously gave a coherent strategic leadership on a range of planning issues across the South East. But these arrangements have now moved to a more informal footing involving overlapping areas of responsibility in a range of institutions within London and *ad hoc* relations between London and other areas. For example, an advisory interregional forum on planning, linking London with the South-East and East of England regions, was established in 2001. The forum has considered a range of issues, such as housing, where there are areas of agreement and disagreement between different actors. In the London Plan, for example, there is an assumption that the numbers of jobs will exceed the housing available, which implies that the gap will be met from an increase in long-range commuting. Both sides see this as undesirable, and have started to monitor and manage the situation. There have also been disagreements on airport location. By common agreement, the forum could work better and operate more to resolve substantive issues. In the words of an ALG document, 'is not able to grapple effectively with . . . [vital issues] . . . and needs considerable strengthening' (ALG 2002: para. 63).

Has central government become the government of the mega-region? We argue that, because no one organisation can represent the interests of the mega-region and the structure of regional government is fragmented, it falls to central government to move policy forward. In any case, given the scope and scale of the key issues for the economy, there is no way that London and South-East political actors are going to be able to develop such strategies. Mega-regional government, as far as London and the South East is concerned, is more about central government deciding matters and pushing them though, rather than the existing regional players organising themselves as an effective regional lobby group. Central government is the only body with the capacity and resources to promote large projects, including guaranteeing project finance and using legislative power to ensure effective planning. In any case, as Syrett and Baldock argue, central government departments still maintain day-to-day control of many policy issues in London, making the regional–central government conflation apparent from the beginning (Syrett and Baldock 2003). As the economic core of the UK economy, it is likely that the needs of London and the South East would remain a strong influence on central government policy irrespective of whether any regional political institution could identify and articulate a clear interest. The South-East mega-region may be able to get the political outcomes that are desired without really trying because it is systematically 'lucky' (Dowding 1996); for it is the place that simultaneously generates wealth and decides elections, and it is where the political elite live.

While the argument that central government plays a pivotal role in the government of the mega-region is relatively uncontroversial, the precise nature of departmental involvement is less straightforward to identify. The Regional Co-ordination Unit (RCU) was established in 2000 as the corporate centre of the regional Government Office network. It aimed to provide a single contact point between the central government and regional institutions. But the former ODPM, with its planning responsibilities and overall responsibility for the regeneration and redistribution agenda, appeared to be the natural lead department on regional policy until its break-up in May 2006. A wide range of other departments, including the Department for Transport and the Department for Trade and Industry, are also heavily involved in mega-region projects. We explore the role of central government in the mega-region through a high profile and administratively complex case study: the Thames Gateway regeneration project. We also consider the London 2012 Olympic Games, which will promote major development in and around the Thames Gateway area. Although the Mayor of London is the signatory to the Host City Contract with the International Olympic Committee, central government continues to play a key role in the delivery of the Olympic project.

Governance in practice: the Thames Gateway and the 2012 Olympic Games

In 2003, the ODPM announced a £22 billion plan to build 200,000 new homes across South-East England by 2016, to relieve the economic pressures of rising house prices and their impact on labour markets and effective provision of public services. The ODPM plan was centred on the Thames Gateway area to the east of London and on Ashford, Milton Keynes and the Stanstead-Cambridge corridor. It drew regional politicians into a wider policy debate. Kent County Council, which is part of the Thames Gateway area, has campaigned for other public services to accompany these investments, such as schools, roads and leisure facilities. London policy-makers, including the GLA, have approved of these ideas because they address fundamental regional problems such as providing affordable housing and easing pressures on the housing market. When seen against the more modest investment of around £500 million for regeneration in the North through the Housing Market Renewal Initiative, it appears that central government is prepared to make a high level of investment to help solve social and economic problems in London and the South East.

The Thames Gateway, the UK's largest 'brown field' regeneration site, was first identified in the 1995 South-East Regional Planning Framework as an area of substantial growth potential. It extends for 40 miles, on either side of the River Thames, from central London to the coast. The Thames Gateway area incorporates parts of three English regions: London, East of England and the South East, two county council areas: Essex and Kent, and 14 district and borough councils. The additional involvement of central government, the GLA and several Urban Development Corporations make for an institutionally complex, functionally and spatially overlapping, management structure. In addition, the main site for the London 2012 Olympic Games adjoins the Thames Gateway, bringing in more investment and physical regeneration in the short to medium term.

The formal objectives of the Thames Gateway development were defined in the government's regional planning guidance document RPG 9. They included improving economic performance to enhance London's position as a major world city, maximising opportunities for new economic activity and jobs, working with the market to build on existing economic and community strengths; and encouraging a sustainable pattern of development by making the fullest possible use of the many vacant, derelict and under-used sites. At a more practical level, the project serves two important functions in the mega-region. Firstly, it relieves pressure on overheated housing and labour markets in London and provides an alternative growth area to the highly congested belt to the west of the city, between Heathrow and Gatwick. Secondly, it promotes the physical and economic regeneration of areas of Kent and Essex, such as Dartford and Thurrock, which are amongst the most deprived parts of England. Plans for the regeneration of the Gateway area are undoubtedly ambitious. They include the construction of 12,000 new homes, including a new town at Rochester Riverside, half of which are to be completed by 2010. Furthermore, 180,000 new jobs are planned and a series of economic growth areas, envisaged as smaller-scale versions of the Canary Wharf office and retail development in east London, are to be completed by 2031. The Thames Gateway area is also associated with other projects of strategic importance for the mega-region and beyond, including the London 2012 Olympic Games.

Development on such a scale does not come cheaply, particularly since much of the formerly industrial brown-field land needs to be cleared and prepared before new building can take place. Central government allocated £446 million for 2002–2005, including £143 million for North Kent alone. However, Kent County Council anticipated that at least £10 billion would be required to carry out the proposed work in Kent over a twenty year period. Of pressing concern for policymakers was the long-term financial viability of the project. Although public money will undoubtedly lever in resources from the private sector, in particular from property development companies who are already heavily involved in the strategic management of the Thames Gateway, concerns remained that insufficient funds were made available. Cash shortages in central government departments led to delays in infrastructure building and environmental improvements. As a consequence, it has been claimed that house building was already running at 25 per cent below projected levels by July 2002 (*The Guardian* 19 July 2002).

Although the Thames Gateway was promoted by central government as a coherent geographical entity united by a single strategic vision, in reality there are at least three distinct areas: London, Kent and Essex, each with its own management structure and set of public-private partnerships. For example, although house building is of key importance to the project, there are three Regional Housing Boards, each with its own strategic priorities, at work in the Thames Gateway. As one member of the Thames Gateway Kent board said in a research interview: 'Basically what you have are three separate areas, and things are different in all of them. In Kent, you have the County Council and one developer for the whole area, but in Essex the county [County Council] is working with three, four different [development] partners''. A limited degree of co-ordination for the whole of the Thames Gateway area has been provided by a joint operating committee, including the chairmen and chief executives of the three Regional Development Agencies involved and representatives from the three area management boards. However, real strategic oversight is provided directly from central government. The ODPM, through its regional agents, the Government Offices, was closely involved in setting targets for house-building, and effectively controls the purse-strings for the whole area (Musson *et al.* 2004). In spite of the complex system of strategic decision making, house building has remained the rationale of the Thames Gateway project, and is seen as offering the best solution to the chronic shortage of affordable accommodation in London. Furthermore, a Cabinet committee, chaired by the Prime Minister, provides inter-departmental co-ordination at ministerial level to ensure that rapid and effective progress is made.

Public policy in the Thames Gateway seeks to create an infrastructure framework to facilitate private sector investment. In some senses, it can be seen as an extension of the logic of the London economy, as firms relocate to custom developed sites and new housing developments on the underdeveloped eastern fringes of the city. However, the grand scale of the Thames Gateway project, which seeks to connect London's economy to deprived areas of the mega-region, creates a far more complex set of institutional relations that have influence far beyond London, Kent and Essex. The high profile Thames Gateway project dominates national housing budget allocations, even though similar problems of affordable housing stock exist across the whole of southern England. Furthermore, the interests of London, in particular relating to key worker housing, have tended to dominate the rest of the Thames Gateway. As such, the project can be seen as a development for London, rather than the creation of new, sustainable communities in deprived areas of Kent and Essex. The economic imperatives of London, defined by central government and articulated through the Thames Gateway project, are projected beyond the city into the surrounding mega-region.

Although the Thames Gateway had long been seen as a major initiative within regeneration policy circles, public and media interest has generally been limited to projections for new houses and jobs. When London was announced as host city for the 2012 Olympic Games in July 2005, it became clear that significant additional investment in the infrastructure and built environment of east London would follow, along with an intensification of wider interest in the Thames Gateway sub-region.

The main Olympic Park, including an 80,000-seat stadium, an athletes' village for 17,000 competitors and at least seven other major sports stadiums, was planned for the Lower Lea Valley, which lies just outside the Thames Gateway area. From the outset, the London 2012 Olympics were seen to offer unprecedented opportunities for regeneration in east London in a way that tessellated with existing projects already underway elsewhere in the area. For the Mayor of London, Ken Livingstone, the Olympics were the once-in-a-lifetime opportunity, offering the possibilities for transformation not seen since the Victorian age (Vigor *et al.* 2004). But in spite of the excitement and activity surrounding the London Olympic Games, systems of governance have mirrored other projects such as the Thames Gateway. As with other areas, the interests of London are separate from those of the mega-region, and central government has played the key role in financing and managing a project of national importance.

The Olympic Delivery Authority (ODA) was established in March 2006 to oversee infrastructure preparations for the London Olympic Games, such as stadium building and transport planning, as well as ensuring the legacy of the Olympic Park after the Games. The ODA works in close collaboration with the London Organising Committee for the Olympic Games (LOCOG), which is responsible for more commercial aspects of staging the event, such as ticket sales and merchandising. Under the chairmanship of Lord Coe, LOCOG maintained a high profile during the bidding stage. However, the ODA was afforded a powerful role in the London Olympics Act (2005), which defined its powers and paved the way for preparations to start. In addition to its land and property, planning and transport functions, the ODA is required to consult and co-operate with existing institutions of London governance including the Mayor, the GLA and Transport for London. Significantly, central government retains the power of veto over these arrangements through the Secretary of State for Culture, Media and Sport. As the London Olympics Act states: 'In exercising its functions the [Olympic Delivery] Authority shall have regard to any guidance given by the Secretary of State, and comply with any direction given by the Secretary of State. A direction may, in particular . . . require the Authority to obtain the Secretary of State's consent before taking action of a specified kind' (House of Commons 2005). Furthermore, with only £875 million of the projected £4.9 billion cost of hosting the games to be met through London council taxes and other existing funding allocations, central government will also retain overwhelming financial control over the Games (*Financial Times* 21 August 2005).

In many respects, the strong role of central government in managing the London Olympic Games is unsurprising. Unlike earlier attempts to bring the Olympic and Commonwealth Games to Manchester, the London 2012 bid was always framed in a national context. LOCOG publicity material called on supporters to 'Make Britain Proud', while the official bid document emphasised the legacy of the Games beyond London throughout the whole of the UK. Furthermore, the spatial proximity of the Olympic Park to an existing major regeneration project in the Thames Gateway and the potential impact of the Games on the national economic core of the South-East mega-region made strong central government involvement almost inevitable. Given the history of fragmented governance in the South-East mega-region, it is also unsurprising that the interests of the South East beyond London are not represented in either the management structure or the organisational objectives of the ODA or LOGOC. Although the London Olympic Games may have a significant impact on the infrastructure and economies of areas beyond London, existing governance structures deal primarily with the urban core.

Conclusion

London is economically and politically exceptional in the UK. It is more internationally connected than any other city or region, while the industries on which its prosperity is founded are markedly different from those found elsewhere. In some respects, the governance of London has long reflected its exceptional nature. In spite of the functional interdependence between London and other areas of South-East England, structures of governance have tended to be fragmented. Central government is closely involved in London, through projects that are frequently portrayed as being of national as well as local importance. Although the first elected mayor and regional assembly in England were established in 2000, these new institutions emphasise the differences between London and elsewhere in the mega-region. As such, the South-East mega-region is far from being the type of autonomous political space associated with other global city-regions. Rather, its economic power and institutional complexity promote fragmented local governance and a strong role for central government.

The case of the South-East mega-region has implications for the creation of city-regions elsewhere in England. It is apparent that, even where communal policy issues exist, co-operation between institutions cannot be guaranteed. Local political tensions, especially around power and control in new structures of governance, appear to be important in this respect. Furthermore, city-regions cannot be seen as a direct successor to other forms of sub-national governance such as elected regional assemblies. The role of central government in the South-East mega-region shows that when new scales of governance are created, existing structures of power and control have an enduring influence.

References

Allen, J., Massey, D. and Cochrane, A. (1998) *Rethinking the Region*, London: Routledge.

Amin, A., Massey, D. and Thrift, N. (2003) *Decentering the Nation*, London: Catalyst.

ALG [Association of London Government] (2002), *Draft London Plan – ALG Views*, London: Association of London Government.

Beaverstock, J., Smith, R. and Taylor, P. (2003) 'The global capacity of a world city: a relational study of London', in E. Kofman and G. Youngs (eds), *Globalisation: Theory and Practice* (2nd edn), London: Continuum.

Buck, N., Gordan, I., Hall, P., Harloe, M. and Kleinman, M. (2002) *Working Capital*, London: Routledge.

Castells, M. (1996) *The Rise of the Network Society, Vol. 1: The Information Age*, Oxford: Blackwell.

Core Cities Group (2001) *Challenges for Cities in the 21st Century*. Accessed on 24 May 2006 at http://www.corecities.com/coreDEV/Publications/CoreCitiesProspectus.PDF

DCLG [Department for Communities and Local Government] (2006) *The Greater London Authority: The Government's Final Proposals for Additional Powers and Responsibilities for the Mayor and Assembly*, London: DCLG.

Dowding, K. (1996) *Power*, Buckingham: Open University Press.

Financial Times (2005) 'Secret report shows Olympic shortfall to reach £3bn', 21 August 2005.

Gordon, I., Fainstein, S. and Harloe, M. (eds) (1992) *Divided Cities: New York and London in the Contemporary World*, Oxford: Blackwell.

The Guardian (2002) 'Housing cash goes into new towns in the South', 19 July 2002.

HBOS (2006) Regional historic house price data. Accessed on 24 May 2006 at http://www.hbosplc.com/economy/includes/RegionalHistoricData06_04_06.xls

London Olympics Act 2005, HC Bill (2005–2006) Chapter 45. London: The Stationery Office.

Jensen, O. and Richardson, T. (2001) 'Nested visions: new rationalities of space in European spatial planning', *Regional Studies* 35, 703–17.

John, P. (1997) 'Sub-national partnerships and European integration: the difficult case of London and the South East', in J. Bradbury and J. Mawson (eds), *British Regionalism and Devolution*, London: Jessica Kingsley.

John, P., Tickell, A. and Musson, S. (2005) 'Governing the mega-region: governance and networks across London and the South East of England', *New Political Economy* 10.1, 91–106.

Kitson, M., Martin, R. and Tyler, P. (2004) 'Regional competitiveness: an elusive but key concept', *Regional Studies* 38.9, 911–99.

LGA [Local Government Association] (2006) *Closer to People and Places: A New Vision for Local Government* (London: LGA). Accessed on 24 May 2006 at http://www.lga.gov.uk/Documents/Publication/peopleandplaces.pdf

Marvin, S., Harding, A. and Robson, B. (2006), *A Framework for City-regions*, London: ODPM.

McGee, T. (1991) 'The emergence of desakota regions in Asia: expanding the hypothesis', in N. Ginsberg, B. Koppel and T. McGee (eds): *The Extended Metropolis: Settlement Transition in Asia*, Honolulu: University of Hawaii Press.

McGee, T. (1997) 'Globalisation, urbanisation and the emergence of global sub-regions', in T McGee and R Watters (eds), *Asia Pacific. New Geographies of the Pacific Rim*, London: Hurst.

McGee, T. and Robinson, I. (1995) *The New Southeast Asia: Managing the Mega-urban Regions*, Vancouver: University of British Columbia Press.

Morgan, K. (2006) 'Devolution and development: territorial justice and the North–South divide', *Publius, The Journal of Federalism*, 36.1, 189–206.

Musson, S., Tickell, A. and John, P. (2004), 'A decade of decentralisation? assessing the role of the Government Offices for the English regions', *Environment and Planning A*, 37.8, 1395–1412.

National Statistics (2004) *Economic Trends* No. 606, May 2004, London: HMSO.

Scott, A. (2001) *Global City-regions: Trends Theory, Policy*, Oxford: Oxford University Press.

Sweeting, D. (2002), 'Leadership in urban governance: the Mayor of London', *Local Government Studies*, 28, 3–20.

Sweeting, D. (2003) 'How strong is the Mayor of London?' *Policy and Politics*, 31, 465–78.

Syrett, S. and Baldock, R. (2003) 'Reshaping London's economic governance. The role of the London Development Agency', *European Urban and Regional Studies*, 10, 69–86.

Tickell, A., John, P. and Musson, S. (2006) 'The North-East region referendum campaign of 2004: issues and turning points,' *Political Quarterly* 76, 488–96.

Tickell, A. and Peck, J. (1996) 'The return of Manchester Men: men's deeds and men's words in the remaking of the local state', *Transactions of the Institute of British Geographers*, 21.4, 595–611.

Travers, T. (2001) 'Editorial: London – better government', *Public Policy and Management* 2–3, 5.

Travers, T. (2002) 'Decentralisation London-style: The GLA and London governance', *Regional Studies*, 36, 781.

Travers, T. (2003) *The Politics of London*, Basingstoke: Palgrave.

Vigor, A., Meen, M. and Tims, C. (eds) (2004) *After the Gold Rush: A Sustainable Olympics for London*, London: Demos and IPPR.

Ward, K. and Jonas, A. (2004) 'Competitive city-regionalism as a politics of space: a critical reinterpretation of the new regionalism', *Environment and Planning A* 36: 2119–39.

West, K., Scanlon, K., Thornley, A. and Rydin, Y. (2003) 'The Greater London Authority: problems of strategy integration', *Policy and Politics* 31, 479–96.

7 Constrained discretion and English regional governance

The case of Yorkshire and the Humber

Simon Lee

Yorkshire and the Humber is not an insignificant political constituency. With a Gross Domestic Product (GDP) of £75 billion, the region's economy is as large as that of the Republic of Ireland, Norway and Singapore (Yorkshire Forward 2005a). With a population of 5 million, Yorkshire is most similar in size among the constituent nations and regions of the United Kingdom (UK) to Scotland (population 5.1 million and GDP £82 billion in 2004), and has experienced similar challenges of long-term deindustrialisation and economic regeneration. However, it is at that juncture that any similarities end. While New Labour's devolution settlement has witnessed the rolling forward of the frontiers of democratic citizenship in Scotland through the restoration of the Scottish Parliament, Yorkshire and the Humber has witnessed only the rolling forward of the frontiers of consumer choice, and administrative decentralisation. Active citizenship and democratic autonomy have been in full retreat in the face of New Labour's nationalisation of policy-making and resource allocation for England. When John Prescott, the Deputy Prime Minister, announced on the 8 November 2004 that the referendum concerning the proposed directly elected regional assembly for Yorkshire and the Humber would not be taking place, it might have been thought that he was signalling the death knell of devolution for the English regions beyond London. In truth, in Yorkshire and the Humber that particular project had long since been stillborn.

This chapter analyses the development of English regional governance by first identifying how New Labour has governed England through a top-down, Treasury-driven statecraft, enshrined in the principles of 'earned autonomy' and 'constrained discretion'. The chapter then details the pattern of regional governance within Yorkshire and the Humber, before outlining the dividend for regional progress that has resulted. The division among the region's political elites about the likely costs and benefits of elected regional government are then identified, together with the political culture of indifference that has resulted. The chapter contends that elected regional government is still necessary, but not for the conventional reasons of democratizing the process of regional planning and economic regeneration. On the contrary, and in the aftermath of the 2001 riots and the July 2005 London bombings, the chapter concludes that decentralisation through the extension of elected government to the English regions could and should be viewed as one catalyst for revitalizing citizenship to accommodate the English nation and its regions' increasingly diverse multiethnic and multicultural communities.

Central government and the English regions: earned autonomy and constrained discretion

Within weeks of New Labour's May 1997 General Election landslide victory, John Prescott had promised that the Government's approach towards the English regions would be characterised by 'five key priorities – integration, de-centralisation, regeneration, partnership and sustainability'. To counter their 'huge disadvantages over the years', it was promised that the English regions would be given 'the tools to do the jobs themselves'. Moreover, the Government would not 'promote the ethic of "de-centralisation from Whitehall, only to see centralisation occurring in the regions'. Prescott gave an assurance that there would not be 'rigid prescriptive formulae from the centre. Innovation and flexibility would be encouraged at all times' because 'One of our most radical commitments is the de-centralisation of power' (Department of the Environment, Transport and the Regions 1997: 1–2).

In practice, New Labour has not delivered de-centralisation of power in England, let alone a genuine politics of autonomy. Prime Minister Tony Blair's chosen model of 'earned autonomy for schools, hospitals, local government and other public services' has enabled 'locally-elected representatives to adopt approaches to public services reflecting their own national priorities and concerns', but only in Scotland, Wales and Ulster (Office of Public Service Reform 2002: 17). As an alternative approach to English statecraft, Blair's model of public services' reform since 1997 has been based upon a clear demarcation between UK Government's provision of an 'overall vision' – i.e. policy design and specification of 'national standards' – and the English regions' delivery of that centrally determined vision through subordinate levels of government 'by devolution and delegation to the front line'. The Blair Governments have nationalised the process both of policy-making and resource allocation in England and its regions. This process has been institutionalised in the biennial Spending Reviews and accompanying Public Service Agreements.

In England alone apparently 'Devolved delivery can only operate with national standards and accountability' (Office of Public Service Reform 2002: 2–3, 28). No explanation has been offered as to why English regional devolution should be confined to administrative decentralisation or why standards, accountability, policy-making and resource allocation have to be nationalised. Consequently, since May 1997, and in common with other English regions beyond Greater London, Yorkshire and the Humber has experienced deficits in policy, resources, institutions, competitiveness, and, above all, active democratic citizenship compared to other parts of the UK (Lee 1999). Decentralisation in the English regions beyond Greater London has been confined to empowerment of the market and the individual as consumer, rather than the individual as an active, participating democratic citizen. In this respect, New Labour's constitutional settlement has been hugely imbalanced and asymmetrical.

Gordon Brown, the Chancellor of the Exchequer 1997–2007, and Tony Blair's successor as Prime Minister, also once promised a 'Politics of Potential' and 'new popular socialism'. These were to be based upon the four foundations of a new redistribution of power, an enabling state, a new constitutional settlement embracing devolved power 'wherever possible' and the reconstruction of the idea of community, as a prerequisite for reinventing government and a new economic egalitarianism (Brown 1994: 114). Brown argued for a broader notion of community that should be separated from the narrower notion of the centralised state, in order to protect individual rights and to enable the community to explore how its affairs might be organised 'in a decentralised way, more sensitively and flexibly'.[1] This was because 'hierarchical and centralised bureaucracies designed in the 1940s and 1950s simply do not do the job in a rapidly changing, information-rich, knowledge-intensive society' (Brown 1994: 119). Subsequently, Ed Balls, before his resignation as Chief Economic Advisor to the Treasury, claimed that the old model of 'command and control' public services had lacked 'devolution, transparency and accountability', suppressed local initiative, possibly constrained innovation and undermined employees' morale, and ignored local need and circumstances, 'potentially leading to the delivery of one-size-fits-all, poor-quality services to diverse communities' (Balls *et al.* 2004: 17, 346).

In practice, Brown and Balls' model of policy-making in England has formed a key part of the *new* command and control system of 'constrained discretion', and top-down, centralizing, 'one-size-fits-all' approaches to policy design and control of resources. The Treasury's principles for policy-making have focused on outcomes as 'the central aim of policy'; an increase in 'operational freedoms and flexibilities' accompanied by 'appropriate minimum standards and regular performance monitoring'; and improved governance through 'clear objectives, appropriate incentives and good performance information in the achievement of higher productivity' (Balls *et al.* 2004: 346). This has amounted to centralised prescription over policy design and resource allocation, with devolution confined to administrative decentralisation. This approach to policy-making has claimed to be 'bottom-up not top-down, with national government enabling powerful regional and local institutions to work by providing the necessary flexibility and resources' (Balls *et al.* 2004: 9). However, the very fact that the Treasury has acknowledged that it, rather than the English regions and localities, has provided the requisite 'flexibility and resources', is indicative of the degree to which centralisation has become institutionalised.

When Gordon Brown addressed the 2005 Sustainable Communities Summit in Manchester, he claimed that regional policy was now entering its third phase. The first two phases had been characterised by 'help directed from the centre', in the interwar period to assist areas of high unemployment and latterly during the 1960s and 1970s to provide large capital and tax incentives. Now, in the new third phase, 'the top-down centralised systems of regional and urban policy – the dirigiste systems of the mid twentieth century' would be set aside in favour of local indigenous capacity' and 'people – their skills, flexibility, their willingness to change, their dynamism'. Brown proceeded to promise that 'the Treasury and central government generally will continue to devolve power away from the centre' (Brown 2005). However, to illustrate this 'true devolution of power', Brown could only cite the examples of the Regional Development Agencies, the Northern Way, the pilot Local Area

Agreements, Sure Start, the New Deal for Communities and the Safer Communities Initiative. He claimed that communities were 'in the driving seat' in Local Strategic Partnerships, albeit 'within a strategic national framework, including challenging floor targets'. Brown's example of 'the devolution of more power to the regions' (the English regions) was the decision (from April 2005) for the Regional Development Agencies to locally administer the Business Link service. Once again, unelected, appointed quangos, directly unaccountable to the regions and communities within which they operate, were being entrusted with new powers.

Throughout Brown's speech, he had spoken about his vision for Britain, but his examples of devolution were almost exclusively examples of the decentralised administration in England that had bypassed the true devolution and extension of citizenship elsewhere in the UK. The common denominator of these English (rather than UK-wide) initiatives was that they had all been designed by UK central government, and had to operate within the 'constrained discretion' demanded by the Treasury. The Treasury has demonstrated this commitment to the principles and practice of constrained discretion through a series of policy statements (Her Majesty's Treasury, Department of Trade and Industry, and Office of the Deputy Prime Minister 2004, 2005; Her Majesty's Treasury and the Cabinet Office 2006). In each of these documents, devolution has been defined as administrative decentralisation, without the involvement of directly elected government.

This preference was reflected in the Labour Party's 2005 General Election manifesto. It promised to embed 'a culture of devolved government at the centre and self-government in our communities' (Labour Party 2005: 103), but omitted any mention of extending political autonomy and citizenship to elected government in England's regions and localities. Instead, the manifesto revisited the idea of 'a new generation of city mayors', a proposal previously rejected by English towns such as Oxford and ridiculed in Hartlepool in May 2002 by the election of H'Angus the Monkey (also known as Stuart Drummond, the mascot of Hartlepool United Football Club), who had campaigned under the slogan 'free bananas for schoolchildren'. For the English regions beyond Greater London, New Labour simply promised to 'devolve further responsibility to existing regional bodies in relation to planning, housing, economic development and transport' (Labour Party 2005: 108). Since, in Yorkshire and the Humber, all of these 'regional bodies' are appointed, unelected quangos, this was simply a commitment to further deepen Yorkshire and Humber's parallel deficits in democracy, accountability, citizenship and political identity.

This agenda was taken forward in the October 2006 White Paper on local government. In introducing it, Ruth Kelly, Secretary of State for Communities and Local Government, claimed that government 'must have the courage at the centre to let go', but then indicated that local authorities will only have the autonomy to choose between three centrally determined leadership models. These are a directly elected mayor, a directly elected executive of councillors, or a leader elected by his/her fellow-councillors' (Department for Communities and Local Government 2006: 4). Furthermore, the 'new settlement between central government, local government and citizens', which promised a radical reduction in national targets and the introduction of a lighter touch inspection system', will in practice mean the retention of around 200 national performance indicators, compared to the present 'between 600 and 1200 indicators' (Department for Communities and Local Government 2006: 4–5, 122). In relation to regional governance, the White Paper promised to deliver 'Strong cities, strategic regions', but then confirmed that this process is being undertaken through a joint review of sub-national economic development conducted by the Department for Communities and Local Government, HM Treasury, and the Department of Trade and Industry (Department of Communities and Local Government 2006: 68). The manner of this review and the confinement of its agenda to questions of economic development suggest that there is little evidence of central government having the courage to let go to, or to depart from the practice of constrained discretion.

Of course, there is a broader politics to this effusive rhetorical commitment to devolution in England but substantive limitation of its development to decentralised administration under the conditions of 'constrained discretion'. It is because the notion of English political identity or consciousness must be denied. When Gordon Brown (2001) spoke in Manchester in January 2001 of 'a Britain of regions and nations', his vision of devolution implicitly only identified Scotland, Wales, Northern Ireland and Britain as nations. It explicitly divided England into administrative regions. Had Brown acknowledged England as a distinct political community, as an MP for a Scottish constituency, Brown's authority to intervene in England's politics either as Chancellor or Prime Minister would have been seriously compromised.

The regional governance of Yorkshire and the Humber

With a population of more than five million and an income of £75,219 million (measured as Gross Value Added at current basic prices) in 2004 (Office for National Statistics 2006: 218), Yorkshire and the Humber possesses both sufficient people and resources to support elected regional government. Yorkshire and the Humber has also been a pioneer in establishing its own regional governance institutions. A non-statutory Regional Assembly for Yorkshire and the Humber was created in July 1996, almost a year before the election of the first Blair Government. The region developed its own sector-based Regional Innovation Strategy from November 1996. Yorkshire and Humberside was also the first English region to launch its own Regional Chamber in March 1998. Such developments were supported by the locally based Joseph Rowntree Foundation, which has funded influential related research, including the report of an Independent Commission on Good Governance in Public Services (2006). Like most English regions, however, there have been powerful constraints on further progress not simply from UK government but also from within the region; at the same time there are important reasons why these constraints need to be overcome.

One of the biggest constraints on the potential for directly elected regional government has been the public's broad cultural identification with Yorkshire as a county. This has not yet extended into a widely shared regional civic identity with

Yorkshire and the Humber. Borne of a long and proud history, Yorkshire can trace the origins of its historic 'Ridings' to their Scandinavian roots in the ninth century. Since August 1975, the people of the county have celebrated 'Yorkshire Day', initiated by the Yorkshire Ridings Society in part to counter any danger of a loss of popular identity following the local government reorganisation of the previous year. 1 August was chosen because it was on that date in 1759 that Yorkshire regiments at the Battle of Minden picked white roses to commemorate the heroism of their fallen comrades.

In contrast, Yorkshire *and the Humber*, and before it Yorkshire *and Humberside*, have only ever existed in the imagination of distant administrators and bureaucrats in Whitehall and Brussels. There has never been any popular local identification with Humberside or indeed 'the Humber' as a political entity. When Humberside County Council, which itself had been created from April 1974 by the administrative reorganisation of English local government, was abolished on April 1996 (to be replaced by four unitary authorities), few tears were shed. In fact, the intervening period had been marked by incessant vandalism to road signage and other references to 'Humberside', and an active campaign for the restoration of the older political constituencies with which people could more readily identify. Local authorities based upon traditional identities such as that of the county and the Ridings have generated popular allegiance, but where administrative reorganisations have created new constituencies, they have generated imaginary rather than imagined communities, and administrative identities lacking genuine popular resonance.

Yet, the people of Yorkshire and the Humber now elect 56 Westminster MPs, 6 Members of the European Parliament, 22 local authorities and in all a total of 847 town and parish councils. At that point, the democratic component of the governance of Yorkshire and the Humber ends. Within the region, the three major actors in the public domain are the Government Office for Yorkshire and the Humber, the Yorkshire and Humber Assembly, and the Regional Development Agency for Yorkshire and the Humber, entitled Yorkshire Forward. In addition, in 2004 Yorkshire Forward formed a partnership with its sister Regional Development Agencies in the North of England, North-East and the North-West Development Agency, to create the Northern Way. This initiative is seeking over a 30 year period to bridge a £30 billion 'productivity gap' between the North of England and the average for England as a whole, by identifying ten investment priorities and dividing the North into eight city-regions (Northern Way 2005)

The common denominator of these regional institutions is that none is directly elected and accountable to the people of the region. All of them are led by politically anonymous figures. Felicity Everiss, the Regional Director of the Government Office, Peter Box, the Chair of Yorkshire and Humber Assembly, and Terry Hodgkinson, the Chair of Yorkshire Forward, remain names virtually unknown outside the opaque circles of decision-making in which they operate, despite the power and influence that they individually and collectively wield. It is also likely that most people within the region would identify Neville Chamberlain as a former Conservative Prime Minister rather than the serving Chair of the Northern Way Steering Group.

The Yorkshire and Humber Assembly has proclaimed itself the 'Voice of the region'. In its September 2005 Annual Review, the Assembly's Chair, Peter Box, even asserted that because of its appointed status as the region's strategic partnership, the Assembly 'can provide democratic legitimacy' (Yorkshire and Humber Assembly 2005: 3). Moreover, in written evidence to a parliamentary select committee, the Assembly claimed that it continued to have 'an important and unique role in ensuring regional accountability and strategic alignment' (Yorkshire and Humber Assembly 2006: 229). However, genuine democratic legitimacy flows from being directly elected and accountable to a specific political community, with the power to remove that body if that is the democratic will of the community. The Assembly does not possess that authentic legitimacy. It is not the voice of the region because the people of Yorkshire and the Humber have not so chosen it, and do not have the power to remove it.

Yorkshire Forward is equally untroubled by the need to be directly accountable to the taxpayers and citizens of the region. In 2004–2005, Yorkshire Forward may have created and safeguarded 27,312 jobs, encouraged 1,179 businesses to start up, attracted £333 million of private-sector finance and supported 66,000 learning opportunities, but those activities have not been subject to the sort of democratic scrutiny made possible by the restoration of the Scottish Parliament or the creation of the Welsh Assembly. Given an income for 2004–2005 of only £308.4 million (including £252.4 million grant-in-aid from the Department of Trade and Industry) (Yorkshire Forward 2005b: 40), even if Yorkshire Forward had been subject to greater regional democratic control and accountability, it would have been of fairly marginal importance. With its budget being not even 1 per cent of the £31.7 billion centrally planned identifiable public spending in the region for 2004–2005 (Her Majesty's Treasury 2005: 91), and less than half a per cent of regional GDP, the opportunity for genuine autonomy over Yorkshire and Humber's economic development would have remained severely constrained by Treasury fiat.

Despite these problems of democratic accountability, the region's policy elite has preferred to remain hidden from view in the opacity of the labyrinthine networks of New Labour's unelected, patronage state, refusing to back the campaign for a directly elected regional assembly. Yet this means that the governance of Yorkshire and the Humber continues to suffer from the worst of all worlds. On the one hand, because policy-makers have to operate within the framework of public service agreements, local service agreements, and a raft of accompanying targets, output measures and performance indicators prescribed by constrained discretion, they lack the power of political autonomy to design a tailor-made agenda for the region. On the other hand, because they lack the legitimacy and visibility that arises from having to undergo the very public test of democratic elections, they also lack the political authority to serve as an effective and legitimate voice for the region. The regional governance of Yorkshire and the Humber continues to manifest the primacy of the technocratic management of territory over questions of democratic accountability and citizenship.

Regression in the region: the dividend from constrained discretion

In the fifth edition of *Progress in the Region*, the annual report drawn up by Yorkshire Futures, the Regional Intelligence Network, an evaluation was made of progress against *Advancing Together*, Yorkshire and the Humber's strategic framework document. Unfortunately, the progress resulting from the policies shaped by constrained discretion, measured against the framework's own benchmarks and performance indicators, was limited. The strategic framework identified six objectives, no fewer than 32 indicators for measuring collective progress, and 33 Regional Sustainable Development Framework indicators (Yorkshire Futures 2005: 8). During 2003 the region had made progress (measured in terms of the applicable baselines) against only 13 of the 32 collective progress indicators. Moreover, in the case of 12 indicators there had been steady or mixed progress, or else it had not been possible to determine progress. Against seven or nearly one-quarter of the indicators, there had actually been deterioration in performance (Yorkshire Futures 2005: 10).

Included among the areas of deteriorating performance were civic participation and governance, which were accorded the third-class status of mere afterthoughts in the pattern of governance enacted by New Labour after May 1997. Thus, it was not until the fourth edition of *Progress in the Region* in 2004 that good governance and civic participation were actually incorporated into the evaluation of the region's progress. Moreover, the technocratic bias in policy-making within the region was illustrated by the Yorkshire and Humber Assembly's gathering of a 'Steering Group of experts on different aspects of Good Governance and Civic Participation' to oversee initiatives to improve progress within the region (Yorkshire Futures 2005: 171). The general citizenry once again was conspicuous by its absence.

In its sixth objective, *Advancing Together* stated, 'People of the region need to feel that they can influence plans that will impact upon them. They need to know that their views are legitimate and will be dealt with in a correct and transparent way' (Yorkshire Futures 2005: 22). However, in terms of good governance and civic participation, *Progress in the Region 2005* identified an 'apparent apathy and perceived lack of influence' among the region's citizens. It was claimed that 'Civic participation should be a key factor in a sustainable society', but against measure after measure of good governance and civic participation, Yorkshire and the Humber recorded a level of engagement below the average for England (Yorkshire Futures 2005: 22). For example, in 2003 only 33.9 per cent of people in Yorkshire and the Humber felt 'able to influence decisions affecting their local area' compared to a mean average for the English regions of 39.3 per cent. Only 32 per cent had participated in civic affairs in the last 12 months compared to an England baseline of 38 per cent. Similarly, only 8.3 per cent had participated in the local community in 2004 compared to an England baseline of 9.8 per cent, while in 2005 only 40 per cent of the region's businesses possessed 'a mission or value statement incorporating the concept of responsible business practice, compared to a 48 per cent baseline for Great Britain as a whole, (Yorkshire Futures 2006: 102).

In relation to Yorkshire Forward, there was a welcome slight increase from 34.4 per cent (in 2004) to 37.6 per cent (in 2005) of stakeholders very or fairly satisfied with the Regional Development Agency's overall performance. However, while only 6.3 per cent of respondents were either fairly or very dissatisfied, the most telling statistic was that no fewer than 40.4 per cent of Yorkshire Forward's own stakeholders stated that they did not know how to answer this question. Indeed, only 22 out of the 35 members of the Yorkshire and Humber Assembly could be bothered to respond to the May 2004 survey of their own institution. While 59 per cent thought the Assembly was either effective or very effective in informing members about the way they might become involved in its work, 14 per cent thought it ineffective or very ineffective. Similarly, while 77 per cent of Assembly members thought its decision-making structures and processes to be inclusive, almost one-fifth (18.1 per cent) thought those processes to be not very or not at all inclusive (Yorkshire Futures 2005: 172). For there to be any dissatisfaction at all among the members of a self-appointed 'voice of the region' would appear to be a clear indictment of processes of government that have not exposed themselves to the democratic rigours of direct elections.

Most tellingly, in 2003 no fewer than 66.1 per cent of people in Yorkshire and the Humber tended to disagree or definitely disagreed that they were able to influence decisions affecting their local area. This figure was above the England average of 60.7 per cent, and meant that the people of Yorkshire and the Humber were in fact in the English region with the weakest sense of political efficacy or empowerment (Yorkshire Futures 2005: 173). *Progress in the Region 2005* concluded that there is 'a lower level of involvement in civic affairs in Yorkshire and Humber than in England as a whole, and the gap is widening'. Despite the introduction of all postal ballots, turnout in elections in the region had also remained low, while 'Informal and formal volunteering rates are lower than in most other regions and below the England average, with the gap widening'. Moreover, 'Overall participation in the local community is low compared to other regions', and 'Trade union membership is declining in the region at a faster rate than in England as a whole' (Yorkshire Futures 2005: 173). The conclusion was drawn that 'The regional partners need to understand the reasons for a decline in general participation in the community' (Yorkshire Futures 2005: 23).

In reviewing this evidence of the state of regional democracy in Yorkshire and the Humber one cannot help but feel that the reason is simple. It is about political power, the power to design policies, allocate resources and set priorities, and the general citizenry's exclusion from the exercise of such power. Regional institutions look to their own *modus operandi*. They operate under a highly centralised national framework, within which they have been excluded themselves from key decisions about the allocation of resources and the design of policy. At the same time, they have been entrusted with delivering against key performance indicators, a task which meets the agenda of central government but does little to revitalise the democratic capacity of the region.

Political constraints and elected regional government

One of the principal reasons for the failure of the region to generate a popular campaign for regional government is that its politicians have remained divided over the issue. Yorkshire and the Humber has generated one of the Labour Party's most powerful and longstanding proponents of directly elected regional government. In John Prescott, MP for Hull East, and Deputy Prime Minister, 1997–2007, the region has possessed one of the Labour Party's longest-standing advocates of regional policy. When launching the Government's White Paper, *Your Region, Your Choice: Revitalising the English Regions* (Office of the Deputy Prime Minister 2002), Prescott reminded Westminster that he had been commissioned in 1982 by Michael Foot to produce an *Alternative Regional Strategy*. Subsequently, Prescott himself commissioned Bruce Millan, a former Scottish MP and European Commissioner for Regional Policy and Cohesion, to chair the Labour Party's Regional Policy Commission. However, the Commission did not advocate directly elected regional government. On the contrary, it instead made the case only for Regional Development Agencies in each of the English regions and for indirectly elected regional chambers (Regional Policy Commission 1996). To that extent, New Labour's programme in government has been consistent with these earlier proposals. Indeed, in introducing the White Paper, Prescott referred only to the strengthening of regional policy in England. Any mention of elected regional government for England was conspicuous by its absence (Office of the Deputy Prime Minister 2002).

It may have taken a Welshman (Prescott was born in Prestatyn, and was first elected as MP for Hull East in 1970) to commission a Scot to draw up the Labour Party's policy on England's regions, but Prescott has not been the sole advocate of English devolution from Yorkshire and the Humber. Most notably, Prescott has received backing from Richard Caborn, MP for Sheffield Central and Minister of State successively at the Department for the Environment, Transport and the Regions (1997–1999), the Department of Trade and Industry (1999–2001) and the Department of Culture, Media and Sport, including the role of Minister for Sport (2001–2007).

However, Yorkshire has also possessed more than its fair share of vocal opponents of directly elected regional government. William Hague, the MP for Richmond, steadfastly opposed Labour's devolution agenda during his tenure as Conservative Party Leader. David Davis, the MP for Haltemprice and Howden and Shadow Home Secretary, has been equally strident in his hostility to elected regional assemblies.

Two influential rising stars of New Labour, the husband and wife team of Ed Balls and Yvette Cooper, MPs for the neighbouring safe seats of Normanton, and Pontefract and Castleford respectively, have shown no public enthusiasm for directly elected regional government. Both have opted to operate through New Labour's preferred policy-making architecture of unelected special advisors and quangos. Thus, Balls served as Economic Advisor to Gordon Brown, then Chief Economic Advisor to the Treasury, before becoming a member of the Steering Group of the Northern Way. Cooper's role as Minister for Housing and Planning in the Office of the Deputy Prime Minister gave her responsibility, by coincidence, for the Northern Way and other intra-regional growth strategies, and the Government Offices for the Regions.

Given Balls' preference for English regional governance through unelected institutions, it is ironic that his meteoric rise as a politician has been threatened, at least temporarily, by the conclusions of an unelected public body. The Boundary Commission for England decided to reduce the number of MPs in West Yorkshire from 23 to 22 by abolishing Balls' constituency, the safe Labour seat of Normanton, which Balls won in 2005 (Boundary Commission for England 2006). Despite this setback, Balls has continued to press for the next phase of English regional governance under New Labour to proceed upon the basis of the strengthening of the powers of the Regional Development Agencies, and the co-ordination and co-operation of local authorities (Balls *et al.* 2006). This was as an alternative to the Centre for Cities proposal for directly elected city-region mayors (Marshall and Finch 2006). Indeed, while acknowledging that 'with greater decentralisation must also come greater accountability for the decisions made—both locally and nationally', Balls has advocated that 'Regional accountability needs to be driven by local leadership, namely county and city-region federations of local authority leaders' (Balls *et al.* 2006: 6).

Despite the antipathy among leading Labour Party politicians from within the region, on 17 March 1999, Yorkshire and the Humber was one of the first English regions to launch a campaign for directly elected regional government. The Campaign for Yorkshire (which later mutated into Yes4Yorkshire), published a Claim of Right asserting 'the right of the people of Yorkshire and the Humber to determine their own domestic affairs should it be their settled will to do so' (Campaign for Yorkshire 2000). Subsequently, the Campaign for Yorkshire held Constitutional Conventions in York in October 2000 and Wakefield in June 2001. It then published its own White Paper on regional government which envisaged that regional government in England would act 'as a REGULATOR, as an imitator/architect of STRATEGY and as a FUNDING body' (capitalisation in the original), with the establishment of a directly elected regional assembly of 'between 30 and 50 members' (Campaign for Yorkshire 2001: 11, 21). However, while it campaigned actively at Westminster, not least through the Campaign for the English Regions, neither the Campaign for Yorkshire nor latterly Yes4Yorkshire was able to generate a genuine popular support for its agenda. This was despite the fact that opinion polls commissioned by the BBC in September 2000 and March 2002 showed 44 per cent and 72 per cent respectively in favour of an elected regional assembly for Yorkshire and the Humber.

However, when the Government gave the people of Yorkshire and the Humber the opportunity to have their say on the Government's proposals for referendums on directly elected regional assemblies, only 1,177 people responded. Of these 833 affirmed their desire for a referendum with 326 against the referendum, but less than half the respondents (i.e. 508 people) stated that they thought there was a strong or very strong level of interest in holding a referendum in the region. Moreover, in the year before the North-East referendum brought to an end the promise of a referendum on a regional assembly for Yorkshire and the Humber, Yes4Yorkshire was met with an equally vigorous Yorkshire Says No campaign, led by its Chairman, John Watson, the former Conservative MP for Skipton and

Ripon. The Yorkshire Says No campaign enjoyed the support of the region's two widest circulation daily newspapers, the *Yorkshire Post* and the *Hull Daily Mail*. For example, the *Yorkshire Post* suggested that 'Those within ministerial circles who favour English devolution are no great political thinkers and their reasons for wanting regional assemblies are poorly thought out' (*Yorkshire Post* 2001).

Consequently, there is little evidence to suggest that, had the electorate of Yorkshire and the Humber been given an opportunity to vote on the principle of a directly elected regional assembly, its verdict would have been any less decisively negative than the 78 per cent 'No' vote recorded by the electorate of the North East. Given the hostility and indifference of the general populace to the proposals, and the consistently low turnouts for local government elections and by-elections, it is unlikely that the turnout would have been as high as the North East's 47.8 per cent. While Yorkshire has maintained its strong cultural identity, there has as yet been no significant spillover into regional political identity or consciousness, let alone active widespread popular support for elected regional government.

Problems of citizenship and the potential of regional government

The pattern of governance that has developed in Yorkshire and the Humber under the Blair Governments has been based upon a strict separation of powers. The power to control and allocate resources and to design policy has been separated from the responsibility for the administration of services and the implementation of policy. The consequence appears to be a growing indifference to the democratic process. Long before devolution was initiated by New Labour, many voters in Yorkshire and the Humber had been effectively disenfranchised by a combination of the first-past-the-post electoral system operating in a region dominated electorally by the Labour Party, and the absence of parties, like the SNP and Plaid Cymru operating in Scotland and Wales, to act as the repository for disillusioned mainstream voters. Thus, although at the 2005 General Election Labour lost seats in the constituencies of Shipley, and Scarborough and Whitby to the Conservatives, and Leeds North-West to the Liberal Democrats, it nevertheless hung on to its remaining seats, giving it 44 out of 56. This represented 79 per cent of the region's seats at Westminster gained with a 43.6 per cent share of the vote. The widely held perception that New Labour has both abandoned Old Labour's traditional principles, and taken its voters in the five Northern English regions for granted, has encouraged disillusioned Labour voters not only to abandon the Party itself but also the democratic process. Consequently, at the 2005 General Election, only 2,199,232 votes were cast in Yorkshire and the Humber, a turnout of just 58.9 per cent, and below the UK average. The highest turnout was only 69.7 per cent (in the Conservative marginal of Haltemprice and Howden held by David Davis), while the lowest turnout was 45.0 per cent in Kingston upon Hull West and Hessle. This was the sixth lowest turnout in the whole of the UK, with John Prescott's constituency ranked only one place higher at 45.2 per cent or the 639th highest turnout (House of Commons Library 2005: 20, 52).

In all parts of the region, the most salient constituency was that of voters who chose not to engage with the democratic process. In total, no fewer than 41.1 per cent or 1.53 million of the region's citizens did not exercise their democratic right. While supporters of the Blair Government might contend that this was indicative of a culture of overall contentment, it might equally be regarded as dangerous evidence of disillusionment, indifference or alienation. The picture has been no better in relation to elections for the European Parliament or local authorities. In the 10 June 2004 elections for the European Parliament, the turnout was a lamentable 42.9 per cent, albeit this was a significant improvement upon the 22.6 per cent turnout recorded at the previous elections in 1999. In local elections, detachment and indifference has been even more marked. In 2003, the average turnout in local government elections in 20 of the region's local authorities was only 35.6 per cent (Yorkshire Futures 2005: 164).

If one takes a wider perspective it should also be recognised that the debate about the need or otherwise for directly elected regional institutions in the English regions has been mistakenly and dangerously separated from parallel debates about race, citizenship, community cohesion, multiculturalism and identity. These debates were given added saliency by the May 2001 Oldham and July 2001 Bradford riots, and given renewed impetus by the London bombings of 7/7 and 21/7. Three of the London suicide bombers were born and bred in Yorkshire. Past debates about devolution in England have understandably focused upon issues relating to greater accountability for institutions and policies affecting economic regeneration and planning. However, too little attention has been paid to the unique challenge confronting English regions such as Yorkshire and the Humber, which is the politics of their multiethnic and multicultural composition.

As recent research has revealed, of the 2.2 million people from abroad who came to live in Britain between 1991 and 2001, no less than 97.4 per cent came to live in England and its regions. With a total migrant population of 235,424 in 2001, or 4.74 per cent of its total population, Yorkshire and the Humber is home to more migrants than Scotland and Wales combined (British Broadcasting Corporation 2005). This illustrates how the challenge of multiculturalism in Britain is not exclusively but predominantly a question for England, its regions and its multiethnic communities. As with the objective of creating a dynamic, innovative, entrepreneurial and prosperous economy, there is no evidence to suggest that a centralised polity in which local and regional autonomy over policy and resources is denied constitutes the best political framework for the creation of a successful, diverse, pluralistic and inclusive multicultural society.

Such rich diversity and plural communities must be given a political voice. Regrettably, since the June 2001 race riots in the Northern English towns of Bradford, Burnley and Oldham, a series of official reports (i.e. Bradford Vision 2001; Oldham Independent Review 2001; Burnley Task Force 2001; and Home Office 2001) has failed to identify the potential relationship between community cohesion, race equality and the political autonomy that can arise from the operation of directly elected political institutions at the regional and local levels. A common flaw of these reports has been their denial of the actuality of devolution to other parts of the United Kingdom and its potential for addressing issues related to race and multiculturalism. Meanwhile, the reports have failed to acknowledge the discrepancy that in England it is UK central government that has been addressing issues of governance and policies relating to communities. Generally, they have failed to explore how a regional democratic process, and genuine autonomy over policy design and resource allocation, might offer a discovery process to revive the public domain of democratic citizenship, participation, legitimacy, scrutiny and accountability.

The report of the Bradford Race Review, which followed the riots of July 2001, argued that 'What is now desperately needed is a powerful unifying vision for the district and strong political, municipal and community leadership'. It further identified that 'so-called "community leaders"' were 'self-styled' and tended 'to retain their power base by maintaining the segregated status quo, even when unrepresentative'. It even identified how ordinary people were 'insufficiently involved in decision-making about policies and programmes intended to meet their particular needs and that is why these fail' (Bradford Vision 2001: 1, 10–11). However, having furnished a forensic analysis of the shortcomings of many of the Blair Governments' failed attempts to deliver a joined-up agenda for community regeneration, the Bradford report then failed to make the connection between unrepresentative institutions, ineffective policies and the potential of genuine political autonomy over policy and resources, whether exercised through local authorities in Bradford or devolved government in Yorkshire and the Humber.

In a similar vein, when addressing the issue of governance, the report of the Oldham Independent Review both bemoaned the lack of 'strategic direction, and a vision for the way it should develop in the future' and emphasised that 'Good citizenship is vital to a stable society'. However, in further stressing that 'The Board of the new Local Strategic Partnership should be tightly drawn to ensure real debate and dialogue, and not just lip service to the idea of partnership' (Oldham Independent Review 2001: 15), the report failed to identify that partnerships that are genuinely local, strategic and joined-up will be impossible as long as localities are themselves the prisoner of a nationalised framework of policy-making and resource allocation that negates citizenship and denies genuine political autonomy.

Similar problems have been evident in the Home Office's policy statements. For example, in January 2005 the then Home Secretary, Charles Clarke, identified the importance in the Government's strategy of increasing race equality and community cohesion, and of 'strengthening society' by 'getting much better at identifying and responding to the specific needs of different communities, in education, health, employment, housing, security' (Home Office 2005: 5). The strategy proclaimed how important it was that 'people from all backgrounds have opportunities to participate in civic society' (Home Office, 2005: 12, 20). However, this agenda excluded the possibility of devolving genuine autonomy over policy and resources in this policy area to directly elected political institutions at the regional and local levels in England. The report duly proceeded to identify a series of related policy initiatives in health, education, housing, local government and neighbourhood renewal but failed to acknowledge that, because of devolution elsewhere, all of these initiatives were national programmes affecting England alone, delivered in the main by an institutional architecture of appointed partnerships and unelected task forces.

The Home Office's strategy suggested that 'national cohesion rests on an inclusive sense of Britishness which couples the offer of fair mutual support – from security to health and education – with the expectation that people will play their part in society and respect others' (Home Office, 2005: 20). This in turn overlooked the fact that because of the nationalisation of policy-making and the centralised prescription over resource allocation embodied in the doctrines of 'earned autonomy' and 'constrained discretion', the people of England, including its many multi-ethnic communities, have been denied the opportunity to 'play their part' in the democratic governance of their own communities. It is futile to repeatedly emphasize the importance of citizenship education in both the compulsory and non-compulsory components of English education, if those very citizens are then denied the opportunity to engage in the democratic process by a centralised prescription over policy and resources that negates the autonomy and citizenship rights enjoyed elsewhere in the UK. Overall, perhaps such departmental perspectives should not be seen as surprising given that the Blair Governments' overall vision of Sustainable Communities and the Northern Way expressly excluded any mention of democratic citizenship (Office of the Deputy Prime Minister 2004a, 2004b, 2004c, 2005).

Conclusion

Under New Labour, the effective nationalisation of policy for England and its regions, through the policy of constrained discretion, and the accompanying micro-management of resource allocation has placed such an emphasis upon results and outputs, through a surfeit of performance indicators and output measures, that the importance of the actual policy-making process itself for sustaining citizenship in communities has been neglected. In particular, for English regions such as Yorkshire and the Humber that now confront new challenges because of the very diversity of their multicultural communities, genuine decentralisation of political power and autonomy over resources has taken on an added importance. Communities need to have the opportunity to re-engage with democracy as a discovery process for democratic citizenship, and its component elements of participation, legitimacy, accountability and transparency.

To continue with the existing and ineffective pattern of governance, whose principles of 'earned autonomy' and 'constrained discretion' have decentralised power only to the individual as consumer, and bestow only an administering role on sub-national governance for services designed elsewhere, will only serve to further alienate the electorate. To advocate an extension of democratic citizenship rights, genuine devolution of power, and autonomy over policy and resources in the English regions, at least as great as that enjoyed by the Scottish Parliament is not to fall into the trap, which the Cantle report identified, of communities continuing to 'look backwards to some supposedly halcyon days of a mono-cultural society, or alternatively look to their country of origin for some form of identity' (Home Office 2001: 9). On the contrary, what is being proposed is a more autonomous and devolved pattern of government that is better attuned to the more pluralistic and diverse multicultural society that England has become.

Note

1 The imprecision of Gordon Brown's original definition of 'community' had led one fellow Labour Party essayist to question whether such imprecision might extend in government into 'a lack of precision over democratic accountability and control', which might in turn undermine any radical transfer of power from the centre to communities (Phillips 1994: 124).

References

Balls, E., O'Donnell, G. and Grice, I. (eds) (2004) *Microeconomic Reform in Britain: Delivering Opportunities to All*, London: Palgrave Macmillan.

Balls, E., Healey, J. and Leslie, C. (2006) *Evolution and Devolution in England: How regions strengthen our towns and cities,* London: New Local Government Network.

Boundary Commission for England (2006) *Final Recommendations for the Normanton, Pontefract and Castleford Constituency*, London: Boundary Commission for England.

British Broadcasting Corporation (2005) *Born Abroad: An immigration map of Britain*, London: British Broadcasting Corporation. Online. Available HTTP: http://news.bbc.co.uk/1/shared/spl/hi/uk/05/born_abroad/html/overview.stm (28 October 2005).

Bradford Vision (2001) *Community Pride not Prejudice: Making Diversity Work in Bradford*. Report presented to Bradford Vision by Sir Herman Ouseley, Bradford: Bradford Vision.

Brown, G. (1994) 'The politics of potential: a new agenda for Labour', in D. Miliband (ed.), *Reinventing the Left*, Cambridge: Polity.

Brown, G. (2001) Speech made at the University of Manchester Institute of Science and Technology, Manchester, 29 January.

Brown, G. (2005) Speech to the Sustainable Communities Summit, Manchester, 2 February.

Burnley Task Force (2001) *Report of the Burnley Task Force*, Burnley: Burnley Task Force.

Campaign for Yorkshire (2000) *Claim of Right*, Sheffield: Campaign for Yorkshire.

Campaign for Yorkshire (2001) *Giving the People a Voice: Campaign for Yorkshire's White Paper on Regional Governance*, Sheffield: Campaign for Yorkshire.

Department for Communities and Local Government (2006) *Strong and Prosperous Communities: The Local Government White Paper*, Cm. 6939-II, London: The Stationery Office.

Department of the Environment, Transport and the Regions (1997) 'John Prescott promises a radical approach to the regions', *Department of the Environment Press Release 194*, 30 May, London: Department of the Environment, Transport and the Regions.

Her Majesty's Treasury (2005) *Public Expenditure Statistical Analyses 2005*, Cm.6521, London: The Stationery Office.

Her Majesty's Treasury and the Cabinet Office (2004) *Devolving Decision Making: 1 – Delivering better public services: refining targets and performance management*, London: The Stationery Office.

Her Majesty's Treasury, the Office of the Deputy Prime Minister, and the Department of Trade and Industry (2004) *Devolving Decision Making: 2 – Meeting the regional economic challenge: Increasing regional and local flexibility*, London: The Stationery Office.

Her Majesty's Treasury, the Department for Trade and Industry, and the Office of the Deputy Prime Minister (2006) *Devolving Decision Making: 3 – Meeting the regional economic challenge: The importance of cities to regional growth*, London: The Stationery Office.

Home Office (2001) *Community Cohesion: A Report of the Independent Review Team Chaired by Ted Cantle*, London: The Home Office.

Home Office (2005) *Improving Opportunity, Strengthening Society: The Government's strategy to increase race equality and community cohesion*, London: The Home Office.

House of Commons Library (2005) *General Election 2005*: Research Paper 05/33, London: House of Commons Library.

Independent Commission on Good Governance in Public Services (2004) *The Good Governance Standard for Public Services*, London: Office for Public Management/The Chartered Institute of Public Finance and Accountancy.

Labour Party (2005) *Britain Forward Not Back: The Labour Party manifesto 2005*, London: The Labour Party.

Lee, S. (1999) 'The competitive disadvantage of England' in K Cowling (ed.), *Industrial Policy in Europe: Theoretical Perspectives and Practical Proposals*, London: Routledge.

Marquand, D. (2004) *Decline of the Public: The Hollowing-out of Citizenship*, Cambridge: Polity Press.

Marshall, A. and Finch, D. (2006) *City Leadership: Giving city-regions the power to grow*, London, Centre for Cities.

Northern Way (2005) *Moving Forward: The Northern Way Action Plan – Progress Report*, Newcastle-upon-Tyne: The Northern Way Steering Group.

Office of the Deputy Prime Minister (2002) *Your Region, Your Choice*, London: Office of the Deputy Prime Minister.

Office of the Deputy Prime Minister (2004a) *Sustainable Communities: building for the future*, London: Office of the Deputy Prime Minister.

Office of the Deputy Prime Minister (2004b) *Creating Sustainable Communities in Yorkshire and the Humber*, London: Office of the Deputy Prime Minister.

Office of the Deputy Prime Minister (2004c) *Making it Happen: The Northern Way*, London: Office of the Deputy Prime Minister.

Office of the Deputy Prime Minister (2005) *Realising the Potential of All Our Regions: the story so far*, London: Office of the Deputy Prime Minister.

Office for National Statistics (2006) *Regional Trends 39: 2006 edition*, London: Office for National Statistics.

Office of Public Service Reform (2002) *Reforming our Public Services: Principles into Practice*, London: Office of Public Services Reform.

Oldham Independent Review (2001) *One Oldham One Future: Oldham Independent Review Panel Report*, Oldham: Oldham Independent Review.

Phillips, A. (1994) 'Whose community? Which individuals?' in D. Miliband (ed.) *Reinventing the Left*, Cambridge: Polity.

Regional Policy Commission (1996) *Renewing the Regions: Strategies for Regional Economic Development*, Sheffield: Sheffield Hallam University.

Yorkshire and Humber Assembly (2005) *Annual Review and Accounts 2004/2005* Wakefield: Yorkshire and Humber Assembly.

Yorkshire and Humber Assembly (2006) *Memorandum by the Yorkshire and Humber Assembly (RG83)* to House of Commons' Housing, Planning and Local Government and the Regions Committee, *Is there a future for regional government?* Session 2005-2006, Volume II Written evidence, HC 977-II, London: The Stationery Office.

Yorkshire Forward (2005a) 'Homepage'. Online. Available HTTP: http:://www.yorkshire-forward.com/www.index.asp (28 October 2005).

Yorkshire Forward (2005b) *Report & Accounts 2004/2005*, Leeds: Yorkshire Forward.

Yorkshire Futures (2005) *Progress in the Region 2005*, Leeds: Yorkshire Futures.

Yorkshire Futures (2006) *Progress in the Humber 2006*, Leeds: Yorkshire Futures.

Yorkshire Post (2001) 'Assembled voices', 12 April.

Part III

Regional development in the UK

8 Devolution and development
Territorial justice and the North–South divide

Kevin Morgan

The longevity of the UK as a stable geo-political entity is perhaps more surprising than we think. If it were being designed afresh the UK would not be a particularly auspicious proposition, with its three-and-a-half nations, multiple religions, plethora of languages, two legal systems, and the whole concoction governed by a highly centralised government in London, a city based in the far South of the largest nation. That the UK – or the United Kingdom of Great Britain and Northern Ireland to be precise – has preserved its territorial integrity since the Irish Free State was established in 1921 is therefore more remarkable than it seems. The fact that this territorial integrity is so often taken for granted, that it should even appear 'natural' to so many British people, speaks volumes for what has been achieved. It could easily have been so different. Indeed, many multi-national states around the world have imploded through economic decline or internecine civil war. In the course of the twentieth century the UK survived a whole series of potentially fatal crises, including two world wars, the inter-war Depression, relative economic decline, and the accelerated closure of coal mines and steel mills which were once considered the lifeblood of Scotland, Wales and the North of England. With the luxury of hindsight, however, we can say that some things clearly work better in practice than in theory (Morgan and Mungham 2000).

Modernist theories of development have long considered territorial attachments to be cultural residues of a pre-modern or pre-capitalist era, primordial attributes that would be supplanted by class loyalties once modernity kicked in. As the 'first industrial nation' the UK was deemed to be a thoroughly modern country in this respect because it seemed to have transcended the territorial political movements that threatened the geo-political integrity of other nation-states and stymied their developmental prospects (Rokkan and Urwin 1982; Morgan 1985). The fact that territorial movements resurfaced with a vengeance in the UK, in the form of Scottish and Welsh nationalism, and under the banner of modernisation at that, exposed the narrow assumptions of modernist development thinking. The advent of nationalism in Scotland and Wales was triggered by two factors – the accelerated closure of heavy industry, which spawned pockets of high unemployment, and 'distant government' as it was felicitously called in the 1970s.

For the past 30 years the twin themes of devolution and development have become ever more entwined in the UK, initially in the form of Celtic nationalism and, more recently, in the shape of northern English regions who feel they are falling further and further behind the more prosperous regions of southern England. These territorial grievances were originally contained by a centrally managed regional policy, the mechanism through which successive governments sought to alleviate inter-regional economic inequalities by re-distributing jobs from growth regions to poorer regions. The flagship of 'territorial justice' in the UK, regional policy was widely perceived to be the quintessential test of central government's commitment to inter-regional equality (even though other forms of public expenditure are equally, if not more, important).

One of the unintended consequences of devolution is that this centrally managed regional policy, the aim of which was to promote economic equity *between* the regions, has been replaced by a devolved regional development policy which aims to promote an economic dividend *within* each region. Even in the unlikely event that devolution yields a uniform economic dividend to all regions, this does nothing to redress the North–South divide, which remains the most serious form of territorial inequality in the UK today. The question of territorial justice, a question that was suppressed and barely discussed in the era of the centralised polity, is likely to become a much more incendiary issue for the polycentric polity that is beginning to emerge in the wake of devolution. To examine these issues in more depth the chapter is structured as follows:

- the first section briefly examines the territorial repertoire of the centralised polity, the heyday of classical regional policy
- the second section examines the promise and practice of devolution, particularly with respect to the 'economic dividend' which is supposedly associated with political devolution
- the third section explores the meaning of 'territorial justice' and examines how it can be secured in post-devolution Britain, where a more polycentric polity is beginning to emerge.

The territorial repertoire of the centralised polity

The stereotyped picture of the North–South divide – consisting of a swathe of prosperous and burgeoning regions in southern England juxtaposed to a deprived and declining set of regions and nations to the North and West – has its economic origins in the collapse of the imperial spatial division of labour in inter-war Britain. Up until then the external success of British capitalism was internally correlated with a spatial division of labour in which the booming heavy industries of coal, steel, shipbuilding and the like were largely concentrated in Scotland, Wales and northern England, or 'Outer Britain' as these areas were instructively called in the inter-war period. The spatial patterns and economic processes of inter-war Britain bequeathed a strong legacy because, for at least two generations, they shaped the official mindset of politicians, planners and policy makers with respect to the nature of the regional problem and its post-war solution.

Nothing symbolised the official thinking better than the Barlow report. Commissioned to examine the problems of a spatially polarised distribution of industry in the late 1930s, the Barlow report created the intellectual framework for post-war regional policy for some 30 years after 1945 (Barlow 1940). At the heart of this pioneering report was the argument that over- and under-development were two sides of the same coin and the solution, as elegant as it was simple, consisted of containing growth in Greater London and diverting it to the depressed areas of 'Outer Britain'.

The Barlow diagnosis spawned the 'donor-recipient' model of regional policy which worked in the following way: prosperous regions like the South East and the West Midlands were encouraged, through a judicious combination of sticks and carrots, to donate surplus growth in the form of branch-plants to recipient regions in the North and West, a model that eventually became untenable when donor regions began to suffer their own unemployment problems in the 1970s. These new structural constraints persuaded the then Labour government to dilute regional policy as discreetly as possible, a trend that was reinforced with alacrity by Mrs Thatcher's Conservative governments (Morgan 1985).

Ever since the high point of regional policy expenditure in the mid-1970s successive governments, Conservative and Labour alike, have sought to belittle the North–South divide. Mrs Thatcher dismissed it as a media invention, as well she might as her government had few votes to lose in the Labour-dominated North of the country. More surprisingly perhaps, Tony Blair also tried to dismiss it on the grounds that it is a simplistic notion which ignores disparities *within* regions (although there is no logical reason to dismiss inter-regional inequalities simply because intra-regional disparities also exist). Most Labour politicians, on the other hand, are less inclined to dismiss it; on the contrary, they fear that London and the southern regions will pull further ahead of their northern counterparts because they are better equipped to exploit the shift to the knowledge-based economy (Mandelson 2001).

One reason why the North–South divide is under-estimated in some quarters today is because regional unemployment rates – the crude but totemic test of regional inequality since the inter-war period – have seemingly converged in recent years. What this complacent interpretation fails to recognise, however, is that unemployment is no longer a reliable guide to the state of the labour market, and certainly not as important as 'economic inactivity', an index which covers conditions like incapacity benefit claimants and premature retirement among others (Green and Owen 1998; Glyn and Erdem 1999; Fothergill 2001). This problem of 'hidden' unemployment is most acute in the former coalfield areas of the North and West of the country; so much so that the real rate of male unemployment in the coalfield regions of England and Wales in mid-2004 was put at 11.1 per cent, more than three times higher than the official rate (Beatty *et al.* 2005).

Although they can be important economic barometers, unemployment and economic inactivity rates are the symptoms of the North–South divide rather than the causes. The causes are to be found in spatially differentiated patterns of income and employment, reflecting the fact that the UK's core developmental assets – senior corporate functions, public and private R&D resources, higher level skills, venture capital funds and political power circuits for example – are heavily biased towards southern England (Massey 1984; Amin *et al.* 2003). This southern-centric bias has a more systemic, if less obvious, effect on the UK's spatial economy. As the UK's most over-developed region, the South East of England is the chief source of inflationary pressures, and UK monetary policy tends to be finely calibrated to the over-heated conditions in this core region rather than the 'under-heated' conditions in the less developed regions of the North. A former Governor of the Bank of England, Sir Edward George, actually conceded this point in a celebrated public relations gaffe. After a speech he had delivered on monetary policy he was asked if he was really saying that job loss in the North was an acceptable price to pay for the control of inflation in the South, and he was reported to have replied by saying 'yes, I suppose in a sense I am' (Morgan 2002).

The political response to the North–South problem is now very different to what it was in the classical era of regional policy, when regional policy consisted of a mixture of financial incentives in the North and development controls in the South. The southern development lobby, the most vocal component of which is the construction industry, opposes any new development controls because the latter are predicated on the antiquated logic of the Barlow report, which assumed a national economy in which investment could be controlled in the South and channelled to the North. In an era of globalisation, it argues, this intra-national trade-off is less likely because, if they are denied a location in the South, spatially mobile firms are likely to migrate to a core region in mainland Europe rather than a peripheral region in the North of England. This European perspective informed the seminal Crow report on housing provision in the South East, a report which explicitly sought to bury the planning mindset of the Barlow report (Crow 1999). The Crow report was the result of a public examination of the demand for new housing in the South East. Government estimates had suggested that 1.1 million new homes would be required by 2016, a figure disputed by the South-East Regional Planning Authority (SERPLAN), which argued that no more than 800,000 new homes should be built or the programme would be unsustainable (Murdoch 2000).

Published in 1999 the controversial Crow report rejected the more modest figure and endorsed the government's 1.1 million projection (Crow 1999). But the real significance of the Crow report is the fact that it introduced a radically different regulatory framework in which to assess the desirability of development controls: if the Barlow report was predicated on a national planning framework, the Crow report was decidedly European in scope and outlook. Steered towards a pro-growth perspective by the Government Office for the South East, the Crow report unashamedly argued that housing provision should serve the economy rather than the environment, and therefore it should help to maintain the momentum of economic growth in the South East. To justify its pro-growth stance the Crow report reminded its audience that the South East might be a high growth British region, but it was a mere thirtieth in the European regional growth league.

A potent symbol of the new regional planning era, the Crow report is one of many signs that economic growth in the South will be fostered rather than frustrated if central government has its way. There appears to be no cause, neither sustainability in the South nor deprivation in the North, that can rival the allure of higher economic growth as the top priority of Labour politicians. Given the profound southern-centric bias to economic growth in the UK it is difficult to see any government intervention being able to redress this bias, even if there were a political determination to do so. The following section will argue that, far from redressing the North–South divide, current regional policy initiatives are likely to exacerbate it because the main message from central government seems to be: 'every region for itself'.

Devolution and the elusive 'economic dividend'

One of the abiding assumptions of devolution campaigns in the UK over the past decade is the notion that regional devolution carries an 'economic dividend'. Rarely examined, and never quantified, this notion has been carefully cultivated by pro-devolution Labour politicians in both the English regions and the Celtic nations. Although the empirical evidence for the notion is highly contentious, what are the theoretical reasons for supposing that there might be such a dividend? In theory we might say that devolution has the potential to confer an 'economic dividend' because of the combined effect of the following: (a) it empowers local knowledge, without which localised learning is of little practical benefit; (b) it allows regions to design and deliver policies that are attuned to their own needs rather than the requirements of a centralised template; and (c) it helps to create the conditions for a more locally accountable and more effective system of governance (Morgan 2001). As we shall see later, however, there are equally compelling theoretical reasons to think that regional devolution carries economic *costs* rather than benefits.

The allure of the 'economic dividend' in the English regions

In the UK the notion of an 'economic dividend' has been most assiduously canvassed in the context of the campaign for regional devolution in the English regions, a campaign heavily influenced by two particular narratives. The first is what we might call the 'Celtic Advantage' narrative, that is the long-established and deeply held belief in the poorer English regions that the Celtic nations had secured tangible economic benefits from administrative devolution, particularly from their territorial ministers sitting in Cabinet and from the Scottish, Northern Irish and Welsh Development Agencies, the first of their kind in the UK. The poor English regions looked with envy as the Celtic nations were able to use their devolved governance systems to mobilise more substantial incentive packages (composed of regional selective assistance grants as well as subsidised land and training programmes), which gave them an edge in the fiercely competitive battle to attract foreign inward investment. The creation of the Celtic development agencies in 1976, that is 23 years before Regional Development Agencies were established in the English regions, enabled Northern Ireland, Scotland and Wales to offer investors lower transaction costs because their agencies acted as 'one stop shops' for all corporate inquiries, a potentially important weapon in locational tournaments for mobile investment. Although these benefits were real enough, it is perhaps understandable if they were exaggerated by the less well-endowed English regions. During the career of the Welsh Development Agency (WDA), for example, Wales became poorer not richer, so much so that its GDP per capita is less than 80 per cent of the UK average, a chastening reminder of the limits to what a Regional Development Agency (RDA) can accomplish on its own account. On the other hand, the economic situation in Wales would almost certainly have been far worse in the absence of the WDA (Morgan 1997b).

An equally important influence on the campaign for regional devolution in England was the European Union. Through their dealings with EU Structural Funds, the regional aid programme for poor regions in Europe, local and regional groups in England became increasingly conscious of their own institutional shortcomings. In particular they were struck by the fact that all innovative regions in the EU enjoy (among many other things) a measure of political devolution. Although this varies significantly from one member state to another, being most pronounced in federal countries such as Germany, this facility was perceived to have given these regions the potential to pursue more robust developmental strategies than was possible in unitary states, where there was little or no institutional capacity for collective action at the regional level (Crouch and Marquand 1989; Rodriguez-Pose 1996). In one variant of this narrative, the 'Innovative Region' narrative, particular attention is drawn to a region's institutional networks for learning, innovation and development, networks which facilitate trust, reciprocity and knowledge transfer (Storper 1997; Morgan 1997a; Cooke and Morgan 1998; Gertler and Wolfe 2002). Although this narrative neither isolates nor extols the role of regional government *per se* in the cocktail of factors which characterise innovative regions, this is precisely what some English advocates of regional devolution have done when they speak of the 'economic imperative' for political devolution (European Dialogue 1993; Murphy and Caborn 1996).

Animated by this intellectual climate a new regional policy coalition was created around John Prescott, the main champion of English devolution in the Labour Party. The vehicle for drafting Labour's new regional policy, and above all for making the *economic* case for regional devolution in England, was the Regional Policy Commission, chaired by the highly influential Bruce Millan, the former EU Commissioner of Regional Policy. The Millan Commission tapped into the key anxieties in England's sub-national economic development community, in particular the sense that regional policy was far too centralised, too top-down in design and delivery, and that this needed to be complemented by a bottom-up perspective. There was also a need to placate the English regions, many of which felt aggrieved and disadvantaged by the Celtic development agencies. Finally, there was a vague, but pervasive view that the English regions would get a better deal from the EU Structural Funds if they had a more coherent institutional voice at the regional level. In response to these anxieties the Millan Commission called for three important institutional innovations at the regional level in England: first, that Regional Development Agencies should be an integral part of English regional policy; second, that development agencies should be created in all regions rather than confined to the assisted area regions; and third, that indirectly elected regional chambers should be created to steer the development agencies and render them accountable to the regions (Regional Policy Commission 1996; Mawson 1997; Harding *et al.* 1999).

All three of these recommendations formed the basis of Labour's legislative agenda when it assumed office in 1997. The standard bearer for this new regional agenda remained John Prescott, the Deputy Prime Minister, and Richard Caborn, his loyal lieutenant at the Department of Environment, Transport and the Regions. The Prescott–Caborn team did more than anyone to propagate the notion that devolution carried an 'economic dividend'. Indeed, the key rationale for creating Regional Development Agencies (RDAs) in England, according to Prescott and Caborn, was to redress 'the economic deficit in the English regions', a reference to the fact that GDP per capita had fallen in every English region between 1992 and 1995 and that in all but two regions it was below the EU average (DETR 1997; Caborn 1999). Prescott and Caborn were acutely conscious of the shortcoming of their regional vision – in the short term the RDAs would add to a burgeoning 'democratic deficit' in the English regions, leaving the new agencies open to the charge of being centrally controlled quangos which were in, but not of, the regions where they operated. But in their longer term scenario, the 'democratic deficit' was portrayed as a transitional problem because, in the fullness of time, the indirectly elected regional chambers would be superseded by directly elected regional assemblies if there was sufficient popular demand (Harding *et al.* 1999).

Of the twin deficits identified above, the 'economic deficit' was always going to be the most intractable for the RDAs to redress. From the outset their main problem has been the chronic disjunction between their powers (which are modest) and their tasks (which are awesome). Raising the level of regional economic prosperity, as measured by GDP per capita, is a particularly difficult task for regional agencies which control less than 1 per cent of public expenditure in their regions. Miniscule budgets, modest powers and a staggering array of responsibilities, straddling economic development, social regeneration, rural renewal and environmental enhancement, suggest that the RDAs are seriously over-extended. In other words it is simply not credible to claim, as Caborn in particular has claimed, that Labour's new regional policy is creating 'empowered communities' in England which have the capacity to 'determine their own future' (Caborn 2000). These grandiose claims were partly predicated on the assumption that the English regions would acquire directly elected regional assemblies, but this vision was soundly rejected when the North-East region voted three-to-one against a regional assembly in November 2004 (Hetherington 2004). Hitherto considered to be the most likely to endorse an assembly, the North-East result will remove regional devolution from the political agenda for a generation at the very least.

Even with the full paraphernalia of regional assemblies it would be difficult to argue that the North–South divide was being addressed by Labour's new regional policy. But to claim, as the government claims, that it is addressing the divide in England through the creation of RDAs is disingenuous because such agencies have been established in every region – and treating unequals equally is not a strategy for promoting equality (Morgan 2002). On the heroic assumption that devolution has a benign effect across the board, then London and the southern regions, with their vastly superior economic advantages, will acquire the regional institutional capacity to help them *sustain* higher rates of growth, with the result that the South becomes even more decoupled from the North. With regional assemblies off the political agenda, at least for the time being, the English regions have lost the opportunity to discover whether devolution yields an 'economic dividend'.

The variable nature of the 'dividend' in the devolved territories

As the UK devolution process is most developed in Scotland, Wales and London, it is here that we should explore the question as to whether any kind of 'dividend' has been secured. Although the economic dimension is the main theme of this section, it is worth emphasising that devolution in Scotland and London was not primarily designed to secure an 'economic dividend'. As a matter of fact only in Wales was the 'economic dividend' elevated into one of the principal goals of devolution, second only to the main goal of creating a stronger 'voice' for Wales in the corridors of power in London and Brussels (Welsh Office 1997; Morgan and Rees 2001). The economic accent of the Welsh devolution campaign helps to explain why *economic development* policy is far more politicised in Wales compared to the other devolved territories. It also helps us to understand why so many *non-economic* policy domains – such as health, education, culture, transport and the environment for example – tend to be framed and evaluated in terms of their economic impact. In the remainder of this section I want to suggest that, while 'devolution dividends' can be discerned in all three territories, it is difficult to identify anything that might plausibly be called an '*economic* dividend' in any of them at this stage. Let us try to distil what seems to be the most distinctive 'dividends' in each of the devolved territories.

In the case of Scotland the campaign for a Scottish Parliament was first and foremost based on a 'claim of right' from a historic nation seeking to regain part of its lost statehood. With primary legislative powers and modest fiscal powers, the Scottish Parliament enjoys far more constitutional powers than the devolved administrations in Wales and London. Bolstering Scotland's constitutional package of powers is a historic financial settlement from central government that is the envy of every part of the UK – which is precisely what renders it vulnerable in the new post-devolution landscape. Given the left-of-centre political orientation of the Scottish Parliament the most important 'dividends' of devolution are to be found in the areas of social inclusion (such as free personal care for the elderly and opposition to student top-up fees) and social citizenship (such as a Freedom of Information policy that is much more robust than the English version). These 'dividends' sprang from policy divergences which reflected the fact that Scotland continues to embrace the social democratic values that the Labour government seems to have diluted in England (Keating 2005).

Nothing radically new has transpired on the economic front, not least because economic development accounts for as little as 5 per cent of the Scottish Parliament's overall budget. The most distinctive aspects of Scotland's economic development are the Business Birthrate Strategy (to increase new firm formation), the Scottish Science Strategy (to accelerate the commercialisation of the science base) and the Fresh Talent Initiative (to recruit the 'creative class' to Scotland). With the exception of the latter, which aims to promote a more entrepreneurial culture as well as redress population decline, these initiatives are legacies of the pre-devolution Scottish Office regime (Adams *et al.* 2005). By their very nature these strategies are designed to transform the cultural underpinnings of the Scottish economy, which is inevitably a long-term endeavour. Attempts to assess the direct impact of devolution on the Scottish economy have found nothing definitive, largely because of two well-known limitations:

- it is difficult to control fully for all influences other than devolution, and this could lead to effects being ascribed to devolution that were caused by other factors
- the timeframe for assessing the impact of devolution is based on just six years of experience, which is far too short a period to witness significant change.

These limitations led one study to argue that devolution may be a very significant political change, but in economic terms it has far less significance because even small changes are difficult to detect in the Scottish economy. Even in the longer term it seems that the impact of devolution on the Scottish economy 'is likely to be complex, subtle and difficult to measure' (Ashcroft *et al.* 2005).

If the economic impact of the devolution settlement is difficult to detect in Scotland, it might be even more elusive in Wales, where there was a much weaker settlement, with no primary legislative powers and no fiscal powers of any kind. Herein lies the great paradox of Welsh devolution: more is expected of the National Assembly for Wales, in terms of its economic impact, even though it has fewer constitutional powers than the Scottish Parliament, and this is entirely due to the different terms on which the devolution campaigns were fought in the two countries. Despite its limited powers the National Assembly has a number of important policy achievements to its credit, two of which deserve to be mentioned. First, it has designed a more robust public health strategy, which is second to none in importance in Wales, a country with the highest rates of limiting long-term illness in the UK, and the latter is one reason why the Welsh rate of economic inactivity is so high. Second, it has sought to incorporate sustainable development principles into all its policies and actions, as it is required to do under section 121 of the Government of Wales Act, the first time any government in the EU was legally required to promote sustainability. The Assembly Government has prioritised public procurement as one of the ways in which it will meet this obligation, an area where it has already won professional awards for its pioneering work. Although these two policy initiatives can legitimately claim to be achievements, as there was no precedent for either prior to devolution, it would be premature to call them 'dividends' because the full benefits have yet to emerge.

On the economic development front the most distinctive policy divergences since devolution are undoubtedly the decision to abolish the economic development quangos and the decision to subsidise the fees of Welsh-domiciled students studying in Wales, a move designed to broaden access to university and to stem the so-called 'brain-drain' of Welsh students to English universities. Of the two decisions the 'bonfire of the quangos' was by far the most controversial, reflecting as it did the centralising instincts of the Labour-controlled Assembly Government, which wanted to exert more political control over bodies such as the Welsh Development Agency and the Wales Tourist Board by merging them with the Assembly's civil service. Though popular with party activists, this decision induced deep disquiet in the business community on two counts: it was announced with zero consultation with any of the Assembly's so-called 'partners' and it fuelled fears about a growing politicisation of economic strategy in Wales (Morgan and Upton 2005). Ostensibly designed to render economic policy more accountable *and* more effective, the 'bonfire of the quangos' has rendered Wales the most state-centric of all the devolved territories in the UK (Cooke and Clifton 2005). For good or ill, the results of these policies will take years to manifest themselves, underlining the point that the impact of devolution is neither clear nor necessarily benign.

Being the only devolved territory in England is just one of the many unique features of London, a city which is undergoing a rate of growth without parallel either in the UK or in any other major European city. Since 1989 its population has increased by nearly 600,000, the equivalent of the capital absorbing a city the size of Sheffield, an increase fuelled in equal measure by natural increase in population and inward migration from overseas. With a current population of over 7.4 million, London's population is projected to exceed 8.1 million by 2016, the urban equivalent of absorbing a city the size of Leeds in the next decade or so. Equally significant employment growth is also forecast for the period to 2016, in stark contrast to the northern English cities, which prompted Ken Livingstone, the Mayor of London, to claim that 'London's growth is now by far the biggest regional issue and challenge in Britain' (Greater London Authority 2002).

Set up in 2000 the Greater London Authority consists of the London Assembly and the Mayor, a political system in which the latter leads on the 'statutory strategies' of transport, spatial development, economic development, environment and culture. Given the phenomenal pressures of growth it is hardly surprising that the London Plan, the Mayor's spatial development strategy, focuses so much on the challenge of transport and housing in the city. The most widely acclaimed 'devolution dividends' to date are undoubtedly the successful launch of the congestion charge and the renaissance of bus travel. In all probability the congestion charge would not have been introduced without the courage, indeed the audacity, of the Mayor, because it was perceived as too high risk for a risk-averse central government. Since its introduction in 2003, however, up to 70,000 fewer cars travel into central London every year, creating more demand for bus travel, which carried six million passengers in 2004, the highest total for 40 years. These transport policy 'dividends' have made a major contribution to the Mayor's goal of transforming London into a 'sustainable world city' (Greater London Authority 2004).

Re-styling himself as a 'London Nationalist' the Mayor wants London to be able to retain more of its wealth for itself because, as a world city, it makes a major contribution to the UK economy, including an estimated £20 billion a year to the national exchequer (GLA 2002). A key part of this strategy is to persuade other parts of the UK to recognise London's unique status and its unique problems:

> Even if placing a brake on London's economic and population growth was an option, it would be the wrong approach. London is internationally recognised alongside New York and Tokyo as a rare example of a true world city – a unique asset for the UK in an era of globalisation . . . London, sustained by adequate investment in its infrastructure, therefore can and must rise to the challenges posed by growth. But, first, this unique growth of London must be recognised both in terms of UK regional policy and strategies by the city's administrations.
>
> (GLA 2002)

The GLA is in effect saying that devolution can deliver an 'economic dividend' in London if, and only if, central government approves major investment schemes in the city, especially in transport infrastructure and affordable housing. The GLA cites the proposed East–West London CrossRail project as an example of a project which has been under discussion for the past decade. The Thames Gateway region in East London, Europe's largest and most ambitious regeneration scheme, also needs significant investment, says the GLA, if London is to accommodate population and employment growth. Even here then, in Europe's foremost growth zone, the 'economic dividend' of devolution is highly contingent on the actions of others.

The 'dirty little secret' about devolution

Until recently the pro-devolution literature in the UK was quite unequivocal that regional devolution carried an 'economic dividend' and, therefore, that it is 'compelling on both economic and democratic grounds' (Quin 2002). Reflecting on the UK evidence to date we can say that the notion of an 'economic dividend' was constructed in a highly tendentious manner to 'sell' the devolution programme of elected regional assemblies to the northern English regions. The fact that this programme failed to persuade the electorate in the North East, the poorest region in England, signalled in the clearest possible way that the 'economic dividend' was seen for the political rhetoric that it was. If the promise of devolution failed to resonate in the North East, what about the devolved territories where devolution is a practical political reality? A dispassionate analysis of the evidence would suggest that devolution can be credited with a number of positive achievements in Scotland, Wales and London, but nowhere can we discern anything that can plausibly be called a clear 'economic dividend' at this point in the process.

These findings should not really surprise us because the 'dirty little secret' about devolution is that the international evidence base for the supposed 'economic dividend' is at best ambiguous and at worst absent. No one has done more to clarify this point than Andres Rodriguez-Pose and his colleagues at the LSE. In a series of recent papers they have unearthed a fascinating paradox about devolution: they show that a 'devolutionary trend has swept the world', but they also show that this trend does not necessarily promote economic welfare (Rodrigeuz-Pose and Gill 2003; Rodriguez-Pose and Bwire 2005; Rodiguez-Pose and Gill 2005). On the basis of a six-country study they came to the following conclusion: 'Although devolution may indeed be associated with an increased degree of policy innovation, with a better capacity of governments to adapt policies to local needs – provided a developed civil society exists – and with greater transparency, it is difficult to directly associate these factors with increased economic performance' (Rodriguez-Pose and Gill 2005).

This is a profoundly unnerving conclusion when we think that devolution is being canvassed around the world as a step towards higher national economic growth or accelerated regional development. On the other hand, the more we expose the 'dirty little secret' the more we can begin to appreciate the complexities and vagaries of devolution: that it comes in many shapes and sizes, that its outcomes are contingent on many other factors, that its effects on equity, efficiency and development can be positive as well as negative, making bold generalisations both useless and dangerous (Morgan 2004).

Territorial justice in a polycentric polity

With the advent of democratic devolution the UK is making the awkward transition from a centralised to a polycentric polity. Of all the issues that will have to be addressed in the new governance landscape none is perhaps more important, or as challenging, as the issue of *territorial justice*. Although there is no single theoretical definition of territorial justice, it seems difficult to disagree with Harvey's re-statement of Rawlsian theory as 'a just distribution justly achieved' (Harvey 1973). In this final section I want to argue that in two crucial fields – namely regional policy and public expenditure – the UK fails to meet this or any other reasonable definition of territorial justice.

Long considered to be the touchstone of a government's commitment to territorial justice, as we have seen, UK regional policy has undergone major changes in scale and purpose in recent years. In terms of scale it has been significantly reduced relative to the classical post-war era and, in terms of purpose, it has been devolved to Regional Development Agencies to promote economic efficiency *within* regions, as opposed to the classical era, when its aim was to secure economic equity *between* regions. This transformation owes a great deal to the involvement of the Treasury, which successfully 'captured' the regional discourse and re-cast regional policy from a Keynesian welfare policy into a Schumpeterian development tool to enhance the UK's low productivity levels. The initial targets of the Regional Development Agencies in England were largely designed to raise GDP per capita in the regions so that the latter could reduce their 'economic deficits' relative to the EU average, a conception which suggests a system of regional autarky in which each region is a self-contained entity with its own balance sheet. To sustain this conception a new discourse of regional competitiveness has been spawned, at the heart of which is the spurious notion that 'everyone's a winner' (Bristow 2005). This was the discourse which the English Regional Development Agencies imbibed at birth, with the result that every agency planned to grow faster than the national average – a statistical impossibility (Robinson 1999; Tomaney *et al.* 2003).

Even if Labour's new regional policy succeeded in raising GDP per capita in each region, this would do little or nothing to redress the inter-regional inequalities at the heart of the North–South divide. Though it was presented as part of the solution by Labour ministers such as Prescott, devolution was perceived to be a problem even before it was defeated by the voters of the North East. The crux of the problem was ably summarised by the Alliance for Regional Aid when it said:

> The most important concern is the evident confusion between devolution to the regions and regional economic policy. Regional economic policy – that is, policies to narrow regional gaps in prosperity – require targeted measures that discriminate in favour of the weakest areas. Devolution, on the other hand, is about a shift in decision-making to the regions. In itself, it does not necessarily imply any discrimination in favour of the weakest regions or any convergence in their economic well-being. Indeed, if devolution were to imply that all regions were treated equally it would work against the objective of narrowing regional differences.
>
> (Alliance for Regional Aid, 2003)

Under pressure from its industrial heartlands in the North the Labour government eventually conceded that it had to formally acknowledge the problem of territorial justice. A small but significant concession came in 2002, when the Treasury committed the government to a new Public Service Agreement (PSA) target to make 'sustainable improvements in the economic performance of all English regions and over the long term reduce the persistent gap in growth rates between the regions' (HM Treasury 2002). As we can see, there are two targets rolled into one here – promoting growth in all regions *and* reducing the gap between them – and the latter is clearly the more difficult to achieve. Though formally committed to reducing the growth gap between North and South, the government insists that this goal must be achieved by raising the performance of the northern regions and not by containing the growth in the South – the mantra for which is 'levelling up, not levelling down' (HM Treasury 2001). To meet this new commitment the government is turning to the concept of the *city-region* to help the North catch up with the South, though this is unlikely to offset the most powerful spatial trend in the UK today – namely the growing domination of a 'London-centred, super-region' (SURF Centre 2004).

The significance of this commitment to territorial justice may be more apparent than real because, having willed the end, the government has failed to will the means. To achieve above average rates of growth the less prosperous regions will need more positive discrimination in the territorial allocation of public expenditure, but the government has already rejected this view, saying it 'does not accept the proposition that increased public funding to the less prosperous regions is a necessary condition to improve their prosperity' (ODPM 2003).

Putting it bluntly, territorial justice cannot be secured without fundamental reform of the mechanisms through which public expenditure is allocated to the nations and regions of the UK because, currently, these are based on 'a hotch-potch of badly designed formulae' which produce 'severe problems of inter-territorial equity' (McLean and McMillan 2003). The most contentious mechanism is the notorious Barnett formula, a population-based formula for allocating changes in public expenditure between the countries of the UK (HM Treasury 1997). What is most remarkable about this formula is that it has survived at all. When Joel Barnett introduced it in 1978 he had 'assumed its use would be temporary, until a more sophisticated method that took account of needs could be devised' (Barnett 2000). The fact that it is not a needs-based formula helps to explain some of the glaring anomalies – and the sense of injustice – in the current territorial allocation. Barnett himself drew attention to an example of 'terrible unfairness' when he highlighted the fact that GDP per capita in the North East of England was 13 per cent below Scotland when Labour came to power, but per capita public expenditure was 19 per cent higher in the latter (Barnett 2000). In a polycentric polity, where public expenditure flows across different levels of government (as opposed to the internal flows within a single government in a centralised polity) there is a stronger requirement for the territorial allocation system to be re-legitimated, and this in turn can only be done in the context of a more credible needs assessment exercise (Heald *et al.* 1998).

The shortcomings of regional policy and public expenditure mean that the territorial inequalities at the heart of the North–South divide will continue to haunt the new landscape of post-devolution Britain. As a geo-political entity the UK owes its longevity to many factors, not least to a judicious combination of social solidarity and territorial justice in a centralised polity committed to 'one nation' policies. A polycentric polity will unleash new forms of territorial rivalry and, if these 'dark sides' of devolution are to be contained within tolerable limits, a new and stronger system of territorial justice will have to be fashioned. The key question is whether the UK can secure the progressive potential of democratic devolution without sacrificing the 'one nation' ethos of the 1945 welfare settlement.

Acknowledgement

The author would like to thank Professor Charlie Jeffery, who originally commissioned this paper as an article for a special issue of *Publius, the Journal of Federalism* (36, 1, 2006, 189–206), as well as for his judicious management of the ESRC Devolution and Constitutional Change research programme.

References

Adams, J., Robinson, P. and Visor, A. (2003). *A New Regional Policy for the United Kingdom*. London: Institute of Public Policy Research.
Adams, J. and Schmuecker, K. (2005). *Devolution in Practice II: Public Policy Differences in the UK*. London: Institute of Public Policy Research.

Alliance for Regional Aid (2003). *Memorandum to ODPM Select Committee Inquiry into Reducing Regional Disparities in Prosperity.* London: House of Commons.

Amin, A., Massey, D. and Thrift, N. (2003). *Decentering the Nation: A Radical Approach to Regional Inequality.* London: Catalyst.

Ashcroft, B., McGregor, P. and Swales, J. (2005). *Is Devolution Good for the Scottish Economy? A Framework for Analysis.* Swindon: Devolution Briefing No. 26, Economic and Social Research Council.

Barlow, Sir M. (1940). *Report of the Royal Commission on the Distribution of Industrial Population.* London: HMSO.

Barnett, J. (2000). 'The Barnett formula: how a temporary expedient became permanent', *New Economy* 7 (2): 69–71.

Beatty, C., Fothergill, S. and Powell, R. (2005). *Twenty Years On: Has The Economy of the Coalfields Recovered?* England: CRESR, Sheffield Hallam University.

Bristow, G. (2005). 'Everyone's a 'winner': problematising the discourse of regional competitiveness'. *Journal of Economic Geography* 5: 285–304.

Caborn, R. (1999). 'Restarting the regional engine'. *Local Government Chronicle*, 1 April.

Caborn, R. (2000). 'Introduction', in E. Balls and J. Healey (eds) *Towards a New Regional Policy*, 3–5. London: The Smith Institute.

Cooke, P. and Morgan, K. (1998). *The Associational Economy: Firms, Regions and Innovation.* Oxford: Oxford University Press.

Cooke, P. and Clifton, N. (2005). 'Visionary, precautionary and constrained: "varieties of devolution" in the economic governance of the devolved UK territories', *Regional Studies*, 39, 437–451.

Crouch, C. and Marquand, D. (1989) *Britain out of Step in Europe?* Blackwell: Oxford.

Crow, S. (1999). *Regional Planning Guidance for the South East of England.* Guildford: Government Office for the South East.

DETR (1997) 'John Prescott promises a radical approach to the regions', Department of the Environment, Transport and the Regions, press release 194, 30 May (1997).

European Dialogue. (1993). *Power to the People? Economic Self-Determination and the Regions.* London: European Dialogue.

Fothergill, S. (2001). 'The true scale of the regional problem in the UK'. *Regional Studies* 35: 241–46.

Gertler, M. and Wolfe, D. (eds) (2002). *Innovation and Social Learning.* London: Palgrave.

Glyn, A. and Erdem, E. (1999). *The UK Jobs Gap.* Minutes of Evidence, House of Commons Education and Employment Committee.

Greater London Authority (2002). *Planning for London's Growth.* London: GLA.

Greater London Authority (2004). *The London Plan: The Mayor's Spatial Development Strategy for Greater London.* London: GLA.

Green, A. and Owen, D. (1998). *Where are the Jobless?* Bristol: Policy Press.

Harding, A. Evans, R. Parkinson, M. and Garside, P. (1996). *Regional Government in Britain: An Economic Solution?* Bristol: Policy Press/Joseph Rowntree.

Harding, A. Wilks-Heeg, S. and Hutchins, M. (1999). 'Regional Development Agencies and English regionalisation: the question of accountability'. *Environment and Planning C: Government and Policy* 17 (6): 669–83.

Harding, A. (2000). *Is There A 'Missing Middle' in English Governance?* London: New Local Government Network.

Harvey, D. (1973). *Social Justice and the City.* London: Edward Arnold.

Heald, D., Geaughan, N. and Robb, C. (1998). 'Financial arrangements for UK devolution'. *Regional & Federal Studies* 8 (1): 3–52.

Hetherington, P. (2004). 'Defeat halts Prescott's push for devolution' *The Guardian*, 6 November (2004).

H.M. Treasury (1997). Memorandum to House of Commons Treasury Committee, *The Barnett Formula*, HC 341. London: Stationery Office.

H.M. Treasury (2001). *Productivity in the UK 3: The Regional Dimension*. London: HM Treasury/DTI.

H.M. Treasury (2002). *Spending Review: Public Service Agreements White Paper.* London: HM Treasury.

Keating, M. (2005). *The Government of Scotland: Public Policy after Devolution*. Edinburgh: Edinburgh University Press.

Mandelson, P. (2001). *Regional Policy and the North-East Economy*. London: Campaign for the English Regions.

Massey, D. (1984). *Spatial Divisions of Labour*. London: Macmillan.

Mawson, J. (1997). 'The English regional debate', in J. Bradbury and J. Mawson (eds) *British Regionalism and Devolution*. London: Jessica Kingsley.

McLean, I. and McMillan, A. (2003). 'The distribution of public expenditure across the UK regions'. *Fiscal Studies* 24 (1): 45–71.

Morgan, K. (1985). 'Regional regeneration in Britain: the territorial imperative and the conservative state'. *Political Studies* 4: 560–77.

Morgan, K. (1997a). 'The learning region: institutions, innovation and regional renewal'. *Regional Studies*. 31 (5): 491–503.

Morgan, K. (1997b). 'The regional animateur: taking stock of the Welsh development agency'. *Regional & Federal Studies* 7 (2): 70–94.

Morgan, K. (2001). 'The new territorial politics: rivalry and justice in post-devolution Britain'. *Regional Studies* 35 (4): 343–8.

Morgan, K. (2002). 'The English question: regional perspectives on a fractured nation'. *Regional Studies* 36 (7): 797–810.

Morgan, K. (2004). 'Sustainable regions: governance, innovation and scale'. *European Planning Studies* 12 (6): 871–89.

Morgan, K. and Mungham, G. (2000). *Redesigning Democracy: The Making of the Welsh Assembly*. Bridgend: Seren.

Morgan, K. and Rees, G. (2001). 'Learning by doing: devolution and the governance of economic development in Wales', in P. Chaney *et al.* (eds). *New Governance-New Democracy?* Cardiff: University of Wales Press.

Morgan, K. and Upton, S. (2005). *Culling the Quangos: The New Governance and Public Service Reform in Wales*. Papers in Planning Research.

Murphy, P. and Caborn, R. (1996). 'Regional government: an economic imperative', in S. Tindale (ed.), 184–221. *The State and the Nations*. London: IPPR.

Murdoch, J. (2000). 'Space against time: competing rationalities in planning for housing'. *Transactions of the Institute of British Geographers* 25: 03–19.

Office of the Deputy Prime Minister (2003). *Government Response to the ODPM Select Committee Report Reducing Regional Disparities in Prosperity*, Cm. 5958. London.

Quin, J. (2002). 'Introduction', *Democratic Regions*. Campaign for the English Regions. London: CFER.

Regional Policy Commission (1996). *Renewing the Regions: Strategies for Regional Economic Development*. Sheffield: Sheffield Hallam University.

Robinson, P. (1999) 'Comparing the regions'. *New Economy* 6 (3): 176–78.

Rodriguez-Pose, A. (1996) 'Growth and institutional change: the influence of the Spanish regionalisation process on economic performance', *Environment and Planning C: Government and Policy* 14, 1, 71–87.

Rodriguez-Pose, A. and Gill, N. (2003). 'The global trend towards devolution and its implications'. *Environment and Planning C: Government and Policy* 21: 333–51.

Rodriguez-Pose, A. and Bwire, A. (2005). 'The economic (in)efficiency of devolution',
Environment and Planning A.

Rodriguez-Pose, A. and Gill, N. (2005). 'On the 'economic dividend' of devolution', *Regional
Studies.*

Rokkan, S. and Urwin, D. (eds) (1982). *The Politics of Territoriality: Studies in European Regionalism.*
London: Sage.

Storper, M (1997) *The Regional World: Territorial Development in a Global Economy.* Guildford
Press.

SURF Centre (2004). *Releasing the National Economic Potential of Provincial City-Regions: the
rationale for and implications of a 'Northern Way' growth strategy.* An ODPM New Horizons
Study, SURF Centre, University of Salford.

Tomaney, J., Benneworth, P. and Pike, A. (2003). *Memorandum to the ODPM Select Committee
Inquiry into Reducing Regional Disparities in Prosperity.* London: House of Commons.

Welsh Office. (1997). *A Voice for Wales.* Cardiff: Welsh Office.

9 Reconstructing regional development and planning in Scotland and Wales

Greg Lloyd and Deborah Peel

In political terms, devolution in Scotland and Wales has been perceived as contributing to a greater assertion of territorial identity, confidence, and nationhood (McCrone 1994), and the promotion of greater distinctiveness (Bond *et al.* 2003). It has enabled the transformation of established territorial administrations into a new territorial politics (Jeffery 2007). It is part of a European-wide trend of reforming government to accommodate national and cultural diversities; to respond to pressures for democratisation; and to adapt to changing functional economic and social needs (Keating 2006). Devolution also has important implications with respect to promoting new forms of public policy design and implementation (Mooney and Williams 2006). In practice, devolution has been implemented differentially across Scotland and Wales. This is a reflection of specific regional, political, economic, and institutional conditions and capacities (Allmendinger *et al.* 2005). In these circumstances, history and experience may combine to inform different kinds of regional experimentation.

The principal question considered in this chapter is whether the creation of a Scottish Parliament and National Assembly for Wales has enabled Scotland and Wales to better address their respective internal economic and territorial problems. The regional development and planning challenges in Scotland and Wales reflect their specific economic, industrial and corporate histories. The structural forces for change include processes of global competition, industrial and corporate restructuring and emergent patterns of investment and disinvestment. In addition, locational factors, including their respective peripheral locations in the UK and in Europe, have created further cost and accessibility disadvantages. These have combined to create significant challenges. Moreover, changing political economies have had important policy effects in both territories in changing the balance of state-market-civil relations and in promoting a new modernising imperative. These regional development issues have been evident for some time, and, notwithstanding different interventions to address them, have persisted.

The key issue in analysis is whether the devolved institutions have taken the opportunity to reform institutional arrangements and policies to address these challenges – particularly through the formulation of national spatial planning strategies. Such strategies can aim to integrate economic development and land use planning, and innovate around spatial planning arrangements so as to secure broader political ambitions concerning sustainable development. Such ambitions must necessarily relate to the broad ambition of seeking to gain a regional dividend; a concept which refers to the ability of Wales and Scotland to better address the specific economic and spatial imbalances and conflicts within their respective territorial spaces. A regional dividend may be variously understood as bringing together the cohesion expectations of Europe, the stability ambitions of the UK Government, and the economic aspirations of the nation-regions themselves. Following Morgan (2006), however, an assessment of the balance between economic equity and territorial justice between nations and regions in seeking a regional dividend must also be alert to the changing processes and institutional contexts within each particular regional space. In Wales, for example, devolution was initially seen as offering considerable potential for the devising of a more distinctive approach to improve its planning and governance arrangements (Tewdwr-Jones 2001). It promised the opportunity in land use planning to depart from previous conjoined approaches in England and Wales and to construct policies for Wales alone. In contrast, in Scotland, even before devolution there had been separate planning legislation, meaning that devolution allowed for further development from a more advanced starting point.

However, a generally optimistic line of reasoning has been contested; raising questions as to how far the principles of autonomy and modernisation have cascaded down into post-devolution governance arrangements and policy design (McConnell 2006). To what extent, in practice, has devolution enabled a greater scalar and territorial sensitivity in government policy to the different parts of each spatial economy? This chapter seeks to answer this question. The first section considers the changing perceptions of what is involved in regional development and the manner in which regional development problems in Scotland and Wales have been understood in terms of the deficiency model. The second, third and fourth sections then explore the ways in which the devolved administrations have addressed their regional development arrangements, their philosophies of strategic regional governance and ideas associated with spatial planning and territorial cohesion.

Attention is drawn to the emergence of a new spatial awareness articulated directly in the Wales Spatial Plan (Welsh Assembly Government 2004a) and the National Planning Framework for Scotland (Scottish Executive 2004a), as well as indirectly through public policy at large. We argue that these spatial planning approaches illustrate the ways in which both Wales and Scotland are seeking to redress their inherited governance deficits, to devise appropriate strategic planning frameworks to better co-ordinate intra-regional investment and development decisions, and to provide ways of resolving sub-regional conflicts in infrastructure and investment. The new emphasis on spatial planning allows for a stronger appreciation of the uneven circumstances and potentials across each economy. Spatial planning has also permitted the joining up of local strategies and policies. Both Wales and Scotland have benefited from their pre-devolution experiences with respect to economic development, land use planning and partnership working. Both have realised important strategic planning advances. Although at this stage in the life-cycle of devolution it would be premature to interpret the impact of these policy innovations, this chapter explores the ways in which various building-blocks are being laid down in order to secure a potential regional dividend in the future.

Changing perceptions of regional development and the regional problem

Traditionally, the discourse and practice of regional development and planning has served to address perceived differential economic performances within the national (UK) economy (Tomlinson 2005). Key differences relate to relative rates of unemployment, investment, new firm formation and economic growth across the UK (Armstrong and Taylor 2000). Wales and Scotland may be considered emblematic of what was previously understood as the established regional economic problem in the UK. In particular, their relative political, geographical and institutional peripheralities were important considerations in understanding the detailed consequences of geo-political and corporate change (Danson 1997). This meant that there were strong structural considerations behind Wales and Scotland's under-performance when measured against the UK national position. Moreover, within Wales and Scotland there were marked differences in economic activity. Their specific urban-rural morphologies, inherited settlement patterns and transportation networks, and the changing functional relations around metropolitan regions, added more layers to be taken into account when devising appropriate economic governance arrangements (Alden 2003). Before devolution, in the context of a relatively centralised political administration, regional development policies were initially devised to address the performance of lagging regions, among which Wales and Scotland were counted. Such approaches tended to be relatively 'top-down' in approach, although attempts were made to ameliorate this through the introduction of regional and local development agencies (Cooke and Morgan 1998). In effect, regional economic differentials were managed through the provision of various financial and regulatory incentives in order to secure national efficiency gains in labour and investment markets.

Today, however, regional development policies are devised in the context of different state-market-civil relations (Lloyd and Peel 2005), and need to reflect a new scalar sensitivity to the needs of individual regions (Allmendinger and Tewdwr-Jones 2006). Contemporary assessments of what is meant by a regional dividend embrace a broader understanding of territorial well-being, involving its social, economic, environmental, and democratic dimensions. Indeed, devolution is part of the broader reconfiguration of regional sensitivity, which allows for an approach to uneven economic performance in a manner which may be more knowledgeable of the changes taking place. New regionalist thinking has strengthened the arguments for elaborating more coherent institutional frameworks at the regional level. These inform an understanding of the potential that may be secured under devolution for the management of economic and spatial change. Indeed, the different processes of industrial, corporate, and spatial restructuring have questioned the use of the traditional nation-state as the appropriate unit of activity in the context of global competitiveness (Bond and McCrone 2004). This has led to a greater interest in a more explicit regionalism in public policy design and implementation (Barnes and Ledebur 1998), and across Europe ideas of spatial planning and territorial cohesion have informed the preparation of regional spatial strategies (Jensen and Richardson 2006). Significantly, the advocacy of regionalism finds particular receptivity where there is evidence of active nationalist sensitivities (Morgan 2006). This may be considered of particular importance to both Wales and Scotland. Again, their historical experiences and ideological preferences assume some importance in devising their own particular regional economic practices (Skelcher 2000).

At the onset of devolution, notwithstanding the effects of previous regional policy, there was clear evidence of the continuing existence of what was considered to be a regional problem in Wales and Scotland. This persistence of endemic economic structural and locational weaknesses may be understood in terms of geography and accessibility, ineffective policy and agency activity, or deficits in the governance arrangements for regional development and planning practice. It is useful, however, to focus on three principal deficits in economic governance which had developed and which served to limit the ability of pre-devolution Wales and Scotland to realise an effective regional dividend. These provide the metrics for understanding whether devolution could deliver a regional dividend.

First, there was evidence of a territorial deficit. Top-down approaches were based on a selective delineation of areas eligible for UK regional policy assistance and European structural funding. This did not provide a comprehensive coverage of Wales and Scotland but concentrated on providing financial support in those areas experiencing relatively concentrated unemployment. These included the former mining valleys in Wales, and the heavy industrial zones of West Central Scotland. Regional assistance did not take account of the emerging patterns of investment elsewhere in the economy, and the inter-relations between the different processes of change. This territorial deficit was further accentuated by the dysfunctional jurisdictions of the various development agencies and local authorities. In effect, regional interventions were not connected in policy or institutional terms, nor were the areas over which they were implemented necessarily coterminous with local government boundaries or land use development planning arrangements. In Tayside, for example, the local development agency operated with three local authorities and two strategic development plans. In Fife, in contrast, the local development agency worked alongside one local authority and one strategic development plan. This resulted in a selective and fragmented map of sub-regionalism both in Wales and Scotland (Lloyd 1997). Fragmentation meant that there was a tendency to secure local dividends through individual area-based initiatives and development projects, which diluted the realisation of an overall potential regional dividend. Devolution offered the potential to be relatively more sensitive to the composition and relations of each territorial system.

Second, there was evidence of a parallel institutional deficit in the arrangements for economic governance. The Regional Development Agencies tended to operate in relative isolation from local authorities, and there was little evidence of comprehensive joint working around industrial interventions and local level land use planning. There were some important exceptions to this, for example with respect to the design and implementation of individual urban regeneration projects and partnerships between development agencies and local authorities. Yet, these important urban schemes were local in scale. Furthermore, the generally disjointed institutional arrangements were exacerbated by relatively limited integration between individual policy sectors, such as health, education and economic development, the fragmented provision of strategic infrastructure provision, and the management of different land use planning jurisdictions (Tewdwr-Jones 2002). In essence, individual initiatives and activities were not connected to wider thinking and practice. For example, decisions around the provision of industrial land for inward investment were not necessarily linked to the allocation of the required residential land, the provision of supporting services, and infrastructure. It follows that the limited inter-organisational working did not facilitate a comprehensive institutional framework. In addition, the lack of institutional integration was exacerbated during the 1980s and 1990s, when the hollowing out of the state and the expansion of the quasi-state led to further fragmentation in regional governance (Sullivan and Skelcher 2002). A case in point is the break-up of the responsibilities for water and sewerage in the mid 1990s. In Wales, the sector was privatised, and in Scotland new agencies were created to provide a separate infrastructure provision that was nonetheless fundamental to both economic development and land use planning agendas. The institutional deficit further eroded the capacity to realise more holistic objectives.

Finally, there was a strategic deficit. Bruton and Nicholson (1985) pointed to the limited strategic planning practice and management evident in regional development and planning arrangements in the UK. Attempts at regional experimentation in land use planning for Scotland through the development of a strategic planning framework suggested an attempt to build an appropriate apparatus to deal with sub-national issues. National Planning Guidelines as well as regional reports demonstrated a tradition of strategic thinking in policy and planning (McDonald 1977). This experiment in 'active regionalism' crossed over between the emerging 'corporate' thinking in local government and the then prevailing statutory land use planning system. In effect, it represented an early argument for enabling effective integrated working across the public sector as a whole. However, notwithstanding the positive steps to develop a strategic approach to inform local interventions and integrate land use planning with economic development, this learning experience was not allowed to flourish. Changes in political priorities and local government reorganisation served to limit the full potential of the strategic planning idea. This was subsequently identified as creating a 'strategic vacuum' in sub-national policy and practice in Scotland which further weakened the potential of economic development and regional planning initiatives (Lloyd 1997). Harris *et al.* (2002) identified a similar outcome in Wales. This strategic deficit in regional development and planning practice prior to devolution was particularly evident in terms of restricted institutional capacity, learning, and leadership in both Wales and Scotland.

Any discussion, however, around a deficiency model can only offer a partial interpretation. Clearly, these deficits were not free-standing, and tended to be self-reinforcing and intertwined in practice. In effect, the territorial, institutional and strategic limitations of regional development and planning governance arrangements prior to devolution restricted potential achievements in employment creation, inward investment, and new firm formation. Moreover, the emphasis on securing local dividends further limited achieving an overall effect. This argument tends to diminish the learning effects arising from the regional and strategic planning processes that had taken place. There were valuable lessons gained through strategic planning innovation, yet the potential was circumvented by changing political and ideological contexts. Clearly, the strategic approach associated with land use planning guidance and the work of development agencies created an awareness of how this could be further developed. Devolution may be viewed as representing an important political innovation which has brought with it a relative autonomy to address the regional problem, and to secure a dividend through more sensitive and improved working. It offered an opportunity to devise more appropriate regional and economic governance arrangements to address these institutional, strategic and territorial deficits; and to more clearly assert the new political objectives which were associated with devolution.

Developments in strategic regional governance

One of the key issues following devolution was the extent to which institutional arrangements in strategic regional governance were sufficiently developed to address these perceived deficiencies. Prior to devolution, the arrangements for managing both Scotland and Wales in terms of their respective spatial economies were broadly similar. Both operated within the broader Westminster framework, yet there were certain differences. These arrangements comprised the (then) Scottish Office and Welsh Office, their respective Regional Development Agencies and local authorities. As already noted, the development agencies were responsible for local and regional economic development within Wales and Scotland, and local authorities discharged the statutory land use planning functions. Prior to devolution, these tended to be relatively parallel activities, and there were some marginal differences in practice between Wales and Scotland. Following devolution, while these elements have remained broadly in place, there would appear to be evidence of more joined-up relations between land use planning and economic development activities (Lloyd and Peel 2005). Different historical experiences and practices have meant that there are some continuing differences between the threading of economic development and land use planning in the two countries. Yet in both Wales and Scotland innovation to develop national spatial planning and a focus on the political objective of sustainable development have represented common themes.

Prior to devolution, both Wales and Scotland relied heavily on their respective development agencies to direct economic development policy (Morgan and Henderson 1997). The Welsh Development Agency, the Development Board for Rural Wales, the Scottish Development Agency, and the Highlands and Islands Development Board were specifically designed to better focus on the needs of their respective regional territories. These were established in the 1960s and 1970s and had matured over time in response to changing economic and territorial conditions

(Cooke 1989). Importantly, the use of the regional development agency approach at that time reflected a renaissance in broader UK-wide regional economic planning practice (Glasson 1992).The Regional Development Agencies were intended to provide an informed 'bottom-up' complement to broader UK wide regional policy. In particular, these arrangements may be seen as a direct attempt at securing a more territorially and institutionally sensitive response to the then prevailing conditions in Wales and Scotland.

Over time, changes were made to the remit and activities of the individual development agencies. In Scotland, for example, the Scottish Development Agency was re-launched as Scottish Enterprise, and the Highlands and Islands Development Board as Highlands and Islands Enterprise. The nomenclature reflected the prevailing neo-liberal ideas of the 1990s, and, although the Welsh Development Agency retained its original name, all of the agencies underwent significant operational changes to assert a stronger emphasis on business development and entrepreneurship. Following devolution, the development agencies have been retained, although there are ongoing managerial changes to their scope and operation.The Welsh Development Agency, for example, has been internalised into the Welsh Assembly Government (Cooke and Clifton 2005).The Scottish equivalents remain as stand-alone agencies but are increasingly being reviewed in terms of their administrative structures, funding and relations with broader planning and governance arrangements.

The experience of the development agencies prior to devolution was important. In general terms, their activities tended to concentrate on specific activities or areas. For instance, the Welsh Development Agency developed an emphasis on the attraction of inward investment to enhance overall regional economic performance. The exclusively economic focus on individual initiatives and selected sites tended to ignore the associated environmental and land use planning contexts (Phelps and Tewdwr-Jones 1999). Meanwhile, the Scottish Development Agency designed and managed a limited number of area-based initiatives across urban lowland Scotland, such as in Glasgow and Dundee. These represented specific urban regeneration and economic development projects. As a consequence, in practice the regional dividend consisted of securing a number of selected local dividends (Tewdwr-Jones 2002; Danson *et al*. 1993). Prior to devolution, the development agencies did not secure a comprehensive approach to their regional constituencies. Nonetheless, the work of the development agencies demonstrated the importance of promoting partnership working with other bodies, local authorities and the private sector.This further encouraged an awareness of the advantages of promoting a strategic approach to economic development and land use planning agendas. This has emerged as a bedrock for the subsequent development of strategic thinking following devolution.

In terms of land use planning, there were some differences between arrangements in Wales and Scotland prior to devolution. This reflected the fact that Scotland had its own statutory land use planning legislation, while Wales was conjoined with that of England. In both Wales and Scotland, however, local authorities discharged their land use planning responsibilities through the preparation of

development plans and the exercise of regulations over land and property development. This system was designed to be discretionary and plan-led, and promoted an
emphasis on the local. The development plan was intended to provide the basis for
'consistent decision making' in different localities and, in preparing them, local
planning authorities had to take account of national policies, specific local characteristics, and the views of the various constituencies of interest. Development plans
operated at two complementary levels – the strategic and the local. Development
plans have remained central to the respective planning systems notwithstanding the
post-devolution interest in the modernisation of the land use planning system, and
the move to establish spatial planning frameworks. The development plans remain
as an important bulwark of governance arrangements in both Wales and Scotland.

Historical experiences and practices are important in enabling both Wales and
Scotland to capitalise on the opportunities afforded them through devolved governance. Of particular interest here is the earlier development of strategic planning
as a context to the emphasis on land use planning practices. Arguably this experience with strategic agendas has informed the subsequent post-devolved innovation
in spatial planning. Initially the Scottish Office led the way with respect to defining a strategic planning approach through its preparation of National Planning
Guidelines in 1974 (Lloyd 1997). These were introduced to address the supra-local
planning and development issues associated with onshore investments around
offshore oil and gas activities. Over time, however, the advantages of providing a
strategic context within which local land use planning decisions could be exercised
were recognised. As a consequence, the strategic approach was extended to other
key development sectors, such as retailing, housing and agriculture.

The strategic planning approach subsequently matured into the Scottish Planning
Policy Statements which still assert a portfolio of planning policy guidance on
selected topics that are considered to have a strategic interest. The emphasis on a
national strategic perspective reflected a concern to address the dynamics of corporate and industrial restructuring in Scotland. It was held that a strategic planning
approach – a national indicative plan – would strengthen existing regional planning
practice. The strategic planning approach had been taken up also in England and
Wales. Prior to devolution, planning policy for Wales was provided through the joint
Department of the Environment/Welsh Office planning policy guidance note
series. Indeed, in 1996, Wales began to develop separate planning policy guidance to
better reflect its specific planning conditions. The recognition that a strategic framework could provide greater certainty for local land use planning, and provide
opportunities for more integrated working with, for example, economic development activities, was an important lesson for subsequent practice.

The National Assembly of Wales inherited most of the duties, powers, and
responsibilities which were formerly held by the Secretary of State for Wales. While
it has no powers to make or amend primary legislation, it can make and amend
policy and secondary legislation, which is of significance to the implementation of
the land use planning system. It operates within legislation designed for England
and Wales, although Section 6 of the Planning and Compulsory Purchase Act 2004
provides the opportunity for the Welsh Assembly Government to devise land use

planning arrangements appropriate to its territorial needs. There was an early recognition of the need for a strategic planning framework for the Welsh economy, which would secure wider integration of agencies, sectors and local planning. The legislative provision allowed the Welsh Assembly Government to innovate with respect to spatial planning and devise local planning measures deemed more appropriate to its scale, territory and development conditions.

In Scotland, the Scottish Executive assumed responsibility for land use planning, and has the opportunity to devise primary legislation. Following devolution, the new Scottish Executive embarked on a modernisation of its land use planning system. This was part of a strategy to promote the long-term growth of the Scottish economy, encourage private sector investment and business activity, provide support for productivity growth, and foster an enterprise culture. The Scottish Executive made a clear commitment to improving the land use planning system in order to strengthen the involvement of communities, to speed up decisions, to better reflect local views, and to allow for quicker public sector investment decisions. This built on a consultation paper published just prior to devolution which flagged up the importance of land use planning in the new public policy agenda. It asserted that a key priority was to modernise the system to enable it to secure the political objective of sustainable development. In short, the received wisdom at this time suggested strongly that there was considerable scope for the improved management of the land use planning process (Peel and Lloyd 2006). A subsequent consultation paper sought to address concerns relating to the revitalisation of the system. This addressed the perceived inability of the planning system to be positive and proactive and to make adequate provision for land and property development and secure appropriate public involvement. Significantly, the process of change emphasised the lack of effective strategic planning in the land use planning process (Scottish Executive 2001). Subsequently, the Scottish Executive sought to reform the shape and structures of planning across a range of scales of intervention and activity, and to address strategic spatial planning and local development management arrangements (Peel and Lloyd 2007). This led to the Planning etc. (Scotland) Act 2006 which put in place a number of measures to make the links between economic development and land use planning stronger.

Overall, it is clear that the respective land use planning experiences and circumstances in Wales and Scotland prior to devolution were followed by different innovations and changes after devolution. This reflects the importance of territorial sensitivity as the devolved administrations have devised measures to better reflect their specific circumstances. A common theme, however, has been the shared perception of a need for a strategic framework. The opportunity provided by devolution to address major territorial and institutional deficits has been acknowledged and has led to significant developments in the framework of strategic regional governance.

Strategic visions: co-operation and competition?

The next key issue is the general philosophy that has informed strategic regional development in each country. In many ways they appear to have converged in Scotland

and Wales. For example, it would appear that partnership working has been a common theme to both Scotland and Wales. The development of policy has been the subject of intense processes of consultation and collaboration. In addition, the ambitions of modernisation have prompted a more inclusive and participatory development of policy priorities in meeting the objectives of sustainable development (Scottish Executive 2005; Welsh Assembly Government 2004b). There has been an explicit adoption of sustainable development as a political ambition, and this has served to influence the design of other policies concerned with securing economic development, promoting social inclusion, and sustaining environmental quality. An important mediating process has been the modernisation of the arrangements for devolved governance (Welsh Assembly Government 2005; Scottish Executive 2005). This has involved measures to promote greater integration in the delivery of public services (Scottish Executive 2004b; Welsh Assembly Government 2004b). Such positive attempts to champion an approach to regional distinctiveness and performance, together with efforts to facilitate a relatively more inclusive approach to policy formulation are characteristic of the post-devolution period in both Wales and Scotland.

The devolved institutions in Scotland and Wales also appear to have adopted broadly similar approaches in a variety of other ways. Both, for example, have moved to promote the branding of a national identity for international purposes, differentiated by the distinctiveness of their respective histories, cultures and interpretation of identity (Ellis 2003) This assertion of distinctiveness has been evident in a variety of policy areas (Welsh Assembly Government 2005; Scottish Executive 2004b, 2007). There has also been an explicit attempt to recast the identity of government and promote it as following a more collaborative approach to public administration. In Wales, there has been an emphasis on establishing a new form of democratic government during the immediate post-devolution period. This was subsequently followed by a concern with the appropriate design and delivery of public services. In introducing the Welsh Assembly Government's (2004b) vision for public services, for example, the First Minister for Wales distinguished between two basic models held to be appropriate for designing efficient and effective local governance. These models of institutional structures and processes promoted the competing ideas of collaboration and competition. The preferred approach in Wales has been that which promotes scale economies through more effective co-operation and co-ordination between public sector agencies. In Scotland, a similar concern with promoting a collaborative notion of public administration and delivery of services at the local level led to the introduction of community planning. This illustrates a change to local governance based on joint working and integrated practices for the delivery of local services (Illsley and Lloyd 2000). This community planning approach built on earlier experiences in local government of strategic thinking.

In both Wales and Scotland, the influence of modernisation on regional development and planning has also been illustrated in approaches to devising economic governance arrangements. Thus, the Welsh Assembly Government (2005) revisited its strategic framework for economic development to reflect three dimensions. First, it set out to reassert its aspirations for securing growth and development in the Welsh economy, particularly with respect to creating employment and quality jobs.

Second, it merged the principal agencies of economic governance and reduced the quasi state (Welsh Assembly Government 2004b). Third, it made an explicit attempt to integrate economic development policy with social and environmental policy. The Scottish Executive's (2004b) framework for economic development similarly asserts priorities for education, transportation and electronic infrastructures, enterprise support, and attracting foreign direct investment (Lloyd and Peel 2005).

However, a note of caution needs to be struck. Although these developments would appear to be very similar, they have been characterised in different ways (Cooke and Clifton 2005). The Scottish approach, for example, has been described as a relatively 'visionary' one when compared to Wales which is seen as involving a relatively more 'precautionary' economic development strategy. This reflects the different emphases placed on reconfiguring the arrangements for economic governance structures. In Scotland, the development agency structures have remained institutionally fragmented and geographically competitive, thereby suggesting a different trajectory of economic governance. Whilst the Welsh Development Agency was a single institution, the Scottish arrangements comprised two broad enterprise networks which were made up of a number of smaller local enterprise companies. The funding and policy support in the Scottish case tended necessarily to be more intra-organisationally competitive. This has raised questions about the integrity of securing a territorial regional dividend through such institutional structures and cultures.

By 2006, however, it should be noted that the development agency arrangements in Scotland had attracted intense Parliamentary scrutiny and were subject to considerable media speculation about its performance, structures, expenditure and capacities to deliver a regional dividend. This illustrates the extent to which the aspirations of devolution demand a balanced appreciation of structural, substantive, procedural, and cultural dimensions in order to deliver a regional dividend in practice. Attention is now turning in Scotland to following the Welsh model of integrating the development agency arrangements into the Scottish Executive so as to secure a more collaborative approach. Questions remain, however, as to how any emerging form can best serve the interests of urban Scotland as well as the Highlands and Islands.

Spatial planning: foundations for a regional dividend?

Finally, we turn to the issue of how approaches in Scotland and Wales since devolution have addressed ideas of national spatial planning and territorial cohesion. Of course, devolution as a whole is bound up with shifting understandings of scale (MacLeod and Goodwin 1999), the re-thinking of territory (Brenner 1999), and the modernisation of land use planning (Lloyd 1997). In part, this scalar turn may be explained in the light of the arguments pertaining to globalisation (Giddens 1998), the influence of European spatial planning (Faludi and Waterhout 2002); and arguments promoting a new localism (Stoker 2003). Here, then, scale has a direct impact on how policy priorities are articulated, and how the territorial deficit may be addressed. What is significant in this context though is that modernisation and scalar shifts in institutional behaviour have been complemented by the concept and practices of spatial planning.

Although spatial planning is a contested concept, it goes further than traditional land use planning in that it seeks to secure wider territorial, institutional and policy connectivities. Faludi and Waterhout (2002), for example, have asserted its importance in Europe in shaping policy thinking and new governance arrangements within member states. Importantly, while it has been well received in the UK it has been interpreted and put into practice in marginally different ways. Both Wales and Scotland have positively embraced the spatial planning idea, but they have articulated it in ways that reflect their particular circumstances.

In Scotland, the influence of spatial planning is very evident in the evolution of the National Planning Framework (Scottish Executive 2004a). This innovation is principally associated with the modernisation of the land use planning system (Lloyd and Peel 2005). The first National Planning Framework sought to analyse the underlying trends in Scotland's territorial development, identify the key drivers of change and the emerging challenges, whilst not directly seeking to resolve the dilemmas faced in policy and spending decisions (Scottish Executive 2004a). In terms of substance, therefore, the first National Planning Framework was intended to promote a spatial vision for the management of economic growth and the promotion of social justice in Scotland over the period to 2025. Significantly, this was organised around the principal cities and advocated a city-regional perspective that was intended to be less competitive (Peel and Lloyd 2005). It complemented the economic development strategy and asserted the importance of place, and priorities for investment in strategic infrastructure. Importantly, however, it was non-prescriptive and sought to encourage wider public policy debate about Scotland's territorial development. It thus represented a clear attempt to address the perceived territorial, institutional and strategic deficits in that it acknowledged the connectivity between Scotland's different geographical sub-regions and sought to link these in an organised way based on functional spatial perspectives.

The Planning etc. (Scotland) Act (2006) is critical to this process of active regionalism since the statutory reforms of the land use planning system have explicitly sought to strengthen the National Planning Framework to place it at the pinnacle of a new development planning hierarchy in Scotland. The new Framework will have a statutory status, and its final form will be deliberated in the Scottish Parliament. This new iteration is intended to address the major developments and infrastructure needs for the different parts of Scotland.

The origins of the Welsh Spatial Plan similarly lie in the post-devolution institutional restructuring of the Welsh Assembly Government. The details of its elaboration (Harris *et al.* 2002) suggest that its lineage and ambition rest on a concern with devising appropriate governance arrangements. While both the Welsh and the Scottish spatial documents offer a (re-)diagnosis of their respective regional problems, the explicit reference to devolution in the Welsh Spatial Plan powerfully underscores the importance of this new landscape of governance in being able to take charge of the cure:

> Devolution has given us the opportunity to shape distinctively Welsh answers to Welsh questions with more power to guide action, both directly and indirectly.

To do this we need to cooperate across traditional boundaries and compartmentalised thinking – whether sectoral or geographic. We recognise that 'one-size' solutions do not fit all parts of Wales. We need to identify the most flexible approach for each individual area within our overall strategy. Differing structures may also be needed as those that work in, for example, health, may not be suited to addressing another issue, like transport.

(Welsh Assembly Government 2004a: 3)

In the Welsh context, spatial planning is interpreted as a tool and an activity for reconciling the different policy and institutional strands which impact on the sub-regional geographies of Wales. It asserts a common purpose and sets out a strategic framework to guide future development and policy interventions 'whether or not these relate to formal land use planning control' (ibid: 4). Research suggests that this interpretation of spatial thinking extends across a host of cross-sector issues at both a territorial and a local level (Harris and Hooper 2004). This suggests a more holistic approach to addressing institutional, strategic and territorial deficits. In similar fashion to the Scottish National Planning Framework, the Wales Spatial Plan seeks to provide an understanding of the Welsh local contexts, and to create a framework to promote integrated development and decision making.

Spatial planning seeks to promote a robust framework within which lower order and scalar decisions can be articulated. The different starting points and the ways in which the spatial planning documents were prepared in Wales and Scotland reflect in part their respective deficits in economic performance, territorial articulation, institutional arrangements, and the prevailing devolved responsibilities to manage the sub-regions. Devolution has enabled Wales and Scotland in their different ways to take these on board and to provide a more strategic approach to their planning and development agendas. The overall funding arrangements for the provision of infrastructure are central to this, and can provide a context to the multiple levels, interests and sectors involved in economic development and local land use planning. Essentially, spatial planning can provide the organising frame of reference to secure a more even pattern of economic development and performance, and the more efficient use of resources to facilitate the political ambitions for sustainable development.

Conclusion

This chapter has argued that the reconstruction of regional development and planning in Scotland and Wales following devolution has been strongly influenced by changing ideas of regional development and a re-interpretation of the regional problem. Prior to devolution, regional development policy was focused on the search for a regional dividend, predicated on addressing an established deficiency model in economic governance from a UK-wide perspective. However, over time, the diagnosis of the regional problem has changed as has the nature of the response. Devolved institutional governance is part of the new active regionalism.

Put bluntly, in managing the post-war regional imbalances, the UK settlement moved from a relatively passive policy and agency approach to a more active model filtered through devolution. Devolution in Scotland and Wales has been associated with a rescaling of political and governance responsibilities that has allowed a focus on spatial planning (Alden 2001). The devolved administrations in Wales and Scotland have used the arguments around state modernisation, the new regionalism and new understandings of regional development to justify the need for a spatial plan covering the whole of their territories; to popularise the importance of a national strategic vision; to champion strategic infrastructure investments and sustainable development; and to assert efficiency and democratic gains. This catalogue of aspirations represents what may be considered to be a re-conceptualisation of regionalism and of seeking to secure a regional dividend. This has to take account of the exogenous conditions stemming from a range of global and European forces, and the impacts of a more fluid economic environment that emphasises flows and spatial connectivity over a relatively more fixed and place-centred approach. Endogenous developments are as important. Here, the spatial planning idiom seeks to provide a more adaptive and strategic form of governance that asserts the importance of connectivity between sub-regions, individual places, and cross-border relations. Consequently, Wales and Scotland have addressed the deficit model in light of their specific conditions, an assessment of their respective regional problems, and their different constructions of what is meant by a regional dividend. Understanding the regional problem and devising responses to it has not taken place in a vacuum, and is also influenced by the wider discourse and intellectual concepts with respect to sustainable development and territorial cohesion.

We have argued that devolution, together with its legacy of territorial, strategic and institutional deficits, has led to Wales and Scotland progressively revising their individual responses to securing a new regional dividend. This is reflected in terms of their new responsibilities and powers to rethink strategic regional governance. This is evident in the changing philosophies informing their respective regional development strategies and the design of their spatial plans. Viewed from within Wales and Scotland, devolution would appear then to have offered the Welsh Assembly Government and the Scottish Executive an opportunity to address their structures and processes of governance, the realities of place, and uneven economic performance in their own distinctive ways. Yet, the different approaches adopted by Wales and Scotland to the deficits associated with economic governance arrangements and ways of working illustrate the lack of clarity around how a comprehensive, strategic and national approach to the UK economy as a whole can, or should, be secured.

References

Alden, J. (2001) 'Devolution since Kilbrandon and scenarios for the future of spatial planning in the United Kingdom and European Union', *International Planning Studies*, 6(2). 117–32.

Alden, J. (2003) 'The experience of Cardiff and Wales', in Salet, W., Thornley, A. and Kreukels, A. (eds) *Metropolitan Governance and Spatial Planning: Comparative Case Studies of European City-regions*, London: Spon, 77–90.

Allmendinger, P. and Tewdwr-Jones, M. (2006) 'Territory, identity and spatial planning', in Tewdwr-Jones, M. and Allmendinger, P. (eds) *Territory, Identity and Spatial Planning. Spatial Governance in a Fragmented Nation*, London: Routledge 3–21).

Allmendinger, P., Morphet, J. and Tewdwr-Jones, M. (2005) 'Devolution and the moderni-sation of local government: prospects for spatial planning', *European Planning Studies* 13(3), 349–70.

Armstrong, H. and Taylor, J. (2000) *Regional Economics and Policy* (3rd eds), London: Blackwell.

Barnes, W. R. and Ledebur, L. C. (1998) *The New Regional Economies. The US Common Market and the Global Economy*, London: Sage.

Bond, R., McCrone, D. and Brown, A. (2003) National identity and economic development reiteration, recapture, reinterpretation and repudiation, *Nations and Nationalism*, 9(3), pp. 371–91.

Bond, R. and McCrone, D. (2004) 'The growth of English regionalism? Institutions and identity', *Regional and Federal Studies*, 14(1), 1–25.

Brenner, N. (1999) 'Globalisation as reterritorialisation: the re-scaling of urban governance in the European Union', *Urban Studies*, 36(3), 431–51.

Bruton, M. and Nicholson, D. J. (1985) 'Strategic land use planning and the British devel-opment plan system', *Town Planning Review*, 56, 21–41.

Cooke, P. (1989) 'Locality, economic restructuring and world development', in Cooke, P. (ed). *Localities. The Changing Face of Urban Britain*, London: Unwin Hyman 1–44.

Cooke, P. and Morgan, K. (1998) *The Associational Economy*, Oxford: Oxford University Press.

Cooke, P. and Clifton, N. (2005) 'Visionary, precautionary and constrained "varieties of devo-lution" in the economic governance of the devolved UK territories', *Regional Studies*, 39(4), 437–51.

Danson, M. (1997) 'Scotland and Wales in Europe', in Thomas, H. and MacDonald, R. (eds) *Nationality and Planning: The cases of Scotland and Wales*, Cardiff: University of Wales Press 14–31.

Danson, M., Lloyd, M. G. and Newlands, D. (1993) 'The role of development agencies in regional economic development', in Hart, M. and Harrison, R. (eds) *Spatial Policy in a Divided Nation*, London: Jessica Kingsley Publishers 162–75.

Ellis, S. G. (2003) 'Why the history of the "Celtic Fringe" remains unwritten', *European Review of History,* 10(2), 221–31.

Faludi, A. and Waterhout, B. (2002). *The Making of the European Spatial Development Perspective: No Masterplan*, London: Routledge.

Glasson, J. (1992) 'The fall and rise of regional planning in the economically advanced nations', *Urban Studies* 29, 505–31.

Giddens, A. (1998) *The Third Way: The Renewal of Social Democracy*, Oxford: Policy.

Harris, N. and Hooper, A. (2004) 'Rediscovering the "spatial" in public policy and planning: an examination of the spatial content of sectoral policy documents', *Planning Theory and Practice*, 5(2), 147–69.

Harris, N., Hooper, A. and Bishop, K. D. (2002) 'Constructing the practice of "spatial plan-ning": a national spatial planning framework for Wales', *Environment and Planning C: Government and Policy*, 20, 555–72.

Illsley, B. and Lloyd, M. G. (2000) Collaborative planning for community agendas in Scotland? *Journal of Planning and Environment Law*, July, 678–83.

Jeffery, C. (2007) 'The unfinished business of devolution: seven open questions', *Public Policy and Administration*, 22(1) 92–108.

Jensen, O. and Richardson, T. (2006) 'Towards a transnational space of governance? The European Union as a challenging arena for UK planning', in Tewdwr-Jones, M. and Allmendinger, P. (eds) *Territory, Identity and Spatial Planning. Spatial Governance in a Fragmented Nation*, London: Routledge 47–63.

Keating, M. (2006) 'Nationality, devolution and policy development in the United Kingdom', in Tewdwr-Jones, M. and Allmendinger, P. (eds) *Territory, Identity and Spatial Planning. Spatial Governance in a Fragmented Nation*, London: Routledge 22–34.

Lloyd, M. G. (1997) 'Structure and culture: regional planning and institutional innovation in Scotland', in Thomas, H. and MacDonald, R. (eds) *Nationality and Planning: The cases of Scotland and Wales*. Cardiff: University of Wales Press, 113–32.

Lloyd, M. G. and Peel, D. (2005) 'Tracing a spatial turn in planning practice in Scotland', *Planning, Practice and Research*, 20(3), 313–325.

Lloyd, M. G. and Peel, D. (2006) 'City-regionalism and city-regions in Scotland?', in Tewdwr-Jones, M. and Allmendinger, P. (eds) *Territory, Identity and Spatial Planning*. London: Routledge 285–304.

McConnell, A. (2006) 'Central-local government relations in Scotland', *International Review of Administrative Sciences*, 72, 73–84.

McCrone, D. (1994) *Understanding Scotland: The Sociology of a Stateless Nation*, London: Routledge.

McDonald, S.T. (1977) 'The regional report in Scotland', *Town Planning Review*, 48, 215–32.

Macdonald, R. and Thomas, H. (1997) 'Nationality and planning', in Thomas, H. and Macdonald, R. (eds) *Nationality and Planning: The cases of Scotland and Wales*, Cardiff: University of Wales Press 1–13.

MacLeod, G. and Goodwin, M. (1999) 'Space, scale and state strategy: rethinking urban and regional governance', *Progress in Human Geography*, 23(4), 503–27.

Mooney, G. and Williams, C. (2006) 'Forging new ways of life? social policy and nation building in devolved Scotland and Wales', *Critical Social Policy*, 26, 608–29.

Morgan, K. and Henderson, D. (1997) 'The fallible servant: evaluating the Welsh Development Agency', in Thomas, H. and MacDonald, R. (eds) *Nationality and Planning: The Cases of Scotland and Wales*. Cardiff. University of Wales Press 77–97.

Morgan, K. (2006) 'Devolution and development: territorial justice and the North–South Divide', *Publius: The Journal of Federalism*, 36(1), 189–206.

Peel, D. and Lloyd, M. G. (2005) 'City-visions: visioning and delivering Scotland's economic future', *Local Economy*, 20(1) 40–52.

Peel, D. and Lloyd, M. G. (2006) 'The twisting paths to planning reform in Scotland' *International Planning Studies* 11(2), 89–107.

Peel, D. and Lloyd, M. G. (2007) 'Neo-traditional planning: towards a new ethos for land use planning?' *Land Use Policy* 24(2), 396–403.

Phelps, N. A. and Tewdwr-Jones, M. (1999) 'Competing through planning', *Environment and Planning B,* 26(2), 159–61.

Scottish Executive (2001) *Review of Strategic Planning*, Edinburgh: Scottish Executive.

Scottish Executive (2004a) *National Planning Framework for Scotland*, Edinburgh: Scottish Executive.

Scottish Executive (2004b) *The Way Forward: The Framework for Economic Development in Scotland*, Edinburgh: Scottish Executive.

Scottish Executive (2005) *Modernising the Planning System: A White Paper* (Edinburgh, Scottish Executive).

Scottish Executive (2007) *National Planning Framework: Small country: Big plans* (Edinburgh, Scottish Executive).

Skelcher, C. (2000) Changing images of the state: overloaded, hollowed-out, congested, *Public Policy and Administration*, 15(3) 3–19.

Stoker, G. (2003) *Transforming Local Governance: From Thatcherism to New Labour*, Basingstoke: Palgrave Macmillan.

Sullivan, H. and Skelcher, C. (2002) *Working Across Boundaries: Collaboration in Public Services*, London: Palgrave Macmillan.

Tewdwr-Jones, M. (2001) 'Planning and the National Assembly for Wales: generating distinctiveness and inclusiveness in a new political context', *European Planning Studies*, 9(4), 553–62.

Tewdwr-Jones, M. (2002) *The Planning Polity: Planning, Government and the Policy Process*, London: Routledge.

Tomlinson, J. (2005) 'Managing the economy, managing the people: Britain *c*.1931–70', *Economic History Review*, LVIII, 555–85.

Welsh Assembly Government (2004a) *People, Places, Futures: The Wales Spatial Plan*, Cardiff: Welsh Assembly Government.

Welsh Assembly Government (2004b) *Making the Connections: Delivering Better Services for Wales*, Cardiff: Welsh Assembly Government.

Welsh Assembly Government (2005) *Wales: A Vibrant Economy*, Cardiff: Welsh Assembly Government.

10 Regional development and regional spatial strategies in the English regions

Peter Roberts

This chapter examines the evolution and current state of the relationship between two component parts of the English regional policy and institutional landscape: regional economic development and regional spatial planning. Although these twin aspects of regional policy represent central elements in the package of measures which provides guidance for the future development of the English regions, they are only two of a number of regional or sub-regional strategies present in each region. Reflecting this situation, it can be argued that one of the common problems faced by the two areas of policy under consideration is the lack of an agreed overarching spatial and organisational 'corporate' strategy for a region. One of the consequences of the absence of a corporate regional strategy has been the emergence in some regions of what can best be described as a contested spatial and sectoral agenda. As this chapter will seek to demonstrate, it was predictable that such contestation would emerge, given that the operational capacity to engage in the direction of regional policy has evolved at a somewhat faster pace than regional governance arrangements. Other chapters in this volume reflect more fully on the evolution of English regional governance and the devolution of central government functions (see Chapters 5–7).

By way of contrast with the situation obtaining in the Celtic nations, where generally the establishment of a new set of political institutions has preceded the introduction of new or substantially revised strategic territorial policies, the situation in the English regions is considerably more complex. In some senses this complexity can be seen to reflect the uneven institutional inheritance of the English regions; some regions have a long and rich history of collaboration between local and regional bodies and of collective working, whilst others possess a less substantial foundation upon which to build new organisational and operational capabilities. However, it also reflects the uneven nature of the institutional and political changes which have accompanied the post-1997 territorial governance reforms. As a consequence of this uneven pattern of reform, the Greater London region now enjoys a measure of direct regional government, following the establishment of the Greater London Authority (GLA). This enables the elected Mayor and the GLA to exercise a degree of strategic co-ordination and policy integration across a range of policy areas. Such powers are absent in the other eight English regions, and this lack of political capacity has created a degree of confusion regarding the relative weight and influence exerted by the various regional strategies. Put simply: which of the many strategies in a region takes precedence and how can spatial conflicts between strategies be resolved in order to ensure the most satisfactory outcome?

Although the asymmetric pattern of regional policy and governance across the English regions is in part a product of the uneven process and varied outcomes associated with the post-1997 constitutional reforms, there are also a number of underlying tensions that have not always been resolved by the introduction of strengthened regional arrangements. These tensions can be seen, for example, in the historic divide which exists between regional policies for economic development, transport, housing and land use planning. In one sense the continuing presence of contested areas of policy could be seen to represent the normal situation. However, as will be argued in this chapter, such divides can also be seen to reflect the incomplete nature of the English regional project. These divides were reflected in the proposals for regional devolution presented in 2002 (DTLR 2002), which emphasised the problems associated with the presence of a plethora of (sometimes) competing strategies.

The desirability of dealing with the tensions which exist between the various aspects of regional planning, development and management is not just the expression of an academic desire to produce institutional and spatial neatness. Rather, the continued presence of different policy agendas and different operational priorities can be seen as a cause of excessive resource use which frequently is associated with suboptimal outcomes. The merits of providing greater policy co-ordination and integration at regional and sub-regional levels has been recognised for some considerable time. Keating (1998: 65) notes, for example, that 'even the anti-regionalist Conservative government set up Integrated Regional Offices in England in an effort to co-ordinate central government's own initiatives in planning, infrastructure and development'. Equally, the Regional Co-ordination Unit (2002) and Baker *et al.* (1999) point to the need for greater clarity in terms of the overall spatial pattern of regional development. This can then guide individual elements of policy and implementation. At national level this argument has been applied through calls for the introduction of a spatial strategy for England which could be used to guide regional planning and development (Town and Country Planning Association 2006).

In order to provide a basis upon which to evaluate the recent experience of regional economic development and spatial planning policies in the English regions, the first section of this chapter briefly explores some selected aspects of the history of regional development and planning. This is followed by a closer examination of the aims and objectives of the post-1997 regional reforms, and by an assessment of the consequences of the actions taken to implement the reforms. The third section examines the current state of policy and attempts to identify some of the more important trends. The final section of the chapter offers conclusions and provides some lessons that can be used to help to guide future policy formulation and implementation.

Regional development and planning: origins and evolution

This section explores a number of selected aspects of the evolution of the two key component parts of the English regional institutional landscape: regional economic development and regional spatial planning. Each of these elements has been in evidence for a considerable period of time and, with a number of notable exceptions, each has evolved in a particular and separate manner. Although there have been a number of attempts to bring the two elements together, prior to 1997 such attempts were heavily constrained by the absence of a clear willingness across central government to provide the English regions with the institutional infrastructure necessary to ensure their co-ordination. It is this absence of the necessary institutional infrastructure which has been identified as the primary weakness in the operation of an integrated approach to regional planning and development. Put bluntly, as far as the creation and implementation of an integrated system of regional planning and development is concerned, it has been 'the incomplete, constrained and discontinuous way in which it has been attempted which has been at fault, not its purpose' (RTPI 1986: iii).

The institutional weaknesses evident in the English regions provided much of the motivation for the creation of the current English regional 'project'. This project has its origins in the deliberations of the Alternative Regional Strategy (ARS) group during the early 1980s. The ARS group argued in favour of the comprehensive devolution of functions, powers and resources to the nations and regions of the UK and proposed the establishment of elected regional assemblies (Parliamentary Spokesman's Working Group 1982). The basis for their proposals was an extensive review and critique of previous attempts at providing a lasting system of integrated regional management; this review included an assessment of the weaknesses inherent in a system which separated the powers of planning and development from the political capacity required to ensure effective implementation. Despite the presence of much good technical and professional practice, the pre-1997 regional arrangements lacked meaningful political capacity, even in the Celtic nations where significant initiatives in policy and implementation were prohibited 'if the Imperial core is not prepared to countenance such variations' (Goldsmith 1986: 167).

In seeking to identify the initial reasons for the presence of the institutional divide between the two elements of regional planning and regional development, it is necessary to trace the origins of each element of policy back to the inter-war years. During this period the first explicit measures to guide the economic development of regions were introduced through the designation of the Special Areas and the establishment of a suite of policy measures designed to attract and support economic activities. This line of policy can be traced through successive eras of regional economic policy to the present day, with responsibility for such policy chiefly resting with the Board of Trade/Department of Trade and Industry. A second and parallel line of ancestry can be identified for regional planning, which although it was present as an explicit activity prior to the Great Depression, gained increased recognition and significance as a consequence of the need to regulate the urban development patterns which emerged during the 1920s and 30s. These patterns of development, and especially the so-called 'drift to the south', became the subject of considerable concern and led to the creation of a Royal Commission on the Distribution of the Industrial Population (the Barlow Commission) charged with the task of investigating the causes and consequences of differential regional development.

The Barlow Commission produced a set of policy recommendations which can be seen as an intended integrated package of measures aimed at ensuring the introduction of a greater degree of common purpose for regional economic development and regional planning activities. With the benefit of hindsight the work of the Barlow Commission can be seen to have been flawed in certain respects – especially with regard to the analysis of the nature and consequences of the factors which had stimulated economic growth in certain parts of the UK during the 1920s and 30s, and in relation to the idea of promoting 'regional balance', a term criticised as 'flung around as an all-purpose phrase in lieu of thought' (Hall 1968: 292) Nevertheless, in general terms the objectives of providing greater strategic direction at both national and regional levels in economic development and land use planning were farsighted. Three specific lines of policy were subsequently introduced, two of which can be seen to have survived virtually intact to the present day: the promotion of regional economic development, the control of urban expansion and the control of industrial location. Whilst the first two lines of policy are still very much in evidence and form the substance of this chapter, controls over the location of economic activities were gradually relaxed and eventually abandoned in the early 1980s.

The investigations undertaken by the Barlow Commission established the considerable extent and the complex nature of the inter-relationship between regional economic development and regional spatial planning, although it is significant that little was said in the subsequent report on the question of regional governance; this proved to be a significant omission in the analysis and recommendations. The complexity of the relationship between the two policy fields can be considered in a number of ways: the division of functional responsibility for the two policy fields between different central government departments; the division of responsibility between central and local government; the different priorities accorded to the two policy fields in different regions; and the absence of effective regional governance; or indeed all of these. Irrespective of the reason for the presence of complexity, be it an inevitable consequence of the characteristics of the two policy fields, or an unnecessary self-inflicted complication, the result has been a history of some six decades of attempts to bring the two elements of policy activity together at the regional level in England. Two episodes in the history of policy co-ordination are of particular significance: the attempt during the 1960s to establish a comprehensive system of national and regional planning and development, and the introduction of the integrated Government Offices (GOs) for the English regions in the early 1990s.

The first of these innovations – the creation during the 1960s of a new central ministry, the Department of Economic Affairs, together with Regional Economic Planning Councils and Boards – provided the potential for the closer co-ordination of regional economic development and regional spatial planning policies. The new institutions focused on the preparation of an integrated comprehensive regional strategy in each standard region. However, despite the establishment of appropriate regional institutions for the design and implementation of the two elements of policy, such reforms were not accompanied by any introduction of democratic accountability to existing regional governance arrangements or the introduction of new elected regional institutions. This continuing absence of the necessary institutional infrastructure hindered the full and effective operation of the policy reforms. In simple terms, whilst certain planning and economic development activities were designed and undertaken at the regional level, there was little evidence of the presence of political control and accountability to ensure the conformity of the two separate policy elements with an agreed regional strategic agenda. As a result, as Grant (1982) has argued, regional economic policy has almost always been subject to a high degree of central control, with little freedom allowed regarding expenditure and implementation at the regional level. It is of considerable significance that the first real relaxation of the central control exercised over regional economic policy has been that associated with the creation of the devolved administrations in the Celtic nations and the establishment of the Regional Development Agencies (RDAs) in the English regions.

The second episode of note in the history of the two elements of regional policy was the establishment of the GOs for the regions. The creation of the GOs in 1994 – initially one for each of the then ten standard regions of England, but subsequently reduced to nine when Merseyside was merged with the North West – was intended to provide greater co-ordination in terms of both the design and implementation of public policy in the regions and brought the two elements of policy together. However, especially in the mid-1990s, the GOs enjoyed little real authority over the fundamentals of regional economic development policy, and were only able to influence the design and implementation of policy at the margin. In the case of regional spatial planning policy, the GOs had greater powers, especially given that they were chiefly responsible for a substantial part of the process of preparing Regional Planning Guidance (RPG). After 1997 the remit of the GOs was expanded, but they remained an arm of central rather than regional government.

Overall, what is clear is that the extent of control exercised by separate central government departments over the two elements of regional policy has tended historically to work against their full integration or co-ordination at the regional level. As Heclo and Wildavsky (1981) argued some two decades ago, the 'kinship' patterns in the 'village life' of central government have remained dominant, with the consequence that traditionally many aspects of regional policy have represented central rather than regional preferences, especially with regard to key components of public expenditure. Although the post-1997 reforms have not yet fully achieved the objectives set out in the ARS and other assessments of regional policy (such as that produced by the Regional Studies Association 1983), substantial progress has taken place in terms of reducing the dominance of the centre. However, as is discussed later, further progress is seriously constrained by the continuing absence of directly elected regional or sub-regional government endowed with the powers required to 'bend' both policy formulation and the pattern of public expenditure necessary to allow the achievement of the objectives of policy, including the achievement of better value for money (H.M Treasury 2004). It is the absence of this crucial element of the regional institutional infrastructure which hinders the delivery of what has been described as a desirable arrangement whereby the economic development and spatial planning elements of regional policy should be 'bought together at the regional level as integrated parts of a set of coherent regional strategies'

(Regional Studies Association 1983: 126). The post-1997 reform programme was introduced with the intention of delivering such an arrangement.

The English regional project

The main elements of the post-1997 regional reforms in England have their origins in the various inquiries into the causes and consequences of the regional problem which were conducted by the Labour Party and a number of other organisations and individuals during the 1980s and early 1990s. Although the starting point for the development of modern regional policy can be traced back to the ARS, the original intentions expressed in this document were modified prior to the General Election of 1997. One crucial modification was the separation of the Regional Development Agency function from the creation of elected regional assemblies in all but one English region (the Greater London region), whilst another significant modification saw the perpetuation of the historic divide between regional economic development and regional spatial planning. So, prior to the election of 1997 the Labour Party was in the position of supporting the immediate establishment of Regional Development Agencies (RDAs) in all nine English regions, but it was not committed to the immediate creation of directly elected regional assemblies in all regions. Furthermore, although a number of suggestions and ideas had been developed regarding the future shape and operation of the regional element of the spatial planning system, these ideas had not achieved the status of specific proposals for immediate implementation. Indeed, it can be argued that it would have been somewhat premature to introduce specific proposals for regional planning in advance of a wider general review of the entire spatial planning system.

Following the election of a Labour government in 1997, some of the above noted policy commitments were translated into legislation and guidance. This process of implementation commenced with a number of consultation exercises: on the creation of the RDAs; on the introduction of an elected GLA which would, amongst other matters, take direct responsibility for a RDA for Greater London; and, somewhat later, the reform of the planning system. It is important at this juncture to note that the intended package of measures was initially seen as an integrated programme of regional reforms to be undertaken by a single central government department – the Department of the Environment, Transport and the Regions (DETR) – and was considered to be a priority area for action by the new administration. Although there were a number of elements in the package which were not developed immediately, the general approach was broadly in conformity with the initial political commitment.

The first legislation introduced to implement these acknowledged regional priorities was the Regional Development Agencies Act 1998. This Act required RDAs to contribute to the economic success of their region as part of their wider mandate to support overall regional (environmental, social and economic) development and 'contribute to the achievement of sustainable development' (Regional Development Agencies Act 1998, paragraph 7(e)). In the eight English regions outwith Greater London RDAs were established in April 1999. Given the complexities inherent in the wider debate on regional government and governance, it was decided to create these RDAs in advance of any further consideration of the case for establishing directly elected regional assemblies. In the case of the Greater London region the full establishment of the RDA – the London Development Agency – was delayed pending the outcome of consultations and the creation of the Greater London Assembly. Once established, each RDA proceeded to prepare a Regional Economic Strategy (RES). The preparation of a RES was guided by the DETR in order to produce documents that covered a broad range of issues, such as social inclusion, environmental conditions and economic development. This broad sustainable development agenda offered the potential for either the preparation of a single overarching strategy that could then be used to guide sector or agency-specific documents, such as RES or RPG, or it could be applied indirectly through the negotiation of separate, but broadly conforming, sector or agency strategies. In the event the response to these opportunities was mixed, with some regions adopting the former model – especially, the East Midlands (Benneworth, Conroy and Roberts 2002) – whilst others introduced negotiated variations on the separate strategy approach. This issue will be discussed further later in the chapter.

A second strand of implementation saw the introduction of voluntary regional chambers, with limited powers of scrutiny and a broad mandate to co-ordinate policy development and implementation at the regional level. As has been discussed in more detail in Chapter 5, the various regional chambers started from different positions of strength or weakness, and have subsequently developed along distinctive pathways. The importance of the regional chambers (or assemblies as they were later renamed) is that they also discharge the function of the Regional Planning Body (RPB) responsible for the preparation of Regional Planning Guidance (now called the Regional Spatial Strategy, or RSS). As such, they represent a second element in the collective management and governance of regional development and spatial strategy. As a footnote, it is important to acknowledge that the regional assemblies (RAs) can claim a degree of indirectly elected accountability through their local authority members, although this mechanism for providing democratic accountability can sometimes generate confused spatial priorities and mandates.

The third strand of the regional project saw the strengthening of the GOs located in each of the regions. From their inception in 1994, the GOs have taken a leading role in ensuring the effective delivery of central government policy in the regions. The (then) ten integrated regional offices initially brought together the regional responsibilities of the (then) Departments of Environment, Transport, Trade and Industry, and Employment (in particular the Training, Enterprise and Employment Division). In 1995 the Department of Education was merged with the Department of Employment, and this added a further role for the GOs (Mawson and Spencer, 1997). Over the past decade the GOs have evolved further, with new and extended functions added to the original portfolio; in particular a number of activities related to rural development and to communities have been introduced into the GO portfolio.

Following the 1997 General Election, the GOs were given additional responsibilities for ensuring the harmonisation of regional policies and the delivery of a greater degree of spatial integration. One important aspect of the enhanced role was the requirement that each GO should ensure the preparation of a Regional Sustainable Development Framework (RSDF) in order to 'identify the links between different Regional Development Activities . . . and set a common and agreed high-level vision for promoting sustainable development at the regional level' (DETR 2000a: 7). At the time, the role of the RSDF was unique. Through its promotion of sustainable development the RSDF was seen as best placed to influence and orchestrate the overall environmental, social and economic development of a region. As a result, it was anticipated that some of the longstanding divisions of opinion and priority between the various regional plans and strategies would be resolved or at least minimised. In the event, given that the GOs were authorised to designate a document as a RSDF if it fulfilled a fairly limited set of criteria, the form and content of RSDFs varied considerably between regions: some exhibited an explicit spatial dimension, others were more concerned with sectoral integration (Benneworth *et al.* 2002). As will be discussed later, one region – the East Midlands – used the RSDF as the centrepiece of a wider process of regional strategy making; the RSDF emerged as one of a number of important products from an exercise to develop a generic integrated regional strategy for the East Midlands, which could be used as a common spatial platform upon which a range of plans and strategies could be built (East Midlands Regional Assembly 2000).

Overall, therefore, there have been three strands of reform relating to regional governance and regional development policy: the Regional Development Agencies (RDAs) responsible for Regional Economic Strategies (RESs); the Regional Assemblies (RAs) acting as Regional Planning Bodies (RPBs), responsible for Regional Spatial Strategies (RSSs); and enhanced Government Offices (GOs), responsible for Regional Sustainable Development Frameworks (RSDFs). The main reason for introducing them has been to demonstrate the presence of all of the policy components necessary to ensure the introduction of a highly integrated form of territorial policy development and delivery at the regional level. Such an approach has been considered desirable by academic commentators such as Mawson (1997), Syrett and Baldock (2003) and by the Audit Commission (2004: 53) who refer to attempts to promote economic growth fracturing when they 'hit the ground in departmental silos'. One important weakness in the delivery of the desired outcome is associated with the continuing absence of directly elected regional governments in the eight English regions outwith Greater London. As a recently retired civil servant observed of the situation obtaining in the late 1990s, perhaps there are too many regional strategies and this might work against policy integration in the absence of an agreed set of regional spatial priorities and the continuing presence of considerable central guidance (Ash 1999). Equally, the same author points to the need to ensure that regions are 'given a significant amount of freedom to determine their own futures' (Ash 1999: 25) It is somewhat ironic that having moved from a situation in the early 1990s when insufficient attention was paid to regional matters, the recent plethora of regional initiatives can sometimes be seen as having generated confusion amongst regional stakeholders and actors, including those who have proved to be willing participants in various regional strategy exercises (Baker *et al.* 2003).

Although the model solution – an integrated territorial programme for each region, sub-region or city-region – is unlikely to emerge in the near future (Roberts 2000), it is possible to identify examples of good practice (Bridges *et al.* 2001) and to suggest potential areas for further investigation set within the context of the wider international discussion of regional management. Valuable insights are available from situations in which the local/regional – national spatial management relationship is either a contested matter or is dominated by a single method of approach (Breheny 1996; Papoudakis 2001; Walsh 2000).

Policy and practice in the regions

We need to look first at the Regional Development Agencies (RDAs), where responsibility currently rests with the Department for Trade and Industry. At their inception in April 1999 the RDAs were charged with the preparation of Regional Economic Strategies (RESs) which, in the words of one RDA Chair, would ensure that 'national policies can be joined-up effectively to meet local needs' (Bridge 1999: 18). The Regional Development Agencies Act 1998 specified the duties of RDAs and also granted the Secretary of State considerable power to guide the RDAs in the preparation of their strategies (DETR 1999a), including guidance regarding the approach to, the methodology for preparation and the content of the RES. This initial guidance was later complemented by supplementary guidance (DETR 1999b) which made RDAs aware of the range of issues and implications that central government policy and the activities of other government bodies had for RESs.

Statutory guidance to the RDAs noted that the fundamental purpose of the RES was to 'improve economic performance and enhance the region's competitiveness' (DETR 1999a: 3) and, more specifically, to provide a regional framework for economic development, skills and regeneration. The latter point is important, because although the RES had a specific function to promote and deliver regional economic development, it also had a major role to play in other policy fields and in helping to establish institutional capacity in a region. In addition to these primary functions, the RES was seen as providing a framework for the delivery, hopefully in a co-ordinated manner, of a range of other national and European programmes. A matter of particular note in the context of this chapter was that the RES was required to support and enhance national policies, while addressing the individual needs and opportunities evident in a region; this matter of spatial focus is a significant feature of RES, and it is of crucial concern in terms of the wider regional contribution and relevance of RES *vis-à-vis* other regional plans and strategies.

A further requirement contained in the guidance was that partnership working should be adopted for the preparation of RES. The intention was that the RDAs should proceed through dialogue with relevant organisations and actors and that the RES should emphasise collaboration and co-operation. A specific requirement was that RDAs should interact with other regional organisations that were responsible for preparing complementary regional strategies, including the regional assemblies, and the range of partners who worked with Government Offices. This positioning of RES suggested that the final strategy should have both inner and outer 'faces'. As might have been anticipated, these twin purposes and functions were not always in balance, with the inner 'face' – which chiefly reflected the priorities of the RDA – often dominating the wider spatial and sectional integration purposes of RES.

Following the preparation of the first round of RES (see Bridges *et al.* 2001; Roberts *et al.* 2001; and House of Commons 2004) the RDAs undertook a range of implementation actions and rolled forward their initial RES. Although in most regions the preparation of the initial RES was conducted as a freestanding exercise, further rounds of RES elaboration and modification were generally harmonised with other regional strategy exercises. One important exception to the general pattern of freestanding RES preparation during the initial phase of activity was the approach adopted in the East Midlands region. Here the RES was developed as part of a general regional strategy; the RES itself was considered to be a component part of an overall vision for the region and a key element in a 'corporate strategy' for the region as a whole. The Integrated Regional Strategy for the East Midlands (East Midlands Regional Assembly 2000) provided an agreed common overarching strategy which provided the basis for the preparation of a range of regional and sub-regional plans, including the RES, Regional Planning Guidance (RPG) and the Regional Sustainable Development Framework (RSDF). This integrated strategy approach has been commended as representing good practice (Bridges *et al.* 2001) and has been proposed as a model for the further elaboration of RES and other regional and sub-regional strategies.

This brings us to the second strand of policy – Regional Spatial Strategy – which in the modern era developed in the form of Regional Planning Guidance (RPG). Although the requirement to prepare RPG pre-dates the introduction of RES, the scope and specification of RPG has evolved considerably over the past decade, including the eventual introduction in 2004 of a much more extensive form of regional planning in the shape of Regional Spatial Strategies (RSSs) (ODPM 2004). At the time that the RDAs were introduced, eight of the nine English regions had been provided with RPG; the ninth, London, had special arrangements for strategic planning at the regional level. The documents produced during this initial round of RPG were of variable quality, with some failing to provide sufficient detail, whilst others did not deal with sub-regional issues (Roberts 1996; Baker 1998). In addition, RPG was non-statutory and in some cases this generated considerable disputes regarding its role, validity, and authority.

Following the election of the Labour Government in May 1997, the structure and operation of RPG was reviewed (DETR 1998) and later strengthened. Key elements of the strengthened system included the introduction of a requirement that regional associations of local authorities should prepare RPG in consultation with a wide range of regional stakeholders, the introduction of an examination in public of draft RPG, and the requirement that greater sub-regional detail should be incorporated in the document. A national guidance document on the preparation of RPG was later published by DETR. This new guidance – Planning Policy Guidance 11 (PPG11) (DETR, 2000b) – outlined the broader spatial planning role of RPG in informing the future development of a region and required RPG to incorporate a regional transport strategy. In addition, the new RPG documents were required to be the subject of a sustainability appraisal; a requirement which offered considerable opportunity to ensure conformity between RPG and the other major regional strategies such as RES and RSDF.

A further series of revisions to the regional planning regime were introduced as part of the overhaul of the entire planning system, which resulted in new planning legislation in the form of the Planning and Compulsory Purchase Act 2004. As well as introducing a new statutory system for regional planning in the form of the Regional Spatial Strategy (RSS), the Act enhanced the status of regional plans by requiring that they should also ensure that they are consistent with and supportive of other regional strategic documents and that they should 'articulate a spatial vision of what the region will look like at the end of the period of the strategy and how this will contribute to sustainable development objectives' (ODPM 2004: 2)

The third element of the package of regional measures referred to above is the Regional Sustainable Development Framework (RSDF). As noted in the previous section, the RSDF was introduced in order to provide a high level vision for sustainable development at the regional level. Given the importance attached to the preparation and guidance role of RSDFs, it is somewhat surprising that the requirements issued to help shape the formulation of RSDF did not make explicit reference to the need for regional partners to provide a spatial framework that reflected the regional and local dimensions of the delivery of the vision.

However, notwithstanding the weaknesses which have emerged in some regions as a consequence of the absence of an explicit spatial dimension to RSDF, the very presence of a cross-cutting requirement to attend to sustainable development matters has influenced a number of dimensions of regional policy and strategy. As was observed in relation to both RES and RPG, it has been accepted that most public plans, strategies, programmes and actions should be designed and delivered in a manner which maximises their contribution to sustainable development. Such an intention would imply that all actions in a region should be aimed at common targets and should make use of a single spatial assessment; this has proved not always to be the case in practice. As a consequence, whilst the high level vision expressed by a RSDF may be in accord with the initial intention of the guidance provided by central government, the reality is that integrated implementation may not always follow. This problem is not confined to the preparation of RSDF, with the House of Commons Committee of Public Accounts observing that 'lack of clarity about which national, regional and local organisations have the power to take or veto decisions can strain relationships between organisations that need to work together' (House of Commons 2004: 11). Although there are instances of divergence between RSDF, RES and RSS, there are, as noted earlier, a number of examples of attempts to introduce a co-ordinated approach to regional policy development and delivery, such as the Integrated Regional Strategy prepared by the East Midlands Regional Assembly and its partners. There are also other examples of good practice, including the introduction of cross-strategy shared aims and objectives, the use of joint approaches to policy formulation, and the application of common methods for assessing the extent to which various strategies in a region conform to the requirements of sustainable development.

The latter case is illustrated by the use of a common sustainable development appraisal method for both RSS and RES in Yorkshire. Such examples of good practice illustrate the benefits associated with the introduction of RSDF.

In order to assess the extent to which the various elements of the new regional policy system have succeeded in reducing the differences of direction and purpose which have sometimes existed between regional (economic) development and regional spatial planning, the final part of this section reports the findings of a brief research exercise undertaken in late 2005 and early 2006 which attempted to identify progress in the regions with regard to the preparation of RES and RSS. When considered alongside the results from a similar interview survey conducted by the present author and colleagues in 2000 and 2001, which examined the relationship between the first round of RES and RSDF (Benneworth *et al.* 2002), it is evident that a number of lessons were identified, developed and applied to subsequent rounds of policy formulation and implementation. The survey conducted in 2000-2001 focused on the extent to which the new regional arrangements introduced in the late 1990s and 2000 had allowed the various strands of regional policy to be co-ordinated more effectively than in the past, whilst the 2005-2006 survey concentrated on the extent of co-ordination achieved between RES and RSS. The intention of the more recent research exercise and the analysis presented herein is to support the further development of policy and practice in the English regions.

The findings from the research exercise conducted in 2000 pointed to the difficulties of attempting to co-ordinate or integrate the production of two regional strategy documents – in this case the first rounds of RES and RSDF – when the exercises were conducted to different timetables. To a certain extent this difficulty diminished as a consequence of the realisation that further rounds of strategy production provided an opportunity for a degree of convergence in terms of both sectoral and spatial priorities. Thus, whilst the first RESs were prepared to a fast timetable, which did not allow in most regions for more than one iteration, and did not coincide with the preparation schedule for RSDF, the preparation of second round RES was informed by the already established RSDF as well as by the first or second rounds of RPG/RSS preparation. Table 10.1 indicates that in most regions an opportunity existed to ensure that RES and RSS preparation processes informed each other and that attempts were made to co-ordinate the timetable for the preparation of the two strategies. In most regions the RA and RDA worked together to evolve common foundations for their respective strategies; such joint working can be seen in the use of a common economic evidence base or the use of the same method of sustainable development assessment.

However, despite the frequent mention of attempts at the greater alignment of RSS and RES, including the generation of a common spatial framework, the strategies inevitably diverged in terms of their emphasis. Perhaps the clearest division related to the emphasis placed in RSS on housing and housing land, and the focus in RES on the provision or safeguarding of quality economic activity land. A further distinction in terms of general policy and spatial emphasis can be seen in some regions, with RSS generally emphasising the regeneration of the older urban areas, whilst RES also points to the importance of other sites and the potential for the development of spatial

Table 10.1 Regional spatial strategy and regional economic strategy preparation and priorities

Region	Regional assembly perspective	Regional development agency perspective
North East	RSS and RES priorities similar and attempt to reflect these spatially; some target areas outside of city-regions	Attempting to ensure co-ordination between RES and RSS; priority given to city-region development
North West	Efforts made to align RSS and RES; RSS has used scenarios developed by RES to inform strategy; emphasis on polycentric development	Intention to align RES with RSS and Northern Way priorities; use of city-region model; need expressed for designation of key sites
Yorkshire and Humberside	General alignment of RSS and RES; but RSS uses thematic sub-regional approach; common SEA and other assessments	General close alignment; use of traditional sub-regions and stronger emphasis on transport than in earlier RES
East Midlands	Assembly identifies common philosophy between RSS and RES on regeneration; focus on housing issues; use of common economic evidence base	RDA identifies problem of different timetables for RES and RSS; emphasis on defending quality employment land; sees some inflexibility in planning process
West Midlands	Common approach of RSS and RES; focus in RSS on older urban areas such as Black Country; principles of awareness, alignment, action and advocacy	Positive alignment approach to ensure RES conforms with RSS; focus on development of new economic sectors and this implies spatial shift
East of England	General agreement on overall spatial strategy and statement of synergy produced; does not support expansion of Stansted Airport	RES does not use standard city-region model, but does define own core cities; in favour of Stansted Airport expansion
South West	Express desire to align RSS and RES in reviews; keen to ensure alignment; identifies importance of economic prosperity	No explicit spatial dimension; commonality of approach between RES and RSS; keen to promote convergence between strategies
South East	See RSS providing overall spatial strategy; both RSS and RES use same growth areas; key difference on airports policy	Emphasis placed on ensuring that RES conforms with RSS framework; RES uses three spatial economic zones
London	London Plan identifies key spatial strategy and specifies areas for redevelopment; co-ordination with RSS through Mayor	RES acknowledges London Plan spatial strategy and is generally aligned to the main priorities

Source: Survey conducted December 2005 and January 2006.

economic zones. A particular distinction can be seen between the two strategies in the East of England and the South East; in both cases there is a difference of policy regarding airports policy, with both RES documents emphasising the need for the expansion of airports capacity, whilst the RSSs urge a more restricted approach.

Although the general pattern in the English regions has suggested a growing mutual awareness of the requirements and priorities of the different regional organisations and agencies, there are still many difficulties that await resolution. In the first section of this chapter reference was made to the difficulties associated with the separation of purpose and budget at the regional level which results from the independent operation of powerful central government departments (Audit Commission 2004). One consequence of the continued presence of these central forces is a tension between regional organisations and between their strategies. Despite these tensions, inter-agency strategic working has improved, with benefits for both the collaborating agencies and the region as a whole. Two examples which illustrate the benefits of greater co-ordination can be seen in Yorkshire and the Humber and in the South West. In Yorkshire and the Humber, both the RSS and RES are closely aligned in their priorities for the regeneration of the older urban areas, market towns and seaside towns; this agreed focus allows for economic development, land use, transport and housing policies to be more closely aligned than in the past. In the case of the South West, both the RES and the RSS place considerable emphasis on the need to focus attention on environmental quality; whilst this does not mean that other objectives have been downgraded, it does imply the need for rigorous analysis, policy formulation and implementation in order to ensure that the agreed objective is achieved through the inclusion of appropriate policies in all strategies and subsequent implementation plans.

Another significant aspect of the relationship between the two areas of strategic working has been the identification of common over-arching priorities. For example, there have been attempts made in the three northern regions to conform to the spatial development priorities of the Northern Way (a trans-regional strategy covering the North East, the North West and Yorkshire and the Humber). Equally, the three Northern Way regions, as well as other regions, have used negotiated common approaches to the development and implementation of city-region strategies. In addition to these particular examples, it is also evident that both RES and RSS in most regions have been able to benefit from a more sophisticated institutional choreography than existed in the late 1990s and early 2000s: rather than dancing separate steps to different tunes, the scope and quality of regional partnership working would appear to have improved.

The emergence of an increasing awareness of the importance of regional partnership working would appear to reflect three factors: the growing political and operational maturity of the major actors, the realisation that mutual benefits emerge from strategic agreement (and lobbying) on key issues such as transport investment and housing land allocations, and a greater sense of self-dependence now that it is unlikely that directly elected regional assemblies will be established in the foreseeable future. In short, the initial aspirations of the ARS are now nearer to realisation than might have been expected given the absence of elected regional government.

However, to repeat the message of the report of the Royal Town Planning Institute (1986) on regional planning, the danger is that the present institutional structures may suffer the fate of previous partial regional governance arrangements (Roberts 2000). It is by no means clear, for example, if all of the current organisational arrangements for regional planning and regional economic development will continue in their present form should there be a change of government. Irrespective of this particular concern, it is possible to point to the presence of a longer-term cycle of institutional learning, which reflects the presence of a growing capacity for partnership working and strategic thinking that can trace its origins back to the late 1980s and the introduction of Structural Funds regional programmes (Roberts 2003). Although the present governance arrangements may lack the full mandate that would be conferred through the establishment of a directly elected regional assembly, the present state of affairs represents significant progress compared with the situation obtaining a decade ago.

The recent evolution of regional strategic capacity has not been the product of a single specific policy or action; rather it reflects a combination of inherited and new institutional elements and aspirations. While a considerable number of aspects of the present arrangements, including the revival of regional strategic spatial thinking and action, can be traced back to a common source – the ARS of 1982 – others either have different roots or have multiple sources. For example, somewhat ironically, the abolition of the metropolitan county councils in the 1980s and the need to replace their structure plans with a form of rudimentary strategic spatial plan – Strategic Planning Guidance or SPG – was an important stimulus to change (Thomas and Roberts 2000). The introduction of SPG for the metropolitan county areas both stimulated an interest in strategic spatial thinking in adjacent areas and provided a forum for a limited discussion of wider regional issues. This initial impetus for regional revival was subsequently reinforced by other requirements and innovations, eventually leading to the introduction of RPG and later RSS.

Whilst this may have been a long and sometimes troubled journey towards the present situation, the crucial question to ask is: was the journey worth the effort? On the basis of the evidence from the previous survey referred to in this section (Benneworth *et al.* 2002) and the information from the recent survey reported herein, the answer to this question would appear to be positive. The crucial issue then is how best to ensure the further progress of the regional institutional journey over the coming years.

Conclusion and lessons for future progress

As has been observed a number of times in this chapter, the relationship between the two key elements of the English regional development landscape – regional economic development and regional spatial planning – has not always been smooth. After a number of promising starts during the 1940s and 1960s, initiatives and institutions have either faltered or outrun their frequently insubstantial political mandate. One key weakness has been the absence of directly elected strategic authorities, whilst another has been the fragmentation of responsibilities and of organisational and operational capacity. A substantial evidence base exists which suggests that the lack of elected authorities has exacerbated divergences between the operation of regional spatial planning and regional economic development policies. From the 1960s until the late 1970s, the absence of directly elected strategic author-ities was partly compensated for by the presence of relatively strong local govern-ment, including sub-regional scale county authorities, and through the presence of regional co-ordination arrangements in the shape of Regional Economic Planning Councils and Boards. The creation of directly elected metropolitan county councils in the early 1970s also helped to develop and deliver a degree of co-ordination between the two aspects of policy. The use of sub-regional arrangements in the past has allowed particular issues associated with strategic co-ordination and integration to be addressed, such as the joint planning of land use and transportation (Roberts and Baker 2004), and such arrangements may prove helpful in the future, especially at the city-region level.

The demise of the regional arrangements and the abolition of the metropolitan county councils during the 1980s significantly reduced the level of institutional capability at the regional level. As a consequence of this pattern of inconsistent support for regional and other strategic institutional arrangements, it is hardly surprising that the latest attempt to introduce regional capability has taken time to mature. It is notable, for example, that in many regions the second round of RES preparation has been more in harmony with RPG/RSS preparation than was the case during the first round of strategy preparation. This trend towards institutional and operational convergence can be explained, in part, by the increasing sophistica-tion and 'thickness' of institutional capability, and, in part, by the presence of a grow-ing awareness of the wider benefits that can be gained from the co-ordinated delivery of policy and the merits associated with the adoption of a common spatial framework. Although substantial progress has been made in recent years with regard to the technical and administrative capability of regions, on the basis of past and pres-ent evidence, it is possible that further progress will be inhibited due to the absence of directly elected regional or sub-regional government. This observation is rein-forced by the survey evidence reported herein which indicates that spatial and sectoral co-ordination would appear to be somewhat easier to achieve in London than elsewhere; this experience suggests that moves towards the introduction of elected mayors for the city-regions (Constitution Unit 2006) may go some way towards reducing the problems currently experienced in relation to policy co-ordination. In the past sub-regions (or city-regions) have proved to be useful territorial units for the production of integrated spatial strategies and for the delivery of specific functions (Roberts and Baker 2004). Although the sub-regions which comprise the proposed city-regions represent only part of the territory of their respective standard regions, the relative success of the former metropolitan county councils – they frequently led regional strategy making and delivery – provides a positive precedent (Roberts *et al.* 1999). An equally valuable alternative proposal is that local authorities should be given additional powers to ensure that they can co-operate on economic development, transport and planning matters; this view has been expressed by the Economic Secretary to the Treasury (Webster 2006).

In addition to the desirability of building on the recent achievements associated with the establishment of the RDAs (and their RESs), the strengthened RAs (and their RSSs) and the expanded GOs, it would also appear to be important to introduce further reforms in order to promote greater spatial integration, including the possibility of building on the experience in the East Midlands and introducing single spatial (or territorial) programmes which combine policy priorities and budgets. In order to deliver policies in a more efficient and effective manner it is recognised that unnecessary duplication and overlap between individual programmes should be eradicated. The 'single pot' model used for managing RDA funding at the regional level, and the positive experience of some Local Strategic Partnerships in relation to the benefits of cross-sector partnership working at a local level, offer indications of the potential benefits associated with a single programme approach. An important option is the suggestion that city-regions, working through multi-area agreements, might prove able to implement the single programme model. Such a model would also address the difficulties and inefficiencies associated with the fragmented delivery of policies which were highlighted by the Regional Co-ordination Unit (2002) and the House of Commons (2004).

This chapter has addressed the need to build on the foundations for better regional management which have been established over the past decade. It has examined the causes and consequences of the 'historic fissure' (Baker *et al.* 1999: 763) between regional spatial planning and regional economic development, and it has offered evidence of growing convergence between the two aspects of policy. This convergence is in part a result of the presence of more extensive and mature partnership working than was the case in previous eras, but it also reflects the introduction of a series of technical, administrative and operational innovations which have reinforced the tendency towards convergence and complementarity. Previous studies have shown the importance of reinforcing positive institutional behaviour, and of providing additional powers and resources in order to allow such behaviour to be translated into more extensive implementation (Roberts 2003). The reinforcement of present practice, perhaps through providing further policy freedoms and budget capacity to established regional partnerships or, additionally, through establishing city-region executive authorities with or without elected mayors, would help to ensure the future progress of the current arrangements. An immediate step in this direction is that suggested in the report of the House of Commons Committee of Public Accounts (2004: 6) which advocated 'the establishment of joined-up arrangements for co-ordination and decision taking'.

However, despite the presence of positive signs, significant obstacles still hinder the introduction of joined-up arrangements, including the separation of responsibility at the central government level, the powerlessness of regional assemblies and the continuing presence of competing actors at the regional level. In these circumstances, and given the likelihood that directly elected regional assemblies will not be established in the eight regions outwith London in the near future, making the best of the positive elements of the present institutional arrangements and reinforcing partial regional governance whenever possible would appear to offer the most promising way forward. What must be resisted at all costs is the abandonment of a work in progress which has already provided substantially improved planning, development and management in the English regions. To do otherwise would be to repeat the mistakes of the past.

Acknowledgement

The author wishes to thank Lynne McGowan who assisted in the survey of regional arrangements referred to in the text.

References

Ash, M. (1999) 'Regional structures – coherence or conflict?' *Journal of Planning and Environment Law*, Special Issue on Modernising for the Millennium, October.

Audit Commission (2004) *People, Places and Prosperity*, London: Audit Commission.

Baker, M. (1998) 'Planning for the English regions: a review of the Secretary of State's Regional Planning Guidance', *Planning Practice and Research*, 13, 153–69.

Baker, M., Deas, I. and Wong, C. (1999) 'Obscure ritual or administrative luxury? Integrating strategic planning and regional development', *Environment and Planning B*, 26, 763–82.

Baker, M., Roberts, P. and Shaw, R. (2003) *Stakeholder Involvement in Regional Planning*, London: Town and Country Planning Association.

Benneworth, P., Conroy, L. and Roberts, P. (2002) 'Strategic connectivity, sustainable development and the new English regional governance', *Journal of Environmental Planning and Management*, 45, 199–217.

Breheny, M. (1996) 'The scope of regional planning', paper presented at the RGS-IBG Conference, Glasgow, January.

Bridge, J. (1999) '21st century regions – creating new paradigms', in M. Gardner, S. Hardy and A. Pike (eds) *New Regional Strategies: Devolution, RDA's and Regional Chambers*, London: Regional Studies Association.

Bridges, T., Edwards, D., Mawson, J. and Tunnell, C. (2001) *Strategy Development and Partnership Working in the Regional Development Agencies*, London: Department of the Environment, Transport and the Regions.

Constitution Unit (2006) 'Regional and local government', *Monitor*, 34, 5.

Department of the Environment, Transport and the Regions (DETR) (1998) *The Future of Regional Planning Guidance – Consultation Paper*, London: Department of the Environment, Transport and the Regions.

Department of the Environment, Transport and the Regions (DETR) (1999a) *RDA's Regional Strategies: Building Partnerships for Prosperity*, London: Department of the Environment, Transport and the Regions.

Department of the Environment, Transport and the Regions (DETR) (1999b) *Supplementary Guidance to Regional Development Agencies*, London: Department of the Environment, Transport and the Regions.

Department of the Environment Transport and the Regions (DETR) (2000a) *Guidance on Preparing Regional Sustainable Development Frameworks*, London: Department of the Environment, Transport and the Regions.

Department of the Environment, Transport and the Regions (DETR) (2000b) *Planning Policy Guidance 11 – Regional Planning Guidance*, London: Department of the Environment, Transport and the Regions.

Department for Transport, Local Government and the Regions (DTLR) (2002) *Your Region, Your Choice*, London: The Stationery Office.

East Midlands Regional Assembly (2000) *England's East Midlands Integrated Regional Strategy*, Melton Mowbray: East Midlands Regional Assembly.

Goldsmith, M. (1986) 'Managing the periphery in a period of fiscal stress', in M. Goldsmith (ed.) *New Research on Central-Local Relations*, Aldershot: Gower.

Grant, W. (1982) *The Political Economy of Industrial Policy*, London: Butterworth.

Hall, P. (1968) 'Regional balance', *Town and Country Planning*, 36, 292.

Heclo, H. and Wildavsky, A. (1981) *The Private Government of Public Money*, London: Macmillan.

H.M. Treasury, Department for Transport, Office of the Deputy Prime Minister and Department for Trade and Industry (2004) *Devolving Decision Making*, London: The Stationery Office.

House of Commons Committee of Public Accounts (2004) *Success in the Regions: Fifty – first Report of Session 2003–2004*, London: The Stationery Office..

Keating, M. (1998) *The New Regionalism in Western Europe*, Cheltenham: Edward Elgar.

Mawson, J. (1997) 'The origins and operation of the government offices for the English regions', in J. Bradbury and J. Mawson (eds) *British Regionalism and Devolution*, London: Jessica Kingsley.

Mawson, J. and Spencer, K. (1997) 'The government offices for the English regions', *Policy and Politics*, 25, 71–84.

Office of the Deputy Prime Minister (ODPM) (2004) *Planning Policy Statement 11 – Regional Spatial Strategies*, London: The Stationery Office.

Papoudakis F. (2001) *The Impact of Structural Funds Regulations on Regional Policy Process in Greece*, Edinburgh: University of Edinburgh.

Parliamentary Spokesman's Working Group (1982) *Alternative Regional Strategy*, London: Labour Party.

Regional Co-ordination Unit (2002) *Review of Area-based Initiatives*, London: Regional Co-ordination Unit..

Regional Studies Association (1983) *Report of an Inquiry into Regional Problems in the United Kingdom*, Norwich: Geo Books.

Roberts, P. (1996) 'Regional planning guidance in England and Wales, back to the future?' *Town and Planning Review*, 67, 875–82.

Roberts, P. (2000) *The New Territorial Governance*, London: Town and Country Planning Association.

Roberts, P. (2003) 'Partnership, programmes and the promotion of regional development', *Progress in Planning*, 59, 1–69.

Roberts, P. and Baker, M. (2004) 'Sub-regional planning in England: neglected opportunity or unwanted complexity', *Town Planning Review*, 75, 265–86.

Roberts, P., Thomas, K. and Williams, G. (1999) *Metropolitan Planning in Britain*, London: Jessica Kingsley.

Roberts, P., Bridges, T., Edwards, D., Lloyd, G., Mawson, J. and Tunnell, C. (2001) *Evaluation of Regional Development Agency Strategies and Action Plans*, London: Department for Transport, Local Government and the Regions.

Royal Town Planning Institute (1986) *Strategic Planning for Regional Potential*, London: Royal Town Planning Institute.

Syrett, S. and Baldock, R. (2003) 'Reshaping London's economic governance', *European Urban and Regional Studies*, 10, 69–86.

Thomas, K. and Roberts, P. (2000) 'Metropolitan strategic planning in England: strategies in transition', *Town Planning Review*, 71, 25–49.

Town and Country Planning Association (2006) *Connecting England*, London: Town and Country Planning Association.

Walsh, J. (2000) 'Dynamic regional development in the EU periphery. Ireland in the 1990s', in D. Shaw, P. Roberts and J. Walsh (eds) *Regional Planning and Development in Europe*, Aldershot: Ashgate.

Webster, P. (2006) 'Brown ally attacks plans for powerful city mayors', *The Times* 6 October, 35.

11 Conclusion

UK regional capacity in comparative perspective

Jonathan Bradbury and Patrick Le Galés

That devolution, regionalism and regional development policy in the UK deserve such scrutiny is testament to the significant upheaval that they have represented in both constitutional and governmental terms since 1997. Gone are the days when the view could still go relatively unchallenged that the UK was a unitary and centralised state, mostly homogeneous and integrated despite minor territorial differences. This was always a mistaken view; but devolution and regionalism have comprehensively underlined the need to take the UK's stateless nations and regions seriously. Of course, there is still evidence of the UK in comparative terms having relatively weakly developed sub-national government. Local government in Britain remains the least autonomous of any of Europe's large countries. Institutions of sub-national governance are also highly fragmented, and the Labour Governments of Tony Blair, in England at least, displayed considerable commitments to the detailed micromanagement of policy implementation. Following rational choice theory such fragmentation has generally been seen as a condition of good government. However, for those who assume that at times politics, history, or social relationship matters, fragmentation can lead to weak political capacity to steer, implement or govern. Out of such motivations has arisen the stronger development of devolved and regional government.

The UK's embrace of devolution and regional government is not unique among European states. Regionalism has been an increasingly widespread phenomenon since the 1970s, and the EU system of multi-level governance has provided a further arena for regions to gain competences and resources since the late 1980s. This is as true for larger long-standing member states such as Italy, Spain and even France as it is for new members such as Poland and Romania. Indeed the development of a regional tier of some sort has become a requirement of entry for new member states. The intentions of reform in the UK have also mirrored those in other states: to revise rather than transform the state. There remains a strong assumption that the new regionalism should not ultimately undermine nation states. In the 1980s and 1990s, pressure towards separatism from the Northern League in Italy and the Catalans in Spain received sharp criticism from the European Commission. It was made clear that the EU would neither support nor accept a breaking up of the large member states which made up the bulk of the EU. In embracing devolution and regionalism, the UK state has also generally held highly conservative assumptions that such reform, whilst innovative and important, would not usurp the consolidated state. The 'Europe of the Regions', dreamed of by generations of regionalists, in which larger states should fade away, is not the leitmotif of broader European thinking and has not been so in the UK either.

Nevertheless, devolution and regionalism have brought new dynamics to the governance of the UK, making it one of the most dynamic, differentiated and interesting cases of territorial change in Europe. The degree of devolution in both Scotland and Northern Ireland is relatively very high, and in Wales is still considerably above the forms of administrative regional devolution seen in England or outside the UK in states such as Sweden. In terms of comparative regionalism the UK has been Europeanised in a way which might not have been anticipated by its leaders. The EU context in practice also has provided an environment that encourages its development. UK governments have always promoted an approach to European integration that favours free trade and enlargement rather than market harmonisation and the deepening of supranational powers. However, enlargement has largely brought into the EU small European countries, that have then done well. Ireland, Finland, Denmark and the Czech Republic represent models of small nation states that are successful economically and have relatively well developed welfare states. Paradoxically, the UK has contributed to this, for example, by preventing tax harmonisation, thereby allowing small states to undercut larger states in corporation tax rates. This justifies the argument that a small culturally homogeneous nation state has a better capacity to do well in the EU alone than when it has to operate within the strict financial and in part legal parameters set by Westminster. At the very least, policy divergence from a British/English norm is supported. Britain is not isolated here. Recent developments in Belgium, inspired by pressures from the Flemish, have made the dismantling of the state an increasingly likely option.

The creation of assemblies and Parliaments in Belfast, Cardiff and Edinburgh has been a huge change to the UK's constitutional arrangements. Yet, as Bulpitt (1983) highlighted, the informal arrangements of territorial politics can be quite different from apparent constitutional forms. John agrees, suggesting that territorial politics is 'the arena where spatially located decisions-makers within the territory of the nation state play out their strategies and realise their values and interests. Institutions may give the elites their formal roles; but territorial politics is more often about informal and political relationships that concern economic interests, pressure groups and the political parties, which are different in the various territories of the state' (John 2008, forthcoming).

Bulpitt (1983) himself argued that well before the recent introduction of devolution a central feature of territorial politics in the UK was in fact that central government, overwhelmed by the breadth of its ambitions, had long granted territorial elites considerable autonomy. Nevertheless, this was within a structure of territorial politics characterised by central government maintaining control of key resources that limited effective regional capacity. Equally, the capacity of stateless nations and regions to assert themselves in the UK was constrained by their own weaknesses. Bradbury (2006) has suggested that whilst political devolution threatened a more fundamental transformation of territorial politics, there were also grounds for considering whether it merely provided an arena in which, whilst some more formal power was delegated to the regional level, much effective power was still retained at the centre, and at the same time the capacity of the UK's stateless nations and regions to exploit change remained relatively weak. This suggested the possibility that irrespective of the apparent extensiveness of devolution, and the support potentially provided by EU membership, the development of the UK's stateless nations and regions after devolution still would be marked by adaptation within a gradualist political tradition.

This line of argument merely serves to underline the central question to be addressed in analysis of the early years of UK-wide devolution and regionalism. How transformative were the effects of the Blair Government's reforms on the UK's stateless nations and regions in practice? An answer needs to engage with the integral concerns in considering regional capacity: what has been the ability of the UK's stateless nations and regions to articulate interests and concerns and to meet the perceived needs of their constituent electorates (Keating 1998; Le Galés 2002). We need to reconsider to what extent and in what ways organisational development, institutional processes, politics, public policy and identity politics in the UK's stateless nations and regions developed such capacity in the years after 1997–1999. Conclusions throughout the book have highlighted predominant themes of both change and continuity.

Devolution and political change

The chapters relating to Scotland, Wales and Northern Ireland highlight the considerable changes that devolution ushered in. This is reflected in the development of new and varied institutional capacity, a reflection of the broader development of organisational complexity in advanced societies, relating not simply to formal institutions but also to accepted norms and standards. Beyond the initial creation of the Parliament and the two assemblies, we learn of a seemingly never ending plethora of new agencies, committees, positions such as that of the children commissioner, and new organisations to co-ordinate policy initiatives. The political complexities of Northern Irish devolution are reflected in the creation of a glut of additional special bodies such as the Independent International Commission on Decommissioning and the British Irish Council, and the labyrinthine processes necessary to reach a final agreement that both the DUP and Sinn Féin could agree on. Devolution has also been accompanied by a wide range of reviews, leading to changed rules regarding governance and policy standards, new policy strategies, initiatives, comprehensive agreements and joint declarations. A huge amount of energy has been devoted to creating a different organisational world in Scotland, Wales and Northern Ireland, and devolution has undoubtedly left the UK with a richer and more complex system of governance.

Similarly, in their different ways the newly devolved assemblies in Cardiff and Edinburgh made vigorous efforts to organise themselves in a manner distinct from the political arrangements pertaining in the UK Parliament. In Scotland, there were coalition agreements between Labour and the Liberal Democrats lasting throughout the first two terms. In Wales, Labour held majority power for only a short period between 2003 and 2005; otherwise it governed either as a minority administration or in coalition. Both in Scotland and Wales there were efforts to organise the work of policy-making and scrutiny in a way that gave more power to ordinary elected members sitting on committees. The inclusive approach was highlighted most starkly by the Scottish Parliament's operation of a petitions committee, to allow any concerted feeling among members of the public to be voiced directly to their elected representatives. Devolution was also something of a shock for the civil service, particularly in Wales where a tradition of following central policy quite closely was subverted by the direction of their new political masters.

Devolution clearly also fostered fairly rapid development of the stateless nations as distinct political spaces, characterised by their own political debates and networks, and institutionalised through new rules and norms. Indeed, Wales and Scotland provide wonderful examples of processes of political institutionalisation. Once the new institutions were created, actors used them in creative ways, developing new areas, and inventing new rules for the Parliament/Assemblies and their committees. The more they developed, the more policies started to diverge, the more the overlapping and interaction with central government raised new sets of questions about the autonomy enjoyed under devolution. In matters of public policy, the Scottish Executive and Welsh Assembly Government have both asserted their own priorities, framed within a more explicitly social democrat agenda than in England. Right from the start the Scottish Parliament's decision to diverge from the UK policy, implemented in England, of up-front tuition fees for university students symbolised the potential to develop different policies in Scotland. Intriguingly, while under EU regulations European students too are not charged up-front tuition fees in Scottish universities, English, Welsh and Northern Ireland students who attend have to pay the fees. The provision of free personal care for the elderly in the second term of the Parliament was equally distinct.

In the case of Wales, central departments have specifically had to learn to consider the fact of Welsh secondary powers, and that Wales was likely to use its secondary powers to implement legislation rather differently than in England. The 'bonfire of the quangos' in 2004 raised more than an eyebrow in Whitehall as it so obviously contradicted two decades of the development of quangos and agencies in British public administration. Day-to-day actions by the Assembly and interactions between civil servants or between ministers at the Welsh and UK levels helped to set new ways of doing things which in turn strengthened the institutionalisation process by which devolution could develop further. The making of the second Government of Wales Act in 2006 is a very good illustration of this process. The more active the Welsh Assembly became, using its secondary legislative powers, the more the existing settlement was considered unsatisfactory, giving momentum to the Act that created the capacity for the Assembly to seize new competences. This specifically provides for a further referendum to grant primary legislative powers to the Assembly as and when a majority in the Assembly, with the consent of

Westminster, wish to hold it. It should also be noted that the vigorous promotion of the Welsh language and the requirement of bilinguism to be appointed as a civil servant within the next few years are also likely to create a very distinctive administrative elite which will increasingly bear little resemblance to the Whitehall civil service. This has strong echoes of the role of language in defining a distinct administrative class in Catalonia.

At the most fundamental of levels, the effect of devolution on the politics of Northern Ireland has been the most significant. Despite the new Northern Ireland Assembly being suspended for longer than it has actually sat, the hopes for a settlement between the interests of unionism and nationalism vested in a power sharing devolution throughout the period after 1997 helped to sustain a virtual end to systematic paramilitary and sectarian violence. The communities have remained divided and there continues to be tensions and violence but on nothing like the scale witnessed at the heights of Northern Ireland's troubles. Yet, over a ten-year period, the unionist opponents to finding an accommodation with nationalism – the Democratic Unionist Party – became the leading unionist party, vested with their community's faith in defending their interests, while at the same time themselves becoming accommodated to the idea of power-sharing with Sinn Féin. Equally, the more radical Sinn Féin replaced the SDLP as the main articulators of the aspirations of nationalism, while at the same time there was a tortuous and lengthy process in which the IRA decommissioned its weapons and Sinn Féin itself moved to support the forces of law and order.

Overall, the political process facilitated by the hopes vested in power-sharing devolution can be interpreted as an overwhelming indication of its success. Rick Wilford's charting of the way in which the parties finally moved to a consensus on the St Andrew's Agreement is a reflection of the fact that devolution helped Northern Ireland to move into a new era. The opportunity for developing the capacity of Northern Ireland to generate positive momentum in institutional and governance arrangements and a coherent and distinct domestic public policy agenda to deal with Northern Ireland's problems lies ahead. The achievement of power-sharing devolution is to allow that possibility. The St Andrews Agreement provided 'the best estimates of the UK and Irish governments of the terms upon which Northern Ireland's political and constitutional future could evolve', and the leaders of unionism and nationalism basically agreed.

Despite this catalogue of novel developments, all of the contributors in Part I of the book counsel caution in reading too much into the capacity of devolution to inspire transformative change. Neil McGarvey reminds us that it would be a mistake to consider 1999 as 'year zero' in Scotland; the presence of distinct civic institutions and a distinct Scottish arena of politics and public policy long pre-dated that, although the precise significance of devolution's historical inheritance remains open to dispute. Jonathan Bradbury suggests that this is less the case with Wales, but still the political distinctiveness of Labour Party dominance, and a century of civic and policy institution development, leading to the creation of the Welsh Office in 1964, are reminders that the grounds for establishing how devolution would operate were significantly influenced by pre-1999 developments. Despite the new demands of mixed member electoral systems the Labour Party was able to continue to dominate executive politics in both Scotland and Wales up to 2007, and remained in power in Wales after 2007. Achievement of a 'new politics' of inclusiveness both within the Scottish Parliament and National Assembly for Wales and externally in relations with civic groups, is contested; the role of committees, in particular, has been varied and, as McGarvey suggests, requires renewed sceptical reflection by comparison with Westminster committees, that may have achieved much more than pro-devolutionists ever gave them credit for.

Similarly, processes of institutionalisation have indeed stoked some demands for further constitutional change; in Scotland to develop fiscal devolution; and in Wales to both broaden and deepen legislative devolution and move towards parity with Scotland. Yet, up to 2007 the Labour Party resisted further change in Scotland, essentially declaring devolution to have been more of an event than a process; and in Wales, while there is broadly a cross-party consensus on the desire to gain further powers, opinion polls have not suggested that it receives the clear support of the public. Equally, while both the Scottish Parliament and Welsh Assembly have rapidly established their place at the heart of government in the respective territories there is no discernible impact on identity politics. Levels of sympathy with Britishness and underlying support for the union in both Scotland and Wales have not changed in any significant manner. Finally, there are frequent reminders of the interconnectedness of politics across Britain. Bradbury reminds us, for example, that Wales' attempts to declare itself a GM crops and nuclear-free zone were deeply problematic, given both the formal distribution of competences between levels of government and the operation of private individuals. Yet at the same time devolution in Scotland and Wales was established with remarkably little conflict with or interference from central government. Indeed, the results of central government comprehensive spending reviews meant that they operated in a very benign financial climate. There was relatively little evidence of a new centralism that could have inspired strong early pressures for further devolution.

In addition, there is a need for some reflection on the aspiration that devolution in bringing government closer to the people would have a beneficial democratic effect. This took place against a problematic background. Much has been written lately about not only the limits of UK democracy but also its erosion (Crouch 2004). Have devolved institutions contributed to the democratisation of the UK political system? The answer is far from clear. Certainly, the rate of participation has not markedly increased. Participation in Scottish Parliament elections has been respectable if not spectacular, while turn-out in Welsh Assembly elections has been poor. Only 43 per cent voted in the Assembly elections in May 2007. Indeed there is a sharp contrast between the high levels of political mobilisation in the Welsh political elite to develop policies, reorganise Welsh governance, seek new powers, and promote the Welsh language in a systematic way, and the majority of the population that does not even bother to vote.

In Northern Ireland, too, Rick Wilford cannot but remind us that, irrespective of political developments, Northern Ireland remains a deeply divided society. This is reflected in the continued separateness of many civic institutions between Protestant and Catholic communities. The organisational structures of the Northern Ireland Executive and Assembly are based on the assumption of labelled differences between unionists and nationalists. Governance relationships and directions in public policy will continue to be fought out with a high regard to the territorial group implications of approaches and decisions. The identity politics of unionists and nationalists have if anything been strengthened as the DUP and Sinn Fèin have emerged as their territorial group political representatives, and the constitutional determination of both groups to drive power-sharing devolution towards their ultimate political objectives of, on the one hand unionist commitments to a united UK and, on the other hand, nationalist commitments to a united Ireland remain undimmed. Northern Ireland has not experienced a deeply rooted transformation of social, civic and political life. It has found a political accommodation in power-sharing devolution, a huge achievement in itself and one that might foster the gradual depoliticisation of territorial group loyalties, but in the short term and for some time to come it represents an agreement to differ, that might yet unravel.

After the elections in Scotland and Wales and the events in Northern Ireland during early 2007, there were grounds for believing the political dynamics of devolution might become more distinctive. The elections to the Scottish Parliament led to the extraordinary appointment of Alex Salmond, the Scottish National Party leader, as First Minister in alliance with the Greens. In Wales Labour suffered a historic decline in their vote share and faced the prospect of either forming a coalition with Plaid Cymru or being removed from power altogether by a rainbow coalition led by Plaid Cymru. Labour chose the former, meaning that Plaid Cymru entered office as an equal partner in a two party coalition. With nationalists in office, seeking independence in Scotland, a full devolved legislative Parliament in Wales and a united Ireland in Northern Ireland, there were prospects that devolution might yet break the UK asunder. At the very least it allowed nationalist politicians the opportunity to use the levers of power to prepare the ground for more transformative change in the long term.

Yet, even in this context it is important to cast a sceptical eye over what these developments mean. To a large extent the biggest achievement of devolution has been the establishment of devolution not as the basis of new politics but as one of normal politics; that publics have come fairly rapidly to see devolved government as a focus for the articulation of their interests and concerns and the key instrument for meeting most of their needs. Party performance is therefore judged in fairly orthodox governmental terms; and it has to be expected that the pendulum will swing in voter preferences either to support an incumbent party or to vote for a change. In both Scotland and Wales the Conservative Party is not a credible 'alternative government', the Liberal Democrats in taking the junior coalition partner role have not canvassed for that position and after the 2007 elections recognised the need to review their strategy by sloping off into opposition to Labour in both countries. This leaves only the SNP and Plaid Cymru as the potential leaders of a concerted vote for change in forming an alternative government. Even then the electoral systems deny them the legislative majorities to give effect to their most radical policies; in Scotland virtually ensuring that the SNP administration is limited to the ambition set for them by the public of trying to govern better than Labour and not the one set by themselves to make Scotland independent. Support for the SNP in May 2007 did not reflect a surge in support for independence. Even in Northern Ireland, Sinn Féin's constitutional ambitions will be constrained not simply by the DUP but also by the likely implications of public disapproval if they govern Northern Ireland badly.

English regionalism, change and indeterminacy

When compared to the development of regional government in England, whatever the 'ifs' and 'buts' of devolution in Scotland, Wales and Northern Ireland, the clarity of change and the role of devolved government in these territories are brought into sharper focus. In England, even after ten years of developing a policy of regionalism, its nature, achievements and future remain subject to much more debate. The issue was primarily promoted by John Prescott, the Deputy Prime Minister 1997–2007, who personally campaigned for developments towards elected regional government over several years. Meanwhile the rest of the Labour Government had far more doubts. From a New Labour perspective, as Graham Pearce and Simon Lee both argue, albeit in contrasting styles, the issue of developing regional governance in England had two specific objectives: first, the strengthening of regional competitiveness, and secondly improvements in central government programmes delivery, in particular regeneration programmes. From the Treasury point of view, the key issue was the economic under performance of the Northern regions, which undermined Britain's overall competitiveness. There was little interest in the Labour Government about developing English regionalism for any broader identity politics or democratic purposes.

Consequently, the development of English regionalism occurred on the basis of creating a multiplicity of functionally oriented non-elected bodies. Of course, this did presage considerable change. The Labour Government inherited the Government Offices of the Regions (GOs), created by the Major Government in 1994. To these the Blair Government added nine Regional Development Agencies (RDAs) in 1999, including the London Development Agency, which were strongly business led, together with Regional Chambers (or regional assemblies as they came to be known), which brought together local councillors, and representatives of voluntary groups, business and trade unions, to try to give a bottom-up voice to the region. The assemblies were dominated by representatives from local authorities. The key body of these two was the RDAs. They were granted increased funding in 2001, and were given responsibility for the regional economic strategies to foster competitiveness, to lead regeneration programmes and to deal with anti-poverty programmes through strategic partnerships. Crucially, the funding was directly provided by central government. In April 2005, RDAs were granted new responsibilities including the delivery of the Business Links service, the development of Regional Skills Partnerships, an increased role in supporting business–university collaboration, and responsibility for the socio-economic work of the Countryside Agency.

The resulting troika of key institutions of regional governance built in an organisational complexity to each of the English regions. But each region then had its own special concerns and organisational responses. John *et al.* introduced us to the significance in London and the South-East of the Thames Gateway joint operation committee and the Olympic Delivery Authority, and the co-ordination mechanisms used in order to give some sense of direction in delivering policy. Across the regions the interdepartmental Regional Co-ordination Unit and the English Regions Networks each in their own way held a general significance. In the English regions too a richer and more complex governance emerged after 1999. In the pipe-dreams of John Prescott the destination of such developments was the gradual move towards elected regional government to bring the myriad organisations and purposes of regional governance under a democratically elected body in each region. This ambition came to a head with the staging of a referendum on an assembly for the North East of England in 2004. However, the proposal received an emphatic 'no' vote, and following this humiliating defeat, the process of change came to something of a halt.

Some assessments of the development of regional governance from the point of view of developing regional capacity have been optimistic. As Jones *et al.* (2004) and Peter Roberts in this volume have reported, regional governance in the East Midlands has been a good example of how co-ordination can work. All of the institutions of regional governance draw on an integrated regional strategy, and RDA performance has been enhanced by introducing sub-regional strategic partnerships to deliver the RDA's strategy on the ground. Both Pearce and Roberts give some support for the view that regional governance in England has made significant developments. Mawson (2006) perhaps strikes the most optimistic tone in suggesting that despite the failure of the North-East referendum to achieve elected regional government, regional governance has been gradually consolidated, and policy co-ordination is emerging at the regional level. This is not the result of a planned approach but rather the product of gradual build-up of each of the institutions and trial and error in co-operation. RDAs have had both their powers and budgets increased. Government Offices for the Regions have grown to employ 3,300 staff, with combined running costs of about £150 million. They are the regional arm now of ten central departments and their regional directors now play a major role in supporting RDAs, bringing together regional directors of various public agencies, and framing regional priorities. Mawson also suggests that despite their obvious weaknesses, Regional Assemblies have played a role in the preparation of various regional strategic documents. In 2004 the 'Planning and Compensation Act' confirmed their role as Regional Planning Boards. Regional governance could yet provide the basis of the logical move towards elected regional government in the mid-long term.

However, most assessments of the development of regional governance have been pessimistic. Harding *et al.* (2005) concluded that the performance of each of the institutions of regional governance in England was 'very moderate'. They were dominated by central government departments, and while they had learned to work together to agree strategies they were unable to provide coherent regional leadership on strategic priorities. Their effectiveness was undermined by the problems of understanding the division of responsibilities between them, and of making sense of the large number of programmes and strategies being developed by different organisation in each region. There was 'a tendency by the agencies, in extremis towards institutional self protection' when the problems of trying to achieve co-ordination proved problematic. Of course, such criticism should take into account the constraints they faced. For example, the performance of RDAs was under-mined by the resources at their disposal and they are still at a relatively early stage of development. Yet, given such problems both of resource and performance it is difficult to give wholehearted support to the notion of effective consolidation of regional governance when it has been marked by such fragmentation.

The circumstances surrounding the referendum on an elected assembly for the North East were also problematic. The proposed assembly was relatively weak in its powers and therefore had questionable benefits for governance; whilst it was easily attacked by its opponents on the grounds of cost. There was no general enthusiastic support in the Labour Government for success in the referendum, and Prescott was left to push for a yes vote on the grounds of North-East identity, which however strong culturally was very problematic politically, given the divisions between different local authority areas in the region. The defeat in the referendum left the whole regional government agenda in jeopardy, and it is noteworthy that whilst the Conservative Party feel obliged to accept devolution in Scotland, Wales and Northern Ireland, they assume no such practical entrenchment for the existing institutions of English regional governance let alone any sympathy for elected regional government. Consequently, by 2007 there was in fact a big question mark hanging over the future of regional governance in England.

Even with Labour still in power serious questions remain about how English regional governance, based on networks of agencies and powerful individuals, that have no direct regional accountability, will develop. Functional rationalisation suggests the logic of building up one of the troika at the expense of the others, with RDAs as the prime candidate for development, but this would increase rather than decrease the apparent lack of bottom-up inclusiveness in making strategies for regional development. The future role of the GOs is also open to question from a regional perspective, in that it is not clear that they represent the interests of the regions in central government and that their achievements in influencing major central departments to spatially differentiate their policies remains very limited. Indeed, the GOs' centralist role is somewhat underlined by the support they receive from those opposed to the creation of elected regional government.

Consequently, English regionalists are somewhat more inclined even than those sceptically reflecting on devolution in Scotland, Wales and Northern Ireland, to observe that but for all the change that occurred in English regional governance after 1997, much stayed the same. Hogwood's pre-1994 characterisation of English regional administration as a mess of central department field offices, quangos and agencies, each with different regional boundaries and regional centres (see Hogwood and Keating 1982) has been replaced by a generally more coherent notion of the areas of regional governance. However, within them there is much underlying continuity in the fragmentation of institutional power, responsibilities and resources. At the level of public attitudes too English regionalism remains a dog that has not barked (Harvie 1991) such that the focus of some in promoting regionalism has returned to the question of what is the region and what is its centre. The city-regions movement, for example, essentially questions the present definition of English regions as consistent with the top-down tradition of centrally defined efficient administrative regions and promotes instead city-regions as part of a bottom-up tradition of defining regions according to areas of popular identity.

For some analysts frustrations at problems in English regionalism meld with perceptions that England generally has been disadvantaged relatively within a form of territorial restructuring that has provided opportunities for significant development of regional capacity in Scotland, Wales and Northern Ireland. Such opportunities have not been granted to England either on an all-England basis or through its regions. Simon Lee comments very starkly on the inconsistencies in Labour's inherently more interventionist approach to government in England compared to elsewhere in the UK. This highlights the fact that the English question in both its forms – what is good for the government of England, and what is fair for the government of England given developments elsewhere in the UK – are more strongly asked in 2007 than they were in 1997. When readers of the *Daily Mail* newspaper regularly express their anger at the perceived English subsidy of Scottish universities to allow Scottish students not to pay tuition fees when the children of English taxpayers do not have such 'free' access to those universities themselves, we should be aware that a new English dynamic has entered the world of UK territorial politics.

Developments and problems in regional development policy

A focus on regional development as a manifestation of regional capacity is, of course, one that concerned both devolved governments in Scotland, Wales and Northern Ireland, and regional governance in England. In the context of globalised markets, territorial restructuring of whatever sort raised questions about the ability of new structures of government to address issues of regional development. In the UK's stateless nations and regions the pre-devolution inheritance was one of fragmentation in policies, deficit in institutional capacity, problems of organisational co-ordination and a lack of strategic planning. The situation was better in Scotland than in Wales, but in both countries much hope was vested in devolution to galvanise a more co-ordinated approach. In particular this focused on a desire to draw economic development and land use planning together into a coherent overarching approach to spatial planning. In England it was expected that making this historic re-connection between different strands of regional development policy would be much more difficult.

Lloyd and Peel explore how in both Scotland and Wales the new devolved institutions oversaw major initiatives in spatial planning to integrate economic development and land use planning. These resulted in the Wales spatial plan and the National Planning Framework for Scotland, both published in 2004, followed in

Scotland by the Planning etc. (Scotland) Act 2006. They were based on strategic visions in both countries that redefined the regional dividend from spatial planning in both process and output terms. It was agreed that policy was to be developed on a partnership basis, and that outputs should not simply focus on narrow economic targets relating to employment, investment and new firm formation. Instead, the regional dividend was conceptualised in broader terms to cover economic development, social inclusion and environmental quality. There was a major focus on the need to integrate the delivery of public services. In the promotion of regional development there was a strong focus on national identity branding and the pursuit of a collaborative approach with the private sector and other agencies. In Wales, there was also a major reform of the Welsh Development Agency. Effectively it was abolished and its functions taken in-house to the re-named department of enterprise, innovation and networks.

Roberts also details significant developments in the English regions. Although it was a tortuous, uneven and slow process many regions achieved some harmony between the regional economic strategies established by the Regional Development Agencies and the regional planning guidance and regional spatial strategies, emanating from the regional assemblies. Best practice actually achieved single spatial programmes that sought to combine policy priorities and budgets, and there was the potential for this to be emulated by other regions. This reflected the co-operation of regional bodies and provided good foundations for a more concerted convergence of economic development and spatial planning ideas. Overall, in all territories the new institutional capacity embraced a more active model of indigenous regional development that sought to bring together different regional development concerns in a more holistic manner. This contrasted sharply with the former practice of a passive agency approach in the context of regional policy essentially led by central government.

However, it is still hard to gauge the progress made in regional development. Approaches in both Scotland and Wales both faced criticism: in Wales for being ultimately too 'precautionary' involving the state too directly in managing the regional economy; and in Scotland for failing to address some of the problems of Scottish Enterprise. Equally, it remains too soon to measure the outcomes, as opposed to the outputs, of strategic policy developments. In England, Roberts remained certain that, except in the case of London, institutional fragmentation and the lack of elected regional authorities meant that, relative to the rest of the UK, English regional development policy still faced major constraints. The new regional development policy has less certain consequences in each of the stateless nations and regions even than the more political and governmental changes effected as part of devolution and regional reform.

Morgan casts a generally more sceptical light over regional development policy by highlighting the fact that the focus on achieving more integrated strategies within the stateless nations and regions of the UK has occurred with too little appreciation of the significance of central government's retreat from responsibility for regional policy. Instead of the central state, as in the classic post-war welfare state era, developing policies for regional development with a responsibility to try and develop territorial equity between the different territories of the UK, the central state has now devolved powers over regional development and invited all territories to consider their own interests, efficiency and competitiveness against each other. Consequently, whatever the successes of regional development policy in any given territory, measured for example in terms of GDP per capita, this has no explicit role in addressing inter-regional inequalities in the UK, more popularly understood as the North–South divide. Put in other terms, however, imaginative devolved and regional government might be in pursuing progressive ideas in regional development, at the state level a broadly neo-liberal political economy that absolves the state of redistributive roles in regional development has continued to hold sway under the Blair Governments. In this context, the new regional development paradigm has potentially divisive rather than progressive implications.

The Blair Governments were not totally insensitive to pressures from Northern English regions to make some intervention in this competitive regionalism. Morgan records that in 2002 the Treasury did formally commit the Government to reduce the gap in growth rates between English regions over the long term. Nevertheless, there was no attempt to contain or redistribute the growth potential of the South East of England; leaving an insistence that the poorer performing regions must simply improve. Equally, there was a steely determination to not reform the territorial allocation of public expenditure, which is based on population rather than needs. However, despite the fact that this means that areas of higher GDP per capita can also receive higher public expenditure per capita, calls for the infamous Barnett formula to be scrapped in favour of a need-based formula have gone ignored by central government. There is a political imperative in this; however rational it might be to create territorial equity across the UK, if this involves reducing public expenditure in Scotland for the benefit of poorer English regions it may create the circumstances for increased political mobilisation around devolution in Scotland. However, if it is not attended to in some way, it may alternatively create the circumstances for increased political mobilisation around the English question. The dilemma of reconciling democratic socialism with democratic devolution is intimately intertwined with the dilemma of reconciling centrifugal and centripetal pressures in territorial politics.

The future of devolution, regionalism and regional development in the UK

Devolved government, regional governance and new paradigms of regional development policy remain at a relatively early stage. They have undoubtedly provided 'shocks' to the system of government, approaches to public policy and means of resolving identity politics both within each of the stateless nations and regions of the UK as well as across the UK as a whole. There have been notable developments in institutions, politics and public policy that have confirmed the UK as an interesting case for scholars and practitioners to follow. Yet there are many indicators of continuity. It remains open to question as to whether in relation to any indicator of change there has been a true transformation of territorial and regional politics (see Bradbury 2006). For the first ten years the UK largely muddled through its embrace of what Morgan has referred to as the rise of a 'polycentric polity' with relatively little fundamental change in the power structure across the state, devolved and regional governance characterised by as many problems as novel achievements.

These issues will have to be returned to regularly. As Derek Urwin (1982) noted, devolution is a historic and threatening departure for the UK. The very fact that the UK is founded on a union of stateless nations and that England as the largest nation has the capacity to be resentful of the costs of union means that despite all of its historic successes, the UK is a fundamentally vulnerable territorial state. Labour Governments are likely to continue to be cautious in managing devolution, but the approach taken by a future Conservative government will be a crucial test. In order to mobilise middle class votes in marginal constituencies in England, it would make sense for the Conservative Party to exploit English resentments either through reducing the representative rights of Scottish and Welsh MPs at Westminster, reform of territorial expenditure or legislative reform.

From the perspective of the stateless nations and regions too there will be pressures that mean that current settlements are unlikely to remain stable. More powers and financial resources will be on the agenda in Scotland and Wales and the management of those demands over time will be crucial and demanding for any UK government. The example of Spain bears witness that it is possible to do it but that it requires considerable energy and political investment. Territorial politics has the potential to become a very divisive issue in UK politics, as contested as in other European states. On a broader level there are also many other economic, cultural and social dynamics that connect with issues of territorial politics. Several authors of the book suggest that overall the UK remains reasonably stable in political, social and economic terms. For an outsider, those classic assumptions are less obvious. The gap in levels of wealth between London and the South East, the Northern regions and Wales persists. Moreover, the social composition of London bears little resemblance to that of Northern cities or the Celtic nations. Profound forces are at play that can potentially erode the nation state and Britain is no exception. Beyond the initial shock of devolution to Britain's apparently robust identity lie many more pressures to come.

For the time being devolution, regionalism and new approaches to regional development have largely succeeded in re-settling the UK's identity politics, provided innovations in the system of government that have largely been welcomed, and have provided the context for improvements in public policy. Cautious analysts would expect future developments to be characterised by further incremental adjustments, debates about specific problems and a gradual increase of regional capacity as part of the dense mix that constitutes UK government and politics. Yet, of course, it is possible that the genie has been let out of the bottle; that separatist nationalism comes to dominate the UK's stateless nations, and that the territorial politics of England comes to be dominated by something altogether more potent than regional governance. This may well be but part of a more general transformation of the UK state, effected by the forces of global economic change, migration, climate change, and social and cultural reconfiguration. If such scenarios are played out it is unlikely that the UK will be on its own.

References

Bradbury, J. (2006) '*Territory and Power* revisited: theorising territorial politics in the United Kingdom after devolution', *Political Studies* 54: 559–582.

Bulpitt, J. (1983) *Territory and Power in the United Kingdom: An Interpretation*, Manchester: Manchester University Press.

Crouch, C. (2004) *Post Democracy*, Oxford: Blackwell.

Harding, A., Marvin, S. and May, T. (2005) *A long-term evaluation of the operation and effectiveness of elected regional assemblies.* Final Report to the Office of the Deputy Prime Minister, 09/05, SURF.

Harvie, C. (1991) 'English regionalism: the dog that never barked', in B. Crick (ed.) *National Identities*, Oxford: Blackwell.

Hogwood, B. and Keating, M. (1982) (eds) *Regional Government in England*, Oxford: Clarendon Press.

John, P. (2008) 'Introduction' to re-print of Jim Bulpit, *Territory and Power in the United Kingdom: An Interpretation*, Manchester: Manchester University Press.

Jones, R., Goodwin, M., Jones, M., and Simpson, G. (2004), 'Devolution, state personnel and the production of new territories of governance in the UK'. *Environment and Planning A.*

Keating, M. (1998) *The New Regionalism in Western Europe: Territorial Restructuring and Political Change*, Cheltenham: Edward Elgar.

Le Galés, P. (2002) *European Cities: Social Conflicts and Governance*, Oxford: Oxford University Press.

Mawson, J. (2006) 'Regional governance and local government, what next?', Paper to the annual general meeting of the Warwick Local Authorities Research Consortium, September 2006.

Urwin, D. (1982) 'Territorial structures and political developments in the United Kingdom', in S. Rokkan and D. Urwin (eds), *The Politics of Territorial Identity*, London: Sage.

Index

Lightning Source UK Ltd.
Milton Keynes UK
13 March 2010
151310UK00002B/24/P